Adobe Creative Cloud

D0905166

Classroom in a Book®

The official training workbook from Adobe

Joseph Labrecque

Adobe Creative Cloud Classroom in a Book

© 2023 Adobe. All rights reserved.

Adobe Press is an imprint of Pearson Education, Inc. For the latest on Adobe Press books, go to adobepress. com. To report errors, please send a note to errata@peachpit.com. For information regarding permissions, request forms, and the appropriate contacts in the Pearson Education Global Rights & Permissions department, please visit www.pearson.com/permissions.

If this guide is distributed with software that includes an end user license agreement, this guide, as well as the software described in it, is furnished under license and may be used or copied only in accordance with the terms of such license. Except as permitted by any such license, no part of this guide may be reproduced, stored in a retrieval system, or transmitted, in any form or by any means, electronic, mechanical, recording, or otherwise, without the prior written permission of Adobe. Please note that the content in this guide is protected under copyright law even if it is not distributed with software that includes an end user license agreement.

The content of this guide is furnished for informational use only, is subject to change without notice, and should not be construed as a commitment by Adobe. Adobe assumes no responsibility or liability for any errors or inaccuracies that may appear in the informational content contained in this guide.

Please remember that existing artwork or images that you may want to include in your project may be protected under copyright law. The unauthorized incorporation of such material into your new work could be a violation of the rights of the copyright owner. Please be sure to obtain any permission required from the copyright owner.

Any references to company names in sample files are for demonstration purposes only and are not intended to refer to any actual organization.

Adobe, Adobe Audition, Adobe Dimension, Adobe Premiere Pro, After Effects, Behance, Classroom in a Book, Creative Cloud, Illustrator, InDesign, Lightroom, Photoshop, Premiere Rush, Substance 3D, Substance 3D Stager, and the Adobe logo are either registered trademarks or trademarks of Adobe in the United States and/or other countries.

Apple, iOS, macOS, Macintosh, and Safari are trademarks of Apple, registered in the U.S. and other countries. Android, Google, and YouTube are registered trademarks of Google Inc. Microsoft and Windows are either registered trademarks or trademarks of Microsoft Corporation in the U.S. and/or other countries. All other trademarks are the property of their respective owners.

Unless otherwise indicated herein, any third-party trademarks that may appear in this work are the property of their respective owners and any references to third-party trademarks, logos or other trade dress are for demonstrative or descriptive purposes only. Such references are not intended to imply any sponsorship, endorsement, authorization, or promotion of Pearson Education, Inc. products by the owners of such marks, or any relationship between the owner and Pearson Education, Inc. or its affiliates, authors, licensees or distributors.

Adobe Inc., 345 Park Avenue, San Jose, California 95110-2704, USA

Notice to U.S. Government End Users. The Software and Documentation are "Commercial Items," as that term is defined at 48 C.F.R. §2.101, consisting of "Commercial Computer Software" and "Commercial Computer Software Documentation," as such terms are used in 48 C.F.R. §12.212 or 48 C.F.R. §227.7202, as applicable. Consistent with 48 C.F.R. §12.212 or 48 C.F.R. §§227.7202-1 through 227.7202-4, as applicable, the Commercial Computer Software and Commercial Computer Software Documentation are being licensed to U.S. Government end users (a) only as Commercial Items and (b) with only those rights as are granted to all other end users pursuant to the terms and conditions herein. Unpublished-rights reserved under the copyright laws of the United States. Adobe Inc., 345 Park Avenue, San Jose, CA 95110-2704, USA. For U.S. Government End Users, Adobe agrees to comply with all applicable equal opportunity laws including, if appropriate, the provisions of Executive Order 11246, as amended, Section 402 of the Vietnam Era Veterans Readjustment Assistance Act of 1974 (38 USC 4212), and Section 503 of the Rehabilitation Act of 1973, as amended, and the regulations at 41 CFR Parts 60-1 through 60-60, 60-250, and 60-741. The affirmative action clause and regulations contained in the preceding sentence shall be incorporated by reference.

Writer: Joseph Labrecque
Adobe Press Executive Editor: Laura Norman
Development Editor: Stephen Nathans-Kelly
Production Editor: Maureen Forys,
          Happenstance Type-O-Rama
Technical Reviewer: Russell Chun
Keystroke Reviewer: Megan Ahearn
Copy Editor: Liz Welch

Proofreader: James Fraleigh
Compositor: Cody Gates,
          Happenstance Type-O-Rama
Indexer: Rachel Kuhn
Cover Illustration: Peter Sunna
          2dpete.com
Interior Designer: Mimi Heft

ISBN-13: 978-0-13-791470-8
ISBN-10: 0-13-791470-9

1 2022

WHERE ARE THE LESSON FILES?

Purchase of this Classroom in a Book in any format gives you access to the lesson files you'll need to complete the exercises in the book.

1 Go to adobepress.com/CreativeCloudCIB.

2 Sign in or create a new account.

3 Click Submit.

● **Note** If you encounter problems registering your product or accessing the lesson files or web edition, go to adobepress.com/support for assistance.

4 Answer the questions as proof of purchase.

5 The lesson files can be accessed through the Registered Products tab on your Account page.

6 Click the Access Bonus Content link below the title of your product to proceed to the download page. Click the lesson file links to download them to your computer.

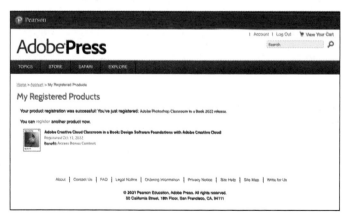

● **Note** If you purchased a digital product directly from adobepress.com or peachpit.com, your product will already be registered. However, you still need to follow the registration steps and answer the proof of purchase question before the Access Bonus Content link will appear under the product on your Registered Products tab.

CONTENTS AT A GLANCE

CONTENTS

GETTING STARTED

Adobe Creative Cloud is a massive collection of professional desktop and mobile applications and web-based services. The software is updated continually throughout each year, receiving new features, performance improvements, and other modifications. Additional connective services like Libraries, file sync, and cloud documents tie everything together in a way that is just not possible through standalone applications.

Whether you're designing with industry-standard applications like Photoshop or After Effects or experimenting with new offerings like XD or Dimension, Adobe Creative Cloud provides everything you need to express yourself creatively across all media.

About Classroom in a Book

Adobe Creative Cloud Classroom in a Book is part of the official training series for Adobe. The lessons are designed so that you can learn at your own pace. If you're new to Creative Cloud design applications, you'll learn the fundamental concepts and features you'll use to design for a wide variety of media. The structure of the book and order of the lessons is derived from my experience teaching these applications to thousands of creative advertising and media design students at the University of Colorado Boulder.

This book also touches on various design principles and concepts using individual lessons as a point of focus. Keep these principles in mind as you work through the lessons and consider how you can apply them across the different applications.

Prerequisites

Before you begin using *Adobe Creative Cloud Classroom in a Book* make sure your system is set up correctly and that you've installed the required software and hardware. You can view updated system requirements here:

helpx.adobe.com/creative-cloud/system-requirements.html

You should have a working knowledge of your computer and operating system. For example, you should know how to use the mouse or trackpad and standard menus and commands. You should also know how to open, save, and close files. If you need to review these techniques, see the documentation included with your macOS or Windows system.

It's not necessary to have a working knowledge of design applications concepts and terminology.

Installing Creative Cloud

You must purchase an Adobe Creative Cloud subscription, or obtain a trial version, separately from this book. For system requirements and complete instructions on installing the software, visit helpx.adobe.com/support.

You can purchase Adobe Creative Cloud by visiting www.adobe.com/creativecloud. Follow the onscreen instructions.

The first lesson in this book delves into everything you need to know to install and manage the Creative Cloud Desktop software.

Using the lesson files

The lessons in this book use supplied source files, including photos, design assets, video clips, audio recordings, project files, and more. To complete the lessons in this book, copy all the lesson files to your computer's storage drive.

Before getting started, you'll need to download the lesson files. You can find instructions for doing so on the first page of the ebook, in the section "Where are the lesson files?," as well as in the "Online content" section.

Important

The media files provided with this book are practice files, provided for your personal, educational use in these lessons only. You are not authorized to use these files commercially or to publish, share, or distribute them in any form without written permission from Adobe Inc., and the individual copyright holders of the various items. Do not share projects created with these lesson files publicly. This includes, but is not limited to, distribution via social media or online video platforms such as YouTube and Vimeo. You will find a complete copyright statement on the copyright page at the beginning of this book.

Any original media such as photographs, videos, and audio recordings referenced in or distributed as part of this book are copyright © 2022 by Joseph Labrecque. Certain additional design assets referenced are derived from direct use of online resources such as Adobe Express or as distributed in applications such as Adobe Character Animator.

How to use these lessons

The lessons in this book include step-by-step instructions. Each lesson stands alone but many build on concepts and workflows from previous lessons. For this reason, the best way to learn from this book is to proceed through the lessons in their written order.

The lessons begin with an overview of a particular piece of design software and how to create a new project in that application. We then proceed by introducing concepts and workflows that are common to the individual application until the project is complete.

Many pages contain additional "sidebar" information boxes that explain a particular technology or offer alternative workflows. It's not necessary to read the content in these sidebars or to follow the workflows, but you may find the content interesting and helpful as it will deepen your understanding and often provide additional context.

By the end of these lessons, you'll have a good understanding of what each Creative Cloud software application does and how to start a new project, and you'll be able to design competently with the particular application each lesson explores.

Nearly every lesson also includes an overview of a relevant design principle. It is good to keep these principles in mind when you're designing, balancing out the technical aspects of the application with a functional understanding of basic design concepts.

Although we only scratch the surface of what you can accomplish with each Creative Cloud application, you won't be left with nowhere to go if you want to learn more. At the close of each lesson, you will find suggestions of where to look next to go deeper with the application we have focused on in that lesson.

Online content

Your purchase of this Classroom in a Book includes online materials provided by your Account page on adobepress.com. These include the following.

Lesson files

To work through the projects in this book, you will need to download the lesson files by following the instructions in "Accessing the lesson files and Web Edition."

Web Edition

The Web Edition is an online interactive version of the book that provides an enhanced learning experience. Your Web Edition can be accessed from any device with a connection to the Internet, and it contains the following:

- The complete text of the book
- Hours of instructional video keyed to the text
- Interactive quizzes

● **Note** If you encounter problems registering your product or accessing the lesson files or web edition, go to www.adobepress.com/support for assistance.

Note If you purchased a digital product directly from www.adobepress.com or www.peachpit.com, your product will already be registered. However, you still need to follow the registration steps and answer the proof of purchase question before the Access Bonus Content link will appear under the product on your Registered Products tab.

Accessing the lesson files and Web Edition

You must register your purchase on adobepress.com in order to access the online content.

1 Go to adobepress.com/CreativeCloudCIB.

2 Sign in or create a new account.

3 Click Submit.

4 Answer the question as proof of purchase.

5 The lesson files can be accessed from the Registered Products tab on your Account page. Click the Access Bonus Content link below the title of your product to proceed to the download page. Click the lesson file link(s) to download them to your computer.

6 The Web Edition can be accessed from the Digital Purchases tab on your Account page. Click the Launch link to access the product.

Additional resources

Adobe Creative Cloud Classroom in a Book is not meant to replace documentation that comes with the software or to be a comprehensive reference for every feature. Only the commands and options used in the lessons are explained in this book. For comprehensive information about application features and tutorials, refer to the following resources.

Adobe Creative Cloud Learn and Support: https://helpx.adobe.com/creative-cloud is where you can find and browse Help and Support content on Adobe.com. On the Learn & Support page, click User Guide for documentation on individual features, or visit https://helpx.adobe.com/creative-cloud/user-guide.html.

For inspiration, key techniques, cross-application workflows, and updates on new features, go to the Creative Cloud tutorials page: helpx.adobe.com/creative-cloud /tutorials.html.

Additionally, you will find links to similar online resources for each application we cover at the conclusion of the relevant lessons.

Adobe Community: Tap into peer-to-peer discussions, questions, and answers on Adobe products at the Adobe Support Community page at community.adobe.com. Click the links for the specific application to visit the corresponding communities.

Adobe Creative Cloud Discover: This online resource offers thoughtful articles on design and design issues, a gallery showcasing the work of top-notch designers and artists, tutorials, and more. Check it out at creativecloud.adobe.com/discover.

Resources for educators: adobe.com/education and edex.adobe.com offer a treasure trove of information for instructors who teach classes on Adobe software. Find solutions for education at all levels, including free curricula that use an integrated approach to teaching Adobe software and that can be used to prepare for the Adobe Certified Professional exams.

Adobe Authorized Training Centers

Adobe Authorized Training Centers offer instructor-led courses and training on Adobe products, employing only Adobe Certified Instructors. A directory of AATCs is available at learning.adobe.com/partner-finder.html.

1 CREATIVE CLOUD DESKTOP AND MOBILE APPLICATIONS

Lesson overview

In this lesson, you'll learn how to do the following:

- Understand what Adobe Creative Cloud is and how it is used.

- Navigate the Creative Cloud Desktop application.

- Install, uninstall, update, and manage desktop software versions.

- Access mobile apps, Creative Cloud Libraries, and the sync folder.

- Browse and manage Adobe Fonts.

- Get familiar with the Behance network and Portfolio services.

 This lesson will take less than 1 hour to complete.

To get the files used in this lesson, download them from the web page for this book at www.adobepress.com/CreativeCloudCIB. For more information, see "Accessing the lesson files and Web Edition" in the Getting Started section at the beginning of this book.

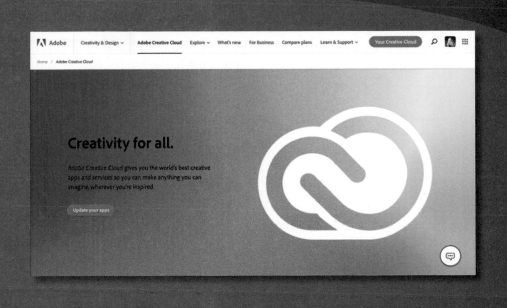

The Adobe Creative Cloud Desktop application functions as a gateway to installing and managing your desktop-based creative applications, accessing related mobile apps, and working with Creative Cloud services, all through a single interface.

Getting started

● **Note** If you have not already downloaded the project files for this book to your computer from your Account page, make sure to do so now, as we'll be using these files in upcoming chapters. See "Getting Started" at the beginning of the book.

Start by ensuring you have an active trial or subscription to Adobe Creative Cloud and have downloaded the exercise files we'll be using later in this book.

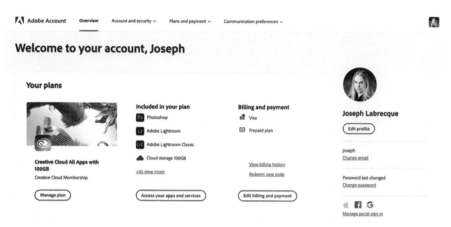

1 Log in to your Adobe account using your Adobe ID to be sure you have an active trial or subscription. You can find this information by visiting https://account.adobe.com.

2 Download the Adobe Creative Cloud Desktop application installer from www.adobe.com/creativecloud/desktop-app.html.

Creative Cloud Desktop

The Creative Cloud Desktop application is a management console for all of your Adobe desktop applications. It also acts as a gateway for you to access mobile software, web-based services, and learning resources.

The application interface

When you launch the Creative Cloud desktop application, you'll be presented with an easy-to-understand interface that includes application management and links to additional mobile applications and web-based services.

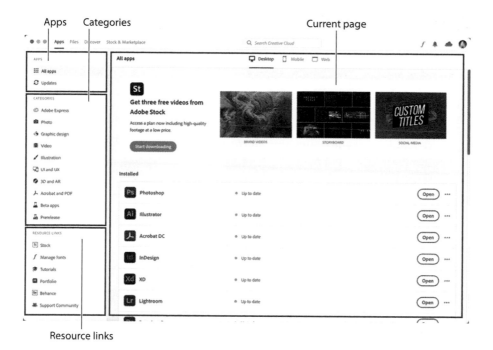

Apps   Categories   Current page

Resource links

You'll see a set of four views accessible from tabs along the top of the application interface. By default, the Apps view ^{Apps} will be active. If it isn't, click the icon to activate this view.

The software interface is simple to navigate and includes the following primary sections in the Apps view:

- **Apps:** This shows a full list of installed and available applications across three categories: Desktop, Mobile, and Web. You can also access updates from the Apps section.

- **Categories:** Applications are grouped into categories. This is often the more direct way to access Creative Cloud applications for specific purposes rather than listing everything at once.

- **Resource Links:** Web-based services like Adobe Stock, Behance, Portfolio, and Adobe Fonts can be accessed here.

- **Current Page:** When you're exploring the various sections of the desktop application, this area displays the sectional content you've chosen to navigate into.

You can also access additional content and services by switching the view along the top of the application interface from the Apps view to another by clicking the desired tab:

- **Files:** Here you'll get direct access to cloud documents and Creative Cloud Libraries.
- **Discover:** Filter by application to discover learning content and other resources.
- **Stock and Marketplace:** This area provides access to Adobe Stock, Adobe Fonts, application plugins, and more.

You will also find quick access to a search, notification, and software preferences in the upper right.

Creative Cloud on the web

You can also access some of these same features on the web by visiting https://creativecloud.adobe.com and logging in with your Adobe ID.

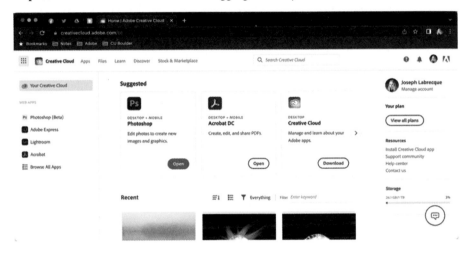

Much of the interface and options are shared with the Creative Cloud Desktop application, but an important distinction is that you are initially taken to a Creative Cloud dashboard. This view presents you with suggested applications, recent files, and direct access to web-based applications like Adobe Express from the left sidebar.

Managing application preferences

The Creative Cloud Desktop application includes preferences that you can set for application updates, notifications, and syncing.

In the upper-right corner of the interface, you can access your Adobe account by clicking the circular photo or avatar ● shown there. An account overview overlay will appear.

Choose Preferences from the overlay menu to open the application preferences dialog box.

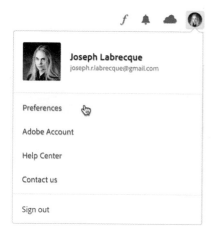

The dialog box has categories along the left side, and details for the selected category are displayed in the wider column to the right.

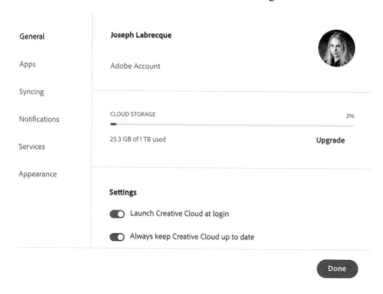

Here are a few items of note in each category that you will want to consider when setting up your preferences:

- **General:** This section displays how much storage you have remaining in the cloud. You can also choose whether to launch this application at system login and whether to keep the desktop app up to date automatically.

  At times, application updates will require that you keep the desktop app updated, so I highly suggest leaving this option activated.

- **Apps:** This is where you determine which applications to keep updated and specify the installation location on your computer for all your applications.

  Some applications will have advanced settings that determine whether to retain old versions and whether to import previous settings to newer installations.

- **Syncing:** This determines the location of your Creative Cloud files sync folder on your computer. You can also pause syncing or throttle download and upload transfer speed from this location.

- **Notifications:** This list of several notification types can be activated or deactivated depending on your personal preference.

- **Services:** Here you'll specify the download location for assets and choose whether to enable Adobe Fonts.

  If you choose to disable Adobe Fonts, all fonts that have been previously downloaded will deactivate.

- **Appearance:** This changes the user interface appearance for the Creative Cloud Desktop application. You can switch between light and dark themes.

Managing desktop applications

The primary use of Creative Cloud Desktop is to access and manage the various software applications that are part of your subscription.

Installing software applications

Before you can use any of the Adobe desktop applications like Photoshop, Illustrator, Premiere Pro, and the rest, you must first install them to your computer.

1 On the Apps tab, click All Apps in the upper left of the interface.

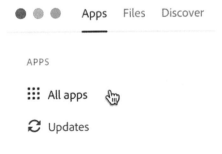

A grid of applications appears.

2 Locate the application you want to install and click Install.

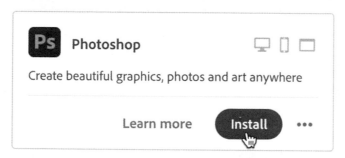

Note If you see a warning icon ⚠ when attempting to install an app, clicking the icon will provide detailed information as to why the software cannot be installed. Normally, this is because you must update your operating system for compatibility.

Creative Cloud will download the application and the installation process will begin.

You can monitor the installation progress directly or proceed to install additional applications while this is happening.

Note You can also locate installed applications in the normal ways in which you locate and launch applications in your operating system of choice. Opening them via the Creative Cloud Desktop application is simply a convenience.

Installing multiple applications will not affect the installation procedures at all.

3 Once the application is installed, click Open to launch it.

Tip If you can't find a specific piece of software, you can click the search icon 🔍 at the top right of the interface to locate and install it.

▶ **Tip** You will also see an application called Lightroom Classic. That is not the application we will be using in this book.

● **Note** Creative Cloud will install Media Encoder automatically when you install Premiere Pro, After Effects, Animate, or any other application that relies on it for media output.

Software applications to install

When working through this book, you'll want to install the following desktop applications:

- **Adobe Lightroom:** Photography management and editing
- **Adobe Photoshop:** Raster image design
- **Adobe Illustrator:** Vector graphic design
- **Adobe InDesign:** Multipage layout for digital and print
- **Adobe XD:** Screen layout and prototyping
- **Adobe Dimension:** Scene-based 3D layout design
- **Adobe Audition:** Audio recording, editing, and mixing
- **Adobe Premiere Pro:** Video sequencing
- **Adobe After Effects:** Motion graphics, video compositing, and effects
- **Adobe Character Animator:** Live, performance-based character animation
- **Adobe Animate:** Multiplatform animation, motion graphics, and interaction design
- **Adobe Media Encoder:** File transcoding and conversion

If you don't have room on your computer to install everything at once, you can always install only what you are using at a given time, removing software that you no longer currently need. As you'll see soon, the Creative Cloud Desktop application makes these actions relatively painless.

Updating software applications

One of the major benefits to Adobe's cloud-based distribution model is that it makes updates available on a regular basis. Some provide important new features and UI improvements, and others are more akin to stability and security updates. In either case, it is a good idea to keep your software updated at all times.

Updates may be installed automatically depending on any preferences you have set. You can also check for updates manually.

1 In the left-hand column of the Apps tab view, choose Updates.

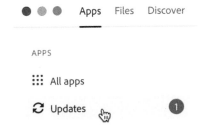

Creative Cloud displays the number of updates currently available in a badge to the right.

2 On the Updates screen, click Check For Updates.

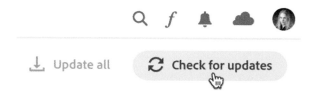

Creative Cloud Desktop will check for any available updates to your installed software applications.

3 If updates are available, they will be listed below, and they often include information detailing what the update contains.

4 Click the Update button to download the update and install it to your system. You can also choose Update All ⬇ Update all to update everything with a single click.

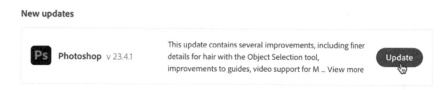

5 Monitor the update process. Sometimes you will receive a prompt that asks you whether you'd like to import settings to the updated version, depending on your chosen preferences.

Once the update completes, you can launch the application and make use of the updated version.

Uninstalling software applications

From time to time, you may need to completely uninstall an application if you no longer use it regularly, or perhaps if you want to free up space on your computer.

While you can do this on the operating system level, it is best to uninstall through the Creative Cloud Desktop application.

1   On the Apps tab, your installed applications are listed in the All Apps sidebar. Click the More Actions ••• option at the right of any installed application to access an overlay menu and select Uninstall.

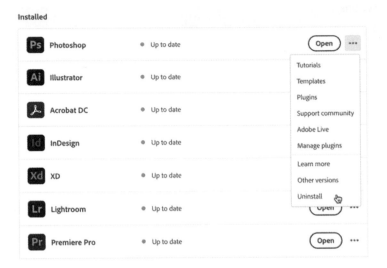

This menu will show more or fewer actions reflecting the chosen application and what is available.

2   Depending on the application being uninstalled, you may get an overlay asking whether you would like to keep or remove preferences during the uninstall process. If you think you might reinstall the application in the future, click Keep to retain your preferences.

Creative Cloud removes the application from your computer, but you can reinstall it whenever you like.

Installing other versions

By default, installing a software application will install the latest version. If you want to install a specific version of most applications, you have to access them through the More Actions menu.

1 On the Apps tab, under All Apps, click the More Actions ••• option at the right of any installed application to access an overlay menu and choose Other Versions.

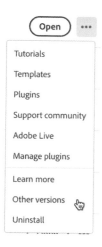

An additional overlay appears. Here you can choose specific versions of the software to install.

2 In the overlay, you can see the latest version highlighted at the top and older versions listed below. Locate the version you want to install and click the Install button associated with that version of the software.

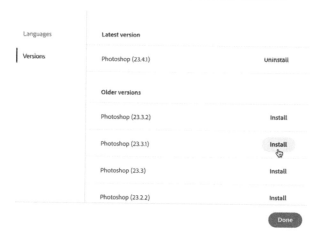

● **Note** For most applications, you can install full-release versions side by side and they will coexist just fine. For instance, Photoshop version 23.4 and Photoshop 22.1 can exist together but versions 23.4 and 23.1 cannot. Other applications do not allow for this.

The version you selected is downloaded and installed.

3 Click Done to exit the overlay.

Desktop software not covered in this book

While this book does cover the major desktop applications available in Creative Cloud, it doesn't include everything that's available.

Here are some applications we will not be detailing in this book:

- **Adobe Lightroom Classic:** Manage and edit photographs in a desktop application.

- **Adobe Bridge:** Preview, organize, edit, and publish your creative assets.

- **Adobe Acrobat:** View, create, manipulate, print, and manage PDF files.

- **Adobe Dreamweaver:** Design web pages using HTML, CSS, and JavaScript workflows.

- **Adobe InCopy:** Provide feedback and edits to InDesign documents.

- **Adobe Substance 3D Collection:** Create 3D art and augmented reality (AR) experiences using an entirely separate suite of software that isn't included in a Creative Cloud subscription but that is available separately.

    We will touch upon this collection in more detail in Lesson 7.

Even though we will not be addressing these applications, that doesn't mean they are not important. Of course, you are free to install and use any application that is available as part of your subscription.

Accessing mobile applications

While the Creative Cloud desktop applications are generally the main focus for subscribers—and they are certainly the focus of this book—some of the mobile apps are valuable and should not be dismissed. In fact, you can use many of them effectively in tandem with their desktop counterparts.

Installing mobile applications

The Creative Cloud Desktop application allows you to easily browse and install Creative Cloud apps to your mobile device.

1   On the Apps tab, under All Apps, you may have noticed a set of three choices along the top center of the Current Page view: Desktop, Mobile, and Web. Switch to the Mobile view by clicking Mobile.

2 Choose a mobile app you would like to install, such as Adobe Express, and click Send Link.

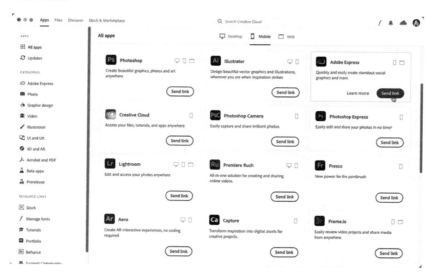

An overlay appears asking that you enter a mobile phone number. This is because Adobe will send a link to install the mobile app to that phone in a text message.

3 Enter your mobile phone number, confirm it, and click Send Link.

● **Note** You can choose to send the link over email by clicking the Email radio button.

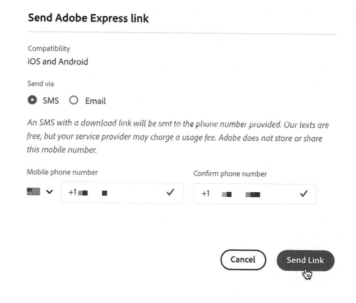

4 Check your mobile device text messages and you will find a new message that includes a link to download and install the mobile app you've chosen from your mobile platform's app store. Click this link.

Follow the instructions presented by the Apple App Store or Google Play Store to complete the installation.

Recommended mobile applications

When viewing the list of mobile apps available, you may feel a bit overwhelmed, since many are named similarly and not every app is as useful as some others.

Here are the mobile apps that I believe are worth looking into for readers of this book:

- **Adobe Express:** Accessible graphic design for digital and print (iOS & Android).
- **Adobe Capture:** Used to capture colors, looks, shapes, materials, and more for use in other software through Creative Cloud Libraries (iOS & Android).
- **Adobe Fresco:** Cloud-based painting, sketching, and drawing application (iOS & Windows).
- **Adobe Lightroom:** Photograph management and editing across devices (iOS & Android).
- **Adobe Aero:** Augmented reality for creating and viewing AR experiences (iOS & Android).

- **Adobe Photoshop:** Cloud-based raster design for the iPad (iPadOS).

- **Adobe Illustrator:** Cloud-based vector design for the iPad (iPadOS).

- **Adobe Premiere Rush:** Cloud-based, short-form video editing and production (iOS & Android).

- **Adobe Photoshop Camera:** A camera app with specialized filters designed in the spirit of Photoshop compositional effects (iOS & Android).

- **Adobe Creative Cloud:** Access your Creative Cloud files and assets on mobile. Includes a set of useful quick actions to remove the background from an image, convert between file types, and so on (iOS & Android).

- **Adobe XD:** Companion app to view and interact with cloud-based prototypes on real hardware as opposed to software-only previews (iOS & Android).

- **Behance:** Access community content and creative livestreams on the Behance social network (iOS & Android).

● **Note** For simplicity, if iOS compatibility is indicated above, this will generally mean iPadOS is also supported.

Creative Cloud services

A Creative Cloud subscription isn't just about installed applications. You'll get access to a number of useful services as well. Many of these work alongside the desktop and mobile software to improve your experience and workflows while others offer complementary services.

Creative Cloud sync folder

When you install the Creative Cloud Desktop application, it creates a folder on your computer named **Creative Cloud Files**. When you place files in this folder, Creative Cloud will sync them to the cloud and across other computers that you are signed into using your Adobe ID.

● **Note** You can change sync settings and the location of this folder in the Creative Cloud Desktop application preferences.

This sync folder functions similarly to other file syncing services such as Dropbox, Microsoft OneDrive, or Google Drive. You add files to one machine, and they are synced to others that are connected by your Adobe ID.

You can access your local sync folder directly from the Creative Cloud Desktop application by switching to the Files tab view along the top of the interface and clicking the Open Sync Folder 🐾 button at the bottom left of the interface.

Creative Cloud Libraries

Creative Cloud Libraries are organized repositories of creative assets that you can access from anywhere. The types of assets you can add to a Creative Cloud Library include colors, color themes, shapes, images, templates, stock photos, audio recordings, looks, materials, and even certain assets particular to specific desktop applications.

You can access your Creative Cloud Libraries directly through the Creative Cloud Desktop application by switching to the Files tab view along the top of the interface and choosing Your Libraries in the left column, or through individual applications that support Creative Cloud Libraries through their own interfaces.

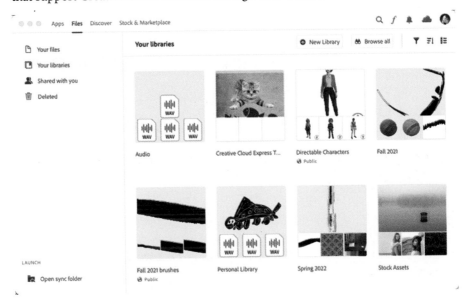

You can gather most assets into a Creative Cloud Library by using the Capture mobile app to capture and organize assets from the world around you. You can also add assets to a Creative Cloud Library from the various desktop applications that directly support them. This is a great way to work with the same assets across multiple applications.

Adobe Fonts

One of the most useful aspects of a Creative Cloud subscription is the ability to browse through and activate thousands of professional typefaces through Adobe Fonts.

You can access Adobe Fonts directly through the Creative Cloud Desktop application by clicking the Adobe Fonts *f* button in the upper right, or via a web browser by visiting https://fonts.adobe.com.

▶ **Tip** The Creative Cloud Desktop application does a good job of managing activated fonts. If you want to browse and activate new fonts, you will do so through the web interface, which includes a set of filters to locate fonts that match specific criteria.

When you activate a font, it will sync across all computers that you are signed into with your Adobe ID and become available for use in any application on your computer—even those that are not part of Creative Cloud.

Activated fonts will even appear in certain web-based services that support them, such as Adobe Express.

Adobe Stock

By browsing the thousands of assets available on Adobe Stock, you can access royalty-free photos, vector illustrations, 3D assets, videos, audio recordings, templates, and more.

Generally considered a separate cost, Adobe Stock works on either a monthly credit pack plan or with a separate subscription plan. Most plans include access to all content capped at a certain number of assets a month, whereas credit packs are best for inconsistent stock needs as more of a pay-as-you-go model. Check out the Adobe Stock FAQ for more details: https://stock.adobe.com/plans#plans-faq.

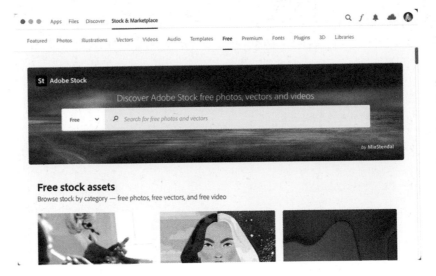

Adobe has also introduced a free collection of assets through Adobe Stock that any-one with a standard Creative Cloud subscription can access and use without paying any additional cost. To access the free collection, simply choose the **Free** option from the search menu before performing a search for assets.

You can further refine your search in the results page to only search for free assets of a certain type, such as free images or free videos. It's a great resource for inspiration or for actual use in your creative projects.

Behance

Behance is a social media platform maintained by Adobe expressly for creatives. Using Behance, members can share their creative work, get feedback from other members, appreciate the work of others, and participate in active livestreams. There is also a job-seeking component for those looking for work. It is a very engaging community!

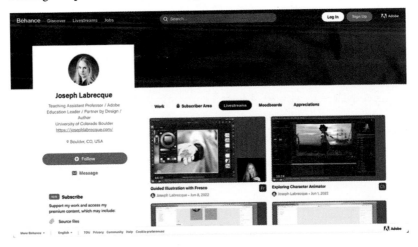

You can access Behance directly from the Creative Cloud Desktop application by switching to the Apps tab view along the top of the interface and choosing the Behance [Be] option listed in the Resource Links in the lower-left corner or through the web browser directly at www.behance.net.

Note You do not need an active Creative Cloud subscription to use this service.

Adobe Portfolio

Portfolio is a professional portfolio website creation and publishing tool that makes it easy for creatives to build a public portfolio showcasing their work. You start with one of the many themes available and then customize it to your liking. You can create up to five multipage Portfolio websites and can even integrate your own domain name.

Note Purchase of a domain name is a separate process and not part of Adobe Portfolio.

The Portfolio editor also has connections to Behance, enabling creatives to easily pull in work from their Behance profile to showcase as part of their portfolio of work.

Note Unlike with Behance, in order to make use of Portfolio, you must have an active Creative Cloud subscription.

You can access Portfolio directly from the Creative Cloud Desktop application by switching to the Apps tab view along the top of the interface and choosing the Portfolio [Pf] option listed in the Resource Links in the lower-left sidebar or through the web browser directly at https://portfolio.adobe.com.

Next steps with Creative Cloud

To further explore the creative options that Creative Cloud has to offer, you can make use of Adobe's help resources available at https://helpx.adobe.com/creative-cloud/user-guide.html.

Review questions

1 What is the Creative Cloud Desktop application primarily used for?

2 If a piece of software cannot be installed, what is the likely solution?

3 What is Adobe Capture used for?

Review answers

1 Creative Cloud enables you to install and manage creative desktop software.

2 You will likely need to update your operating system for compatibility.

3 Adobe Capture is a mobile app used to generate assets from the world around you to be placed in Creative Cloud Libraries for design application access.

2 CLOUD-BASED PHOTOGRAPHY WITH LIGHTROOM

Lesson overview

In this lesson, you'll learn how to do the following:

- Understand the Adobe Lightroom family of software, services, and related utilities.

- Gain an understanding of the design principle "rule of thirds."

- Capture and import photographs into Lightroom.

- Edit photographs using Lightroom presets and properties.

- Create organized albums of photographs.

- Share albums and photographs on the web.

 This lesson will take less than 1 hour to complete.

To get the files used in this lesson, download them from the web page for this book at https://www.adobepress.com/CreativeCloudCIB. For more information, see "Accessing the lesson files and Web Edition" in the Getting Started section at the beginning of this book.

Lightroom can be used across multiple operating systems and device platforms. Every image you capture is synced through cloud-based services, making your photographs available through any version of Lightroom. Any edits you make are infinitely modifiable since they are all completely nondestructive.

Getting started

Start by viewing the photographic image files we will be using in this lesson.

● **Note** If you have not already downloaded the project files for this lesson to your computer from your Account page, make sure to do so now. See "Getting Started" at the beginning of the book.

1 Open the Lesson02/02Start folder to view the set of example photographs being used in this lesson.

This folder contains an assortment of personal photographs taken with a mobile device camera. You can substitute your own photos for every activity in this lesson if you prefer.

2 Close or minimize the window.

Introducing Lightroom

When it comes to getting started with Creative Cloud desktop software, there is often no better place to begin in this current age than with Adobe Lightroom. Nearly everyone has a high-resolution camera built into their mobile device, always at the ready to capture anything at hand.

Lightroom allows users to capture, edit, and share their photographs across mobile, desktop, and web. All photographs are stored in the cloud along with any data pertaining to edits you've applied to the photos. This workflow allows for *nondestructive editing* of photographic data, meaning you can always go back and adjust or undo your individual edits since the original photograph itself is never changed—only the data that surrounds it.

Additionally, Lightroom on iOS or Android is a great place for anyone to start their photographic journey with Creative Cloud, since the mobile version can be installed and used without a subscription.

In this lesson, we'll explore how to capture, organize, edit, and share photographic images across devices and platforms.

Understanding the Lightroom ecosystem

The Lightroom ecosystem encompasses a set of software applications across mobile, desktop, and web and the cloud-based services that bind them all together. This allows you to edit the same photos across multiple devices.

For example, you can capture a photograph on Apple iOS or Google Android and make quick edits that are synced to the cloud. Then you can open the same photograph on your Windows or macOS machine and continue editing, and finally share your edited photo through the same cloud-based services.

Let's have a brief look at the Lightroom family of software alongside some related applications and utilities.

Lightroom Desktop

Lightroom can be installed on either macOS or Windows. It includes the ability to import, edit, organize, and share your photographs. Editing is accomplished through a collection of presets or can be controlled using multiple sliders and other tools within the software. In this lesson, we will focus on the use of Lightroom for the desktop through hands-on activities.

Any edits you make in the desktop version of Lightroom will sync to the cloud and become available on the mobile and web versions of the software. Lightroom desktop includes everything you need to import, organize, edit, and share your photographs.

Lightroom Mobile

The mobile version of Lightroom is available for both iOS and Android. The core of the software is the same as in the desktop version, so behavior is similar, and edits are shared across versions. Many of the same tools and settings are available whether editing and organizing on mobile or desktop, with the mobile version having the additional ability to capture photos directly using the built-in camera.

Any edits made in Lightroom mobile will sync to the cloud and become available on the desktop and web versions of the software. With Lightroom mobile, you can work in either portrait or landscape view.

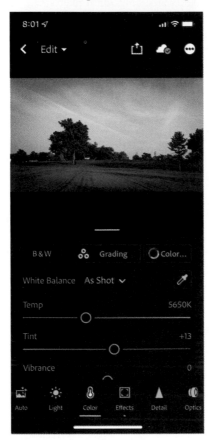

Lightroom Web

There is also a web-based version of Lightroom. This version lacks many of the advanced features available elsewhere but retains the core editing capabilities found in the desktop and mobile versions.

Any edits made in Lightroom web will sync to the cloud and become available on the mobile and desktop versions of the software. Lightroom web is primarily used for quick edits and easy photo access.

Lightroom Classic

The original Lightroom Classic is available on both macOS and Windows and includes several features not available in Lightroom, such as the ability to print your photographs. However, any edits made in Lightroom Classic are only available to the local Lightroom catalog and are not cloud enabled.

Lightroom Classic includes a different way of organizing and a set of features not found in other versions. Many professional photographers still prefer Lightroom Classic due to the organizational workflows that are available and the inclusion of a somewhat more specialized toolset.

▶ **Tip** It is not recommended that you use both Lightroom and Lightroom Classic together, as they have completely different ways of organizing and storing photos.

● **Note** Adobe continues to update Lightroom Classic alongside the other Lightroom products.

Adobe Camera Raw

At the core of each and every version of Lightroom and Lightroom Classic is a utility application called Adobe Camera Raw.

Camera Raw includes many camera and lens profiles and is updated frequently to support newer hardware. Updates can also contain new features and improvements to the RAW image data processing engine.

File formats: JPG vs. RAW vs. DNG

When capturing digital photos, most cameras have settings that determine which file format the camera will use to save image data. The most common format is JPG, since it can be viewed nearly everywhere. JPG is not as desirable for professional work, though, as it is a compressed, lossy format that tosses out a great deal of the original sensor data.

Specific to most cameras is another format for storing RAW data from the sensor. This data is representative of the photograph but must be interpreted by software to be viewed. Nearly every manufacturer has their own specific implementation of RAW data formats and, generally, only their specific software can read their formats. Camera Raw is an exception—it can interpret every major RAW format with ease.

DNG is a format pioneered by Adobe in cooperation with a number of major camera manufacturers. DNG stands for *Digital Negative* and is designed as a manufacturer-agnostic, standardized version of the RAW sensor data. Of course, Camera Raw can handle DNG files as well.

Any of the RAW file formats are preferable to JPG when using Camera Raw since you will have much more data to work with in editing and the interpretation is done by you and not the camera software. However, since RAW files contain so much more data, they are much larger than their JPG equivalents.

Aside from all of the Lightroom products, Camera Raw is also used by Adobe Photoshop, Adobe After Effects, and Adobe Bridge. As you can see in the following figure, the Camera Raw interface looks very similar to what you've already seen in Lightroom.

Adobe Bridge

Adobe Bridge is a powerful organizational tool for various Creative Cloud file types and provides the most direct way of launching Camera Raw.

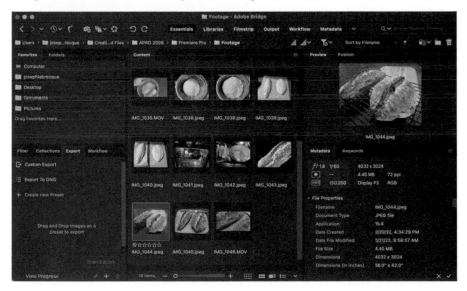

Tip To view
this information in
Lightroom, click the
Info icon 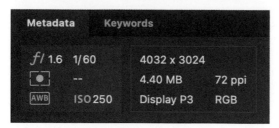 in the lower
right.

One great benefit of using Bridge to view your photos is that you get immediate
access to metadata from the time the photo was taken. This includes f-stop, shut-
ter speed, ISO, and other photographic settings. You can access this information in
Lightroom as well, but there it's more obscure.

Metadata	**Keywords**		
$f/$ 1.6 1/60		4032 x 3024	
	--	4.40 MB	72 ppi
AWB ISO 250		Display P3	RGB

The Lightroom interface

Lightroom exhibits a simple, uncluttered workspace that is focused on your photos.

Detail/Square/Grid view   Edit controls

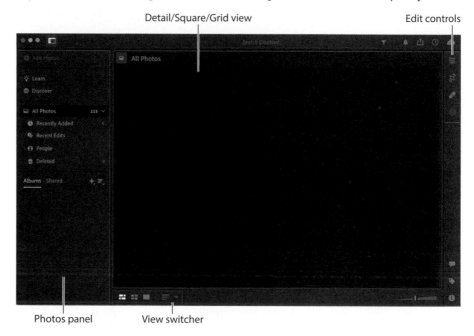

Photos panel   View switcher

You can import, search, and organize albums in the Photos panel on the left side of
the Lightroom workspace. When ready to make edits, the Photos panel collapses
and the various Edit controls emerge from the right.

In the center area, you can display your selected photos in Grid view, Photo Grid
view, or Detail view while editing or when you want to view a single photograph.

We will touch on other important features of the interface as we work through this
lesson.

Design principles: Rule of thirds

The rule of thirds is a compositional rule of thumb that divides an image into nine equal parts via two horizontal lines and two vertical lines—both sets equally spaced—to create a grid of nine squares. The principle states that any major elements of focus should be placed along these lines or across their intersections. In spite of its name, this is really a guideline and not a rule!

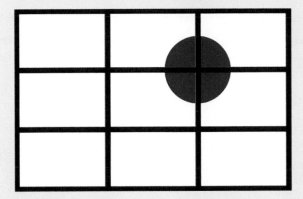

In Lightroom mobile, you can summon a rule of thirds grid when capturing a photograph. In Lightroom desktop, you can enable a rule of thirds grid when cropping using the edit controls.

Importing photographs

When you capture photos using Lightroom mobile on iOS or Android, they will automatically be added to your Lightroom storage and will sync across all devices. If you aren't capturing photos through the Lightroom mobile app directly, you'll need to import them through the Add Photos feature in Lightroom desktop.

Note You can choose to work with the photos in the Lesson02/02Start folder, or you may select your own photographs.

Let's import some photographs into Lightroom.

1 Click the Add Photos option in the Photos panel to begin the import process.

2 Locate the photos to import in the Browse dialog box that appears and click Review For Import.

3 In the confirmation screen that appears, confirm the photos you'd like to import, and click Add *n* Photo(s).

Note There is a checkmark overlay in the upper-left corner of each photo thumbnail that you can use to either include or exclude each image from the import.

The imported photos are added to Lightroom and appear in either Grid view or Photo Grid view.

Note If you'd like to use your own photos, which I recommend, you can import them in the way detailed here or you can capture them through Lightroom mobile and they will automatically sync to the desktop. I've also supplied the set of photos that we are going to be using in this lesson, if you'd like to follow along with the same source files.

You can switch between these views using the controls in the lower-left side of the Photos panel.

Viewing imported photographs

With a fresh set of photographs available within Lightroom, we can now proceed to explore these imported images.

To begin, let's locate an image we'd like to work with using the available filter options. Using the Photos panel, you can filter imported photographs by those recently added or through more stringent criteria.

1 Open the Photos panel if it's not open already.

2 Expand the Recently Added option to filter the group of photos we've just imported. Recently added photo sets are grouped by time. Clicking a set of recently imported photos will make that set visible in Lightroom and hide any others.

● **Note** Filtering will instruct Lightroom to show only photos that meet certain criteria and not others. If you have additional photos, they still exist, of course!

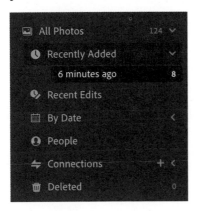

3 Select your import set to continue.

4 Double-click a photo to open it in Detail view.

You can use the controls below your photo to provide a star-based rating that you can also filter by or zoom in to view your photo close up. Other photos will appear along a thumbnail strip below the photo you selected.

Using presets and edit controls

When working on photos in Lightroom, you will likely want to change how your photographs look by adjusting a variety of visual properties.

Presets allow you to apply a series of prepackaged adjustments to your photos, whereas edit controls enable you to make manual edits, crop, reframe, and more.

Using Lightroom presets

Now that we have a photo open in Detail view, we can begin editing the chosen photograph. The quickest way to apply edits to any photo is by selecting a preset.

1 Click the Edit icon ▤ at the top of the right-hand sidebar.

The Edit controls expand and the Photos panel to the left of the interface disappears.

▶ **Tip** To view the Photos panel at any time, click the Photos icon ▣ at the top left of the Lightroom interface.

2 At the very top of the Edit controls, you will find a Presets button. Click this button to display the available presets.

Hovering over each preset will provide a quick preview of what your photograph will look like with the preset applied.

3 To apply a preset, click it and it will highlight in blue.

Note that any of these presets can be removed or swapped out at any time. Again, Lightroom workflows are completely nondestructive!

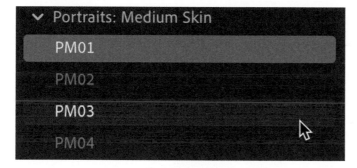

4 Click the Presets button to close the Presets panel.

Preset options

When you first access the Presets panel, you are provided with a list of Premium presets. You also have the option to access any presets you've created by choosing the Yours tab. Or you can access community presets through the Recommended tab.

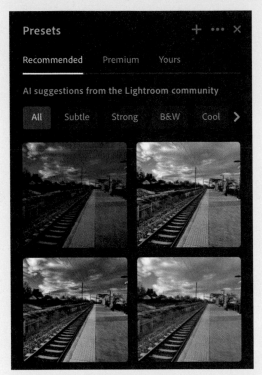

The presets that appear on the Recommended tab are particular to your currently selected photo, making use of Adobe Sensei artificial intelligence.

In addition to presets, there are single-click buttons that allow Auto and B&W adjustments—often a good first step when performing manual edits.

Editing photographs

Editing images in Lightroom can range from adjusting the lighting and color, to cropping or even removing elements from your photos altogether.

This workflow differs from the use of presets because you control every detail yourself.

1 Navigate to Lesson02 > 02Start and open IMG_1016.jpeg in Detail view for editing.

This photograph was taken on a drab winter day in Colorado. It could definitely use some adjustments to make it more vibrant!

2 Open the Edit controls if they are not open already, and familiarize yourself with the Light section.

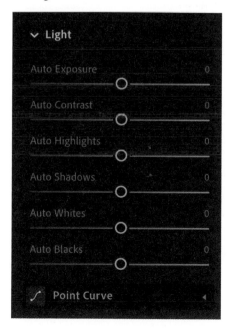

3 Shift the sliders for different lighting properties until the image becomes clearer and less drab. I'm going to pay particular attention to the shadows and highlights for this image. Set the Highlights slider to +16 and the Shadows slider to −26.

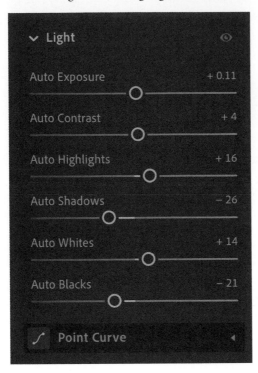

● **Note** Scroll down within the Edit controls to see an even greater assortment of properties you can manage, such as Color, Effects, and Detail.

4 To view the differences between the original and the edits you've made, click the Show Original toggle 🔲 below the Detail view.

Cropping photographs

We'll now crop our edited photo to make the framing tighter and to make use of the rule of thirds to reframe everything in a creative way.

1 Select Crop And Rotate 🔲 and use the overlay that is provided to make the shot tighter and better composed by paying attention to the rule of thirds overlay.

2 Use the handles of each side of the frame overlay and those at its corners to adjust the crop to make the overall composition focus on the set of buildings.

3 When you hover over the photo, a hand icon appears. Drag to reposition the photo so that important elements like the towers align with the rule of thirds grid intersections.

4 Press the Return/Enter key to commit the crop.

Removing objects with the Healing Brush

Using the Healing Brush and associated controls, we can remove unwanted objects from our photos.

1 Select the Healing Brush ✎. You can use it to draw over portions of the photo that you want to remove.

2 Zoom in on a portion of the photo for finer control over the framing of the image and to remove unwanted portions. For this image, zoom onto the flag at the top of the tower to remove it.

3 Adjust the brush size by using the control slider or the square brackets ([]) on your keyboard and brush across an object to select it for removal.

A	B	C	D
Adjust the brush size and zoom in.	Draw over an object to be removed.	Shift the blue markers to adjust the sample area.	The object is effectively removed.

● **Note** Of course, since we are working in a nondestructive environment, we can always bring the object back or adjust in other ways.

The object is removed and you can now adjust the sample area using the same tool if need be by dragging the blue markers that appear. This area determines what is used to replace or repair the brushed-over content.

Using a mask to refine the sky

Masking is an effective way of isolating portions of a photo for enhanced edits within only the masked areas.

We'll use a linear gradient mask to adjust the sky.

1 Click the Masking icon ● to reveal a set of masking tools, including brushes, gradients, and range selection tools.

A list of mask types appears in the Create New Mask sidebar.

2 Click the Linear Gradient option.

3 Drag a mask from the top of the sky until you just start touching the treetops and towers.

4 With a mask created across the sky, use the various property sliders that appear to adjust only the properties of that portion of the image.

● **Note** Masks are great for adjusting the exposure of elements like the sky, which can often be problematic when you're performing overall edits.

▶ **Tip** You can also manage the mask from the Masks panel that appears.

Masking with artificial intelligence

Newer versions of Lightroom come equipped with a set of artificial intelligence–powered masking tools that can be used for selecting the sky or the subject of a photograph.

Leveraging Adobe Sensei AI, these tools can produce much more complex masks than the traditional masking tools such as brushes and gradients.

Organizing and sharing photographs

Aside from the editing tools we explored in the last section, one of the great strengths of Lightroom is the ability for users to organize their photographs into albums and even share photos with the world through the web-based ecosystem.

Creating albums

Albums are a great way to organize your photographs in a meaningful way. You can create albums and name them whatever you like for fast identification.

Let's create a new album and place the photos we've previously imported into it.

1 If you're still viewing the Edit tools, open the Photos panel at the left of the interface.

2 Locate the Albums section toward the bottom of the panel and click the Add An Album button located there.

3 Create a new album by clicking the Create Albums & Folders icon and choosing Create Album from the menu that appears.

The Create Album dialog box appears and prompts you to name the album. You can also automatically include the selected photo as part of the album if you like by selecting the "Include the selected photo" option.

4 Enter a meaningful name in the field provided and click Create.

● **Note** You can also create folders to even further organize related albums together. Albums hold collections of photos and folders contain collections of albums.

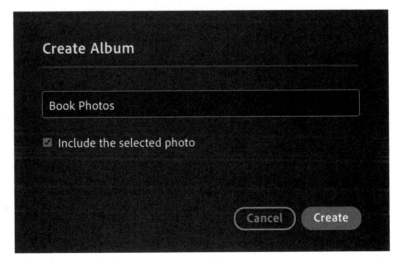

A new album is created. Lightroom will populate it with the selected photo if you chose to add it.

5 Add the remaining photos to the album by dragging their thumbnails onto it and releasing the mouse when the album highlights in blue.

You've now created a new album and populated it with a set of photographs. Choosing the album will display only the photographs that are associated with that album. This is a great way to provide meaningful organization to your photo collection.

▶ **Tip** A single photo can be included in multiple albums, and deleting any album will not delete the photos within it.

Sharing Lightroom content

With Lightroom so focused on providing cloud-based services for photographers, sharing photographic content is an essential part of the experience. Lightroom provides a few approaches available for doing so.

Sharing albums on the web

You can share individual photos, groups of photos, or entire albums over the web.

Let's share an album first.

1 Right-click your album in the Album section of the Photos panel and select Share & Invite from the menu that appears.

The Share & Invite dialog box opens, enabling you to generate a share link, specify privacy settings, and customize the experience.

2　Generate a URL, customize your share options, and click Done when ready. Be sure to copy the generated URL for the next step by clicking the generated link or the clipboard icon next to it.

3　Paste the copied share URL into your web browser. Now you'll be able to view the entire album of photos.

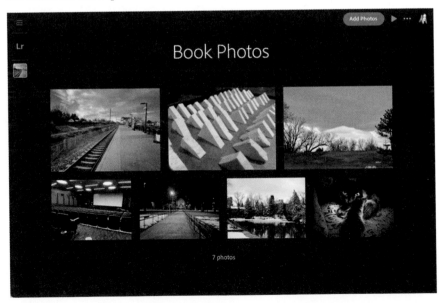

If the link is made public in the share settings, you can send this same URL to anyone you would like to view your album.

Exporting photos

You are also able to export your photos as individual bitmap images suitable for sharing to social media, emailing, and printing.

Let's export a JPG file from Lightroom:

1 Select a photograph you want to export.

2 Click the Share icon 📤 at the upper right of the interface.

The Export section of the overlay opens.

3 Now you can export your selected image in a variety of formats. Click JPG (Large).

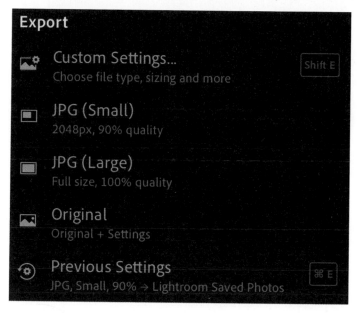

4 Browse to the location on your computer where you want to export the photograph. Click Export.

Lightroom saves the image file to the location you chose during the export process.

Sharing photos on the web

The workflow for sharing photos on the web is very similar to exporting.

Let's share a photo on the web:

1 Select the photo you'd like to share.

2 Click the Share icon 📤 at the upper right of the interface.

3 In the Share section of the overlay that appears, you can share your selected image. Click Get A Link to proceed.

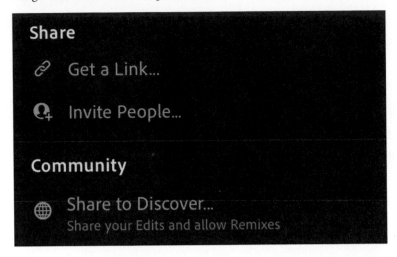

The Share & Invite dialog box appears and presents you with the same options you saw when sharing an album.

4 Generate a URL, customize your share options, and click Done when finished.

Sharing photos as a discoverable remix

Sharing a photograph as a remix will allow the community of Lightroom users to see the specific edits and adjustments you made when developing your photograph. It also allows them to remix the original photo in their own way.

Let's share a photo as a remix:

1 Select the edited photo you'd like to share as a remix.

2 Click the Share icon ⬆ at the upper right of the interface.

3 The Community section of the overlay that appears enables you to share your selected image to the wider community of users. Click Share To Discover to proceed.

● **Note** In order to share in this way, your photograph must have had adjustments made upon it in Lightroom.

Community

⊕ Share to Discover...
Share your Edits and allow Remixes

4 The Share Edit dialog box presents you with options for naming and categorizing your photo edit. Click Enable 'Save As Preset' to allow users to make use of your edits as a preset.

5 Click Allow Remixing to allow users to remix your photograph.

6 Click Share when finished.

Next steps with Lightroom

To further explore the creative options that Lightroom has to offer, you can make use of Adobe's help resources available at https://helpx.adobe.com/support/lightroom-cc.html.

If you'd like to advance in your exploration of Lightroom Classic in a way similar to what we have covered here, check out *Adobe Photoshop Lightroom Classic Classroom in a Book*, also available from Peachpit and Adobe Press.

Review questions

1 What is the primary difference between Lightroom and Lightroom Classic?

2 What is the rule of thirds?

3 What are Lightroom presets?

4 What are albums and folders used for?

5 When you share an album or even a single photo, how can a viewer access it?

Review answers

1 Lightroom Classic includes features that Lightroom does not—such as the ability to print—but can handle only local files since it is not cloud enabled.

2 The rule of thirds is a design principle that divides an image into nine sections as a framing reference.

3 Lightroom presets are prepackaged adjustments that are applied to a photo with one click.

4 Albums contain a collection of photographs and folders contain a collection of albums.

5 They can access it through a link that takes them to that album or photograph via the web version of Lightroom.

3 RASTER IMAGE COMPOSITING WITH PHOTOSHOP

Lesson overview

In this lesson, you'll learn how to do the following:

- Understand the different variations of Photoshop across desktop and mobile.
- Clean up and restore a damaged photograph.
- Manage pixel layers and adjustment layers.
- Work with brushes and colors.
- Enable blend modes and adjust layer opacity.
- Create new documents and make use of presets.
- Import image files into a document.
- Make selections and mask portions of images.
- Add text layers to a Photoshop document.
- Modify character and paragraph attributes.
- Understand the design principle of negative space.
- Create and modify shape layers in a design.
- Export Photoshop authoring files as distributable images.

 This lesson will take less than 2 hours to complete.

To get the files used in this lesson, download them from the web page for this book at www.adobepress.com/CreativeCloudCIB. For more information, see "Accessing the lesson files and Web Edition" in the Getting Started section at the beginning of this book.

Adobe Photoshop is perhaps the most well-known software application in the entire Creative Cloud collection. Photoshop is used across multiple creative industries and is the standard for image correction, manipulation, and compositing.

Getting started

● **Note** If you have not already downloaded the project files for this lesson to your computer from your Account page, make sure to do so now. See "Getting Started" at the beginning of the book.

Start by viewing the finished project to see what you'll be creating in this lesson.

1 Open the Lesson03/03End folder to view the projects we will work with in this lesson.

2 Preview the GreenGrapes.jpg file from this location.

GreenGrapes.jpg is a semi-colorized and restored black-and-white 35mm photograph. We will use a combination of healing tools, layer management, blend modes, and brushes to restore and recolor the image.

3 Close the GreenGrapes.jpg file preview.

4 Preview the GarlicPoster.png file from the same location.

GarlicPoster.png is a promotional poster image that we will design using selection and masking tools in addition to various shape, brush, gradient, and text tools.

5 Close the GarlicPoster.png file preview.

Understanding Photoshop

Photoshop predates Lightroom by nearly two decades. Before Lightroom was released, Photoshop was the primary software application used by photographers to work with digital photography.

With Lightroom focusing on the more photographic aspects of digital imaging since its introduction, Photoshop has increasingly been used for other tasks like photo restoration, manipulation, compositing, and effects. Today, Photoshop serves multiple industries as the standard creative imaging software toolset.

While the primary platform for Photoshop remains the desktop environment, in recent years it has expanded to iPad and even to the web.

Photoshop for Desktop

The desktop version of Photoshop is the most complete and powerful of any version available today. It contains decades of tried-and-true tools and workflows alongside innovative features made possible through Adobe Sensei, Adobe's artificial intelligence remote services.

In becoming adept at using Photoshop, you will be able to express yourself not just with photography, but through a wide array of creative image compositing techniques and toolsets.

Most of this lesson will focus on this version of Photoshop. Although you can complete the exercises using other versions, the interface varies quite a bit between the desktop and mobile—or even web—versions of the software.

Photoshop on the iPad

In bringing Photoshop to iPad, Adobe used the core Photoshop codebase—meaning that Photoshop on iPad *is* Photoshop. This differs greatly from other mobile experiments of the past, which used the Photoshop name but were in actuality completely new creations.

The biggest difference between the iPad and desktop versions of Photoshop is in the user interface. Photoshop for the iPad is meant for use with touchscreen or stylus, in a more condensed, reimagined UI.

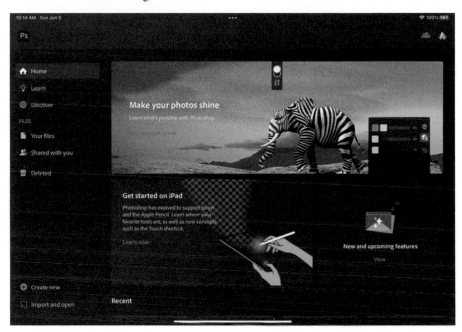

Photoshop on the iPad introduced the need for a cloud-based file format: Adobe Photoshop Document Cloud (PSDC). Any document created on iPad can be opened in any other version of Photoshop without issue, since the same file format and the same codebase are used to interpret it.

While Photoshop on the iPad does not contain all the features of its desktop counterpart, Adobe is adding new features all the time.

Adobe Fresco

Related closely to Photoshop on the iPad, Fresco takes all of the brushing and painting aspects of Photoshop and refines them into a seamless drawing, sketching, painting, and inking experience.

Meant to be used with a stylus like Apple Pencil, Fresco is available on iPad and iPhone as well as a number of Windows-based devices that have stylus or touch support.

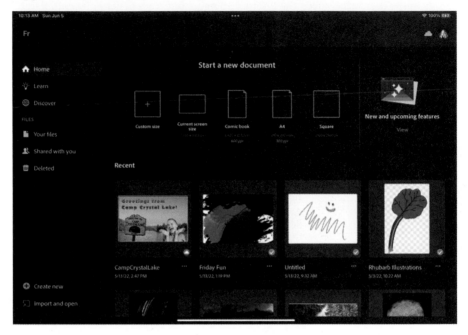

Fresco uses the exact same PSDC file format as Photoshop on the iPad and other versions of the software that leverage the cloud-based document format. Because of this, Fresco can open Photoshop files and files created in Fresco can be opened in Photoshop.

Photoshop on the Web (beta)

Adobe is expanding Photoshop to the web as well. Using a modern web browser, you can open and review Photoshop documents without having the software installed on your computer.

This is great for those running incompatible laptops or even Chromebooks, but keep in mind that Photoshop on the Web is primarily, at this point, designed for viewing and sharing Photoshop documents and is not intended to replace the desktop software.

Note You can view the system requirements for all versions of Photoshop by visiting https://helpx .adobe.com/photoshop/ system-requirements.html.

As of this writing, Photoshop on the Web is a beta release available only to a select segment of Creative Cloud subscribers. Adobe will open it up to additional segments as the beta progresses.

Working with raster images

You will likely come across two different terms when working with photographic images: raster and bitmap. Both terms refer to the types of images that Photoshop is primarily used to create and manipulate. These images are composed of individual pixels arranged in rows and columns to create a single, rectangular picture.

Note We'll compare raster images with vector graphics in Lesson 4.

Raster image at 100%

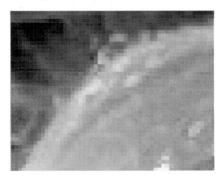

Raster image at 2500%

If you enlarge a raster image or zoom in very far in Photoshop or other imaging software, you will see the individual pixels that make up the image. It's a great little exercise to understand exactly what these images are composed of and how pixels are arranged to form a whole picture.

Manipulating photographic content

Let's dive into Photoshop and get familiar with some of the fundamental concepts of the software such as healing tools, layer management, brushing, and blend modes. We'll do so from a photo-centric perspective to start.

Opening an existing image file

Our first task involves the restoration and colorization of a black-and-white photograph. The first step is to open the existing image file in Photoshop.

1 With Photoshop running and the home screen active, choose File > Open from the application menu.

A file browser appears.

2 Browse to the Lesson03/03Start folder and locate the file named Grapes.jpg.

▶ **Tip** You can also open a file in Photoshop by dragging it onto the home screen from the system file browser.

3 Select the Grapes.jpg file and click Open.

The file opens in Photoshop and appears in the Document window.

Background layers

Whenever you open an existing photograph file such as a JPEG image in Photoshop, it will appear in the Layers panel as a locked Background layer.

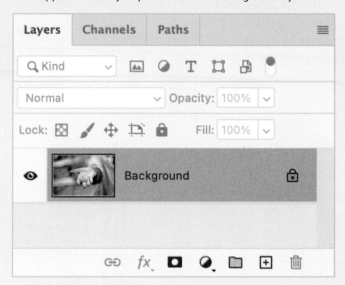

Since JPEG files never have more than a single layer, this layer is treated differently from additional layers you might create in Photoshop. The Background layer is always the bottommost layer, even if you add additional layers to a document, and many regular layer features are not available.

To unlock the layer, click the Lock icon 🔒 to dismiss it. This will make the image editable like a regular pixel layer. With the Background layer unlocked, you can do things like change its stacking order or use features like blend modes on it—just like any other layer.

The Photoshop interface

The Photoshop interface consists of windows and panels, all arranged in a meaningful way through the selection of multiple workspaces. Panels provide access to many of Photoshop's features like color selection, swatch libraries, adjustments, and brushes. Workspaces are different arrangements of panels geared toward certain tasks such as painting, photography, and web graphics.

You can change the current workspace by clicking the workspace switcher ▣ at the upper right and choosing a new one. You can also choose to reset your workspace to the saved layout if you move or close panels unintentionally.

The default workspace in Photoshop is the Essentials workspace. We will be using this workspace as we go through this lesson, so it would be a good idea to switch to it using the workspace switcher and choose Reset Essentials from the menu of available workspaces to ensure that everything appears as expected.

Tools panel — Options bar — Panels

Document window

Let's briefly examine the prominent interface items arranged in the Essentials workspace:

- **Document window:** This window displays the document you are working in. You can open multiple documents at once and switch the active document by using the tabs that appear along the top of this window.

- **Tools panel:** This panel contains the tools available for creating and editing images. Some tools are grouped together, as identified by a small triangle in the lower-right corner. You can access these by holding the mouse button down over a tool group to expose all the tools within.

  You can swap out the tools in the panel by clicking the Edit Toolbar icon ⋯ at the bottom of the panel.

- **Options bar:** Here you will find options for the currently selected tool. The options will change depending on the tool in use.

- **Panels:** A group of panels is stacked and arranged along the right side of the interface. Some of the most important panels we will use in this lesson are the Properties panel—which displays editable properties for selected layers—and the Layers panel—which enables layer creation and management.

You can enable additional panels by choosing the Window option from the application menu. If you ever find an arrangement of panels you particularly like, you can use the workspace switcher to create a new workspace that will then appear in the menu above the default ones.

Removing dust and scratches

The image file we've opened is the digital scan of a 35mm black-and-white film photograph taken in the mid-to-late 1990s. It features an outstretched hand holding an assortment of grapes.

Scratches and dust artifacts

Look over the image and notice there are scratches and dust across the photograph. We will remove these artifacts. Since the removal of artifacts is a destructive act, we want to preserve the original Background layer and work on a copy. That way, we can always return to or reference the original, untouched image.

1 Using the mouse, drag the Background layer from the Layers panel to the very bottom of the panel, where you will find a set of icons. Hover over the New Layer ⊞ icon and release the mouse button.

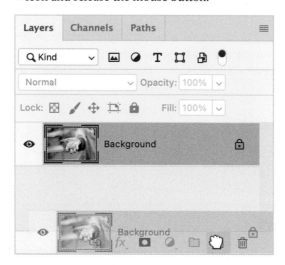

A copy of the original Background layer is created and appears at the top of the layer stack. By default, the layer is named Background copy.

2 Locate the Spot Healing Brush ✎. tool in the Tools panel and select it. This may be grouped along with similar tools like the Patch Tool. Click and hold on a tool group to see all the tools as part of any group.

3 In the Options bar above the Document window, ensure Type is set to Content-Aware and click the Brush Size ⁚₁₅ ˅ icon. Set the Size value to **30 px** in the overlay that appears.

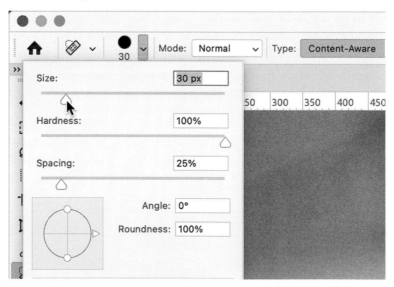

The overlay will disappear once you click anywhere outside of it or press the Escape key on your keyboard.

4 Ensure that the Background Copy layer is selected in the Layers panel and locate the long scratch visible in the lower-left quadrant of the image. Drag the Spot Healing Brush 🖊. tool across the scratch and release the mouse button to replace the scratch with pixels gathered from the Content-Aware spot healing process.

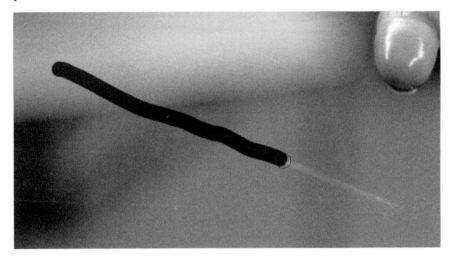

The scratch disappears.

5 Continue seeking out small scratches and dust particles across the rest of the image. Click the smaller ones and drag across larger ones to remove them in the same manner as we did the long scratch.

When you are finished, the photograph should be completely devoid of such imperfections.

● **Note** Content-Aware is a term in Photoshop that refers to the use of Adobe Sensei artificial intelligence processes available in the software to gather information across the image to intelligently replace the removed pixels through AI processes.

▶ **Tip** You can quickly increase or decrease the size of any active brush, including the Spot Healing brush, by pressing the square brackets ([ ]) on your keyboard

Improving a photograph through adjustment layers

While the levels and contrast of the photograph are not terrible as things appear right now, there is normally room for improvement in these areas.

We'll make some improvements to the appearance of the photograph by using adjustment layers.

● **Note** An adjustment layer will affect all layers that appear below it in the Layers panel by default.

1   At the very bottom of the Layers panel, locate and click the Create New Fill Or Adjustment Layer ◕ icon.

In the menu that appears, choose **Levels**.

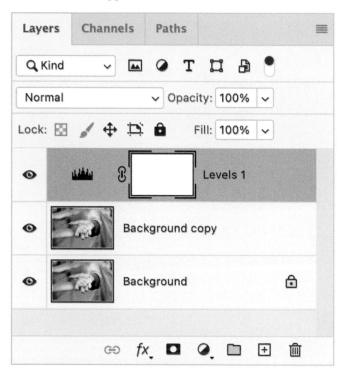

A new adjustment layer named Levels 1 is added to the top of the layer stack.

2 Select the adjustment icon in the Levels 1 layer if it isn't already selected. In the Properties panel, using the three sliders or associated text values beneath the histogram, set the Shadow input level on the left to 40 and the Highlight input level on the right to 238. Leave the center Midtone input value at **1.00**.

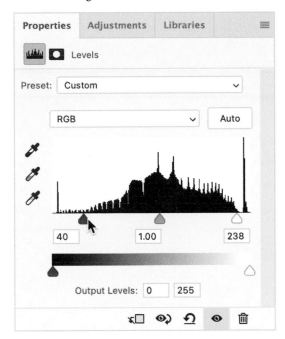

The image now exhibits a greater degree of contrast due to the Levels adjustments.

● **Note** Using adjustment layers is a completely nondestructive way of modifying your images. These layers can be hidden, have their properties modified, and be deleted altogether and the image itself remains unaffected.

Saving as a PSD file

A JPEG file is a flat image with only a single layer. Because we've added both a pixel layer and an adjustment layer to the original image, it can no longer be saved as a JPEG file without flattening the layers.

That is a destructive process, so we will save it as a Photoshop PSD file to keep all our layers intact as we continue our work.

1 Choose File > Save as from the application menu. A large dialog box appears, asking whether we want to save the file on our computer or save it as a cloud document. Ensure the file name is set to Grapes.psd in the Save As input at the top of the dialog.

A large dialog box appears, asking whether we want to save the file on our computer or save it as a cloud document.

Note Adobe wants you to know about the extra features enabled by saving a cloud document. They provide a nice rundown of the advantages in the save overlay; cloud syncing, autosave, versioning, and co-editing are all features available only when you save to the cloud.

2 Click Save On Your Computer.

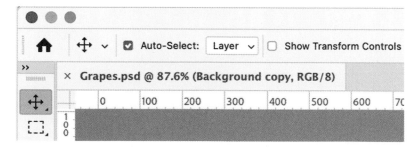

3 Choose Photoshop from the Format menu and navigate to the Lesson03/03Start folder. Click the Save button to save the file Grapes.psd to this location.

The document tab file information changes to reflect that the file is now a PSD—a Photoshop document capable of retaining layers along with many other features of the software.

Using brushes and managing color

With the photograph restored and enhanced, next we'll add a bit of color to the image by painting with brushes.

1 With the Levels 1 adjustment layer selected, click the New Layer ⊞ icon at the bottom of the Layers panel to create a new pixel layer at the top of the layer stack.

▶ **Tip** Transparency is often indicated by a grid of alternating white and gray squares. When you see this pattern, it is likely indicating transparency.

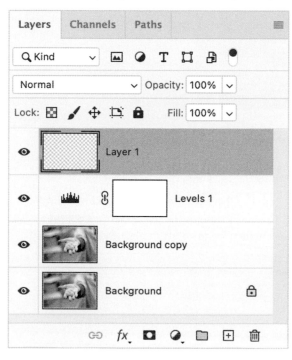

A new layer is created, filled with transparent pixels.

2 At the bottom of the Tools panel, you will find a cluster of color controls. Click the foreground color to activate the Color Picker.

● **Note** The default color choices are black as the foreground color and white as the background color. Most tools will use the foreground color.

3 In the Color Picker, select a green color suitable for the grapes. Enter **#6bda20** as the hex color value and click OK.

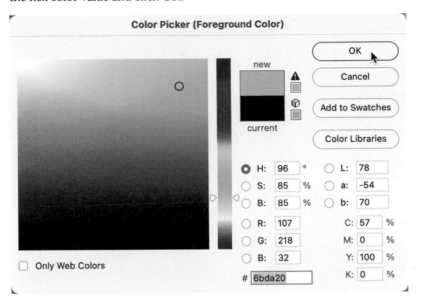

The foreground color is now set to the green color you selected.

4 Select the Brush Tool ✏. from the Tools panel and in the Options bar, click the Brush Size ⦂ icon. In the overlay that appears, select General Brushes > Soft Round and set the Size value to 60 px and adjust the Hardness value to 50%.

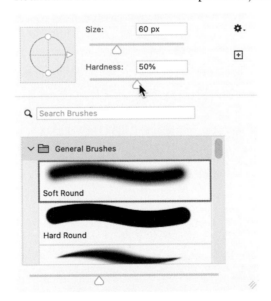

This will set the brush to a suitable size for coloring the grapes, and the edges of the brush will exhibit a medium hardness.

5 Zoom in to **350%** by entering that value into the zoom input at the bottom left of the interface.

6 Hold down the spacebar and drag across the image in the Document window to pan the image, setting the cluster of grapes in the center of your view.

▶ **Tip** Zooming and panning in this way gives you full control over the image and how you work on it with brushes and other tools.

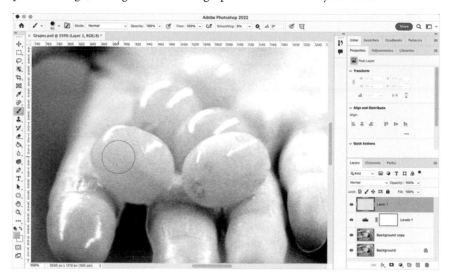

7 Ensure the new Layer 1 pixel layer is selected in the Layers panel and carefully drag across the grapes in order to paint green in the pixel layer.

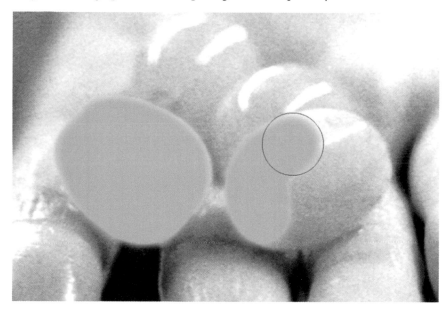

A thick green color now obscures the grapes beneath.

▶ **Tip** Sometimes, coloring a single object or portion of a black-and-white photograph can result in a very striking image. It isn't always necessary to colorize an entire photograph, depending on the project.

8 When finished painting over each grape, zoom back out to see the entire photograph.

The green color in Layer 1 completely obscures the grapes in the photographic layer below.

The colorization process doesn't look very realistic just yet, but we'll fix this in the next section.

Adjusting blend modes

Blend modes are a mechanism that determines how pixels in a layer above will blend and interact with pixels in layers below it. Many different blend modes are available in Photoshop.

We can use blend modes to blend the color we just painted into the photograph in a much more realistic and convincing way.

1 Ensure that the Layer 1 pixel layer containing the painted green color is selected in the Layers panel. At the top of the panel are sets of layer controls and settings. The blend mode is currently set to Normal, meaning that no blend mode is applied. Use the drop-down menu to change the blend mode to Soft Light.

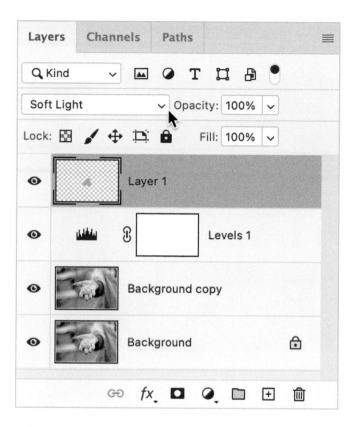

Soft Light works by either darkening or lightening the colors, based on the blend color.

2 Double-click the layer name to edit it. Rename the layer to **Grapes** and press Enter to commit the change.

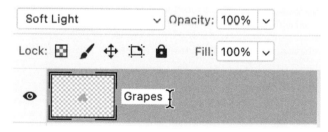

It is important to stay organized by naming your layers.

The grapes no longer look cartoonish but appear somewhat realistic in color. Against the remainder of the photograph, they stand out as an element of contrast and emphasis.

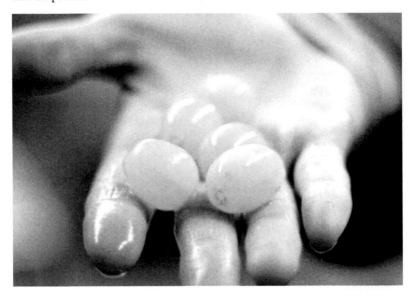

The addition of a blend mode has created a nuanced implementation of our brushed green color by blending in different ways with the pixels in the photograph, depending on their particular light or dark values.

Brushing, blend modes, and opacity adjustments

Let's use everything we've learned about layers, brushing, and blend modes to color the hand as well. We'll take the extra step of adjusting layer opacity.

1   Create a new layer by clicking the New Layer ⊞ icon at the bottom of the Layers panel.

2   Double-click the layer name and type **Hand** for the new name. Press Enter to commit the change.

3   Drag the Hand layer until it appears directly beneath the Grapes layer and release the mouse button.

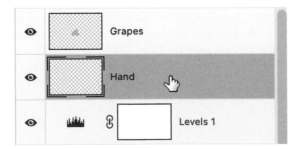

The grape cluster sits above the hand in the photograph, so it makes sense to move the hand color beneath as well.

4   Change the foreground color to a value of **#f4d9be**.

5   Select the Brush Tool ✏ from the Tools panel and paint the areas of the photo that make up the hand.

▶ **Tip** If you make any mistakes, you can always clean up stray pixels with the Eraser tool ✐ afterward.

▶ **Tip** When painting, be sure to zoom in and out as needed for precision, resizing your brush as necessary.

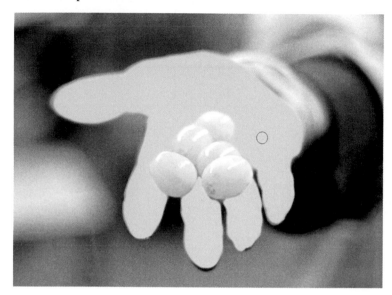

6   In the Layers panel, with the Hand layer selected, set the blend mode to Overlay and adjust the opacity to 50%.

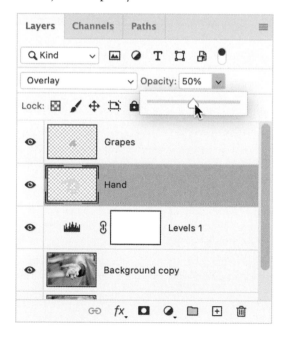

The Overlay blend mode works by multiplying or screening the colors based on the blend color and is perfect for preserving highlights and shadows. The effect is somewhat similar to what we saw with the Soft Light blend mode.

Lowering the layer opacity can help make the colorization more subtle than it would be otherwise. It's often a good idea to play with a combination of both settings for the ideal effect.

► **Tip** The more layers of differing colors you can add, the more realistic the photograph will appear. For instance, you could add in some slightly darker areas to the hand or some variance in the green used across the grapes with these techniques.

You may stop here or continue coloring in additional elements if desired using the same techniques.

Experiment with different blend modes to achieve a greater variety of effects with your own photographs.

Neural filters

Photoshop makes use of artificial intelligence in several ways. We saw an example of this earlier when healing scratches and dust by using Content-Aware settings with the Spot Healing Brush tool.

A set of special filters is available in recent versions of Photoshop called Neural Filters that also leverages AI in some rather spectacular ways. One of these filters enables automated colorization of an entire photograph.

To access this process, choose Filter > Neural Filters from the application menu and locate the Colorize filter in the list of neural filters. Activating the toggle switch will begin the colorization process.

While the colorization is automatic, you can make manual adjustments to influence the AI and produce different results.

Not a bad result! So why did we spend so much time in this lesson to colorize the manual way?

1   Giving a designer or artist complete control over the process allows more room for interpretation and the personal expression of creativity.

2   The traditional process is a great way to learn Photoshop basics: layer management, brushes, adjustment layers, opacity, and blend mode changes. You cannot learn these things by flipping a toggle switch!

Neural filters are somewhat experimental but hold a lot of promise as Adobe continues to improve existing filters and add new ones.

We'll explore more traditional filters later in this lesson.

Exporting as a JPEG file

A Photoshop PSD document is an authoring file, intended to be used by a designer as part of their workflow and not suitable for distribution.

To make our creation viewable by the general user, we'll need to export it in a standard image format.

1   Choose File > Export > Export As from the application menu.

The Export As dialog box appears. This is a special dialog box that enables full control over image export file formats and settings.

2   In the File Settings area on the right, choose JPG as the format.

You'll see many other settings that appear below this choice, all specific to the JPEG file format. We will leave them at the defaults.

3 Click Export in the lower right to open the Save dialog box.

4 In the Save dialog box, browse to a location on your computer to save the JPEG file and click Save.

You now have a JPEG file that can be shared on the web, via email, on social media, or anywhere that accepts standard digital image files.

Resampling raster images

Since we are dealing with raster images, we should make note of some pitfalls to avoid when using them. As we have seen, raster images are composed of rows and columns of pixels. If you resize the image, it must undergo a process called resampling since pixels must be removed or added to each affected row or column.

This isn't as big a deal if the image is resampled smaller, but if you resample a small image to a larger size, the software must make informed guesses as to which color to use on all the new pixels being added. Those guesses are often quite rough since the original data has been lost.

To illustrate this, there is an image file named TinyGrapes.jpg in the Lesson03/03Start folder. It is a version of the image we colorized earlier but resampled down to 250x164 pixels.

If we open this image in Photoshop and choose Image > Image Size, and then bring the width up to 4000 pixels and the height to 2624 pixels, you can see in the preview render exactly why this is a bad idea.

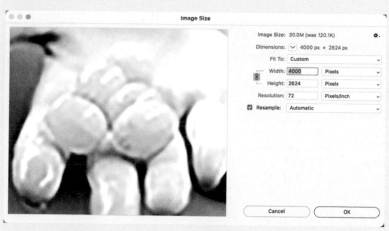

The image looks terrible because we are telling Photoshop to fill in thousands of additional pixels that simply are not present in the image. It uses the existing pixel data to estimate what colors these pixels should be.

The takeaway here is to only resample down and never up, if possible, and remember to always keep copies of your original images as a backup!

Designing a promotional image

The second project we'll be working through in this lesson is the design of a promotional image from a blank document instead of working with existing content as we've done previously.

We'll further solidify our use of layers, brushing, and other common features, and build on that through the use of selections, masking, text, filters, and more.

Creating a new document

▶ Tip If you're not creating a new document, you can open any existing cloud documents from the home screen sidebar by choosing your files. You can even access any photos you have collected in Adobe Lightroom in the cloud by choosing Lightroom photos.

We'll begin by creating a new document from a preset and saving it to our computer.

1   On the Photoshop home screen, click the New File button.

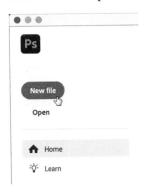

The New Document dialog box appears.

2   From the categories along the top, choose Art & Illustration to view the presets in that category.

3   Select the Poster preset and enter **GarlicPoster** for the document name. Click Create.

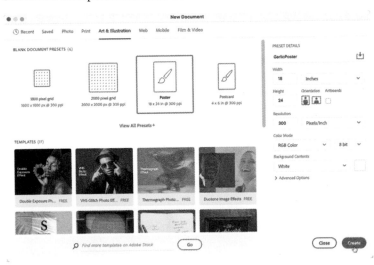

A new document appears in Photoshop that matches the Poster preset specifications of 18x24 inches and 300 pixels per inch—a large enough document to design at high resolution.

4 Let's save the new document. Choose File > Save As from the application menu.

5 Photoshop will offer to save your document to the cloud. Click the On Your Computer button to proceed.

6 In the dialog box that appears, click the Save On Your Computer button.

7 A file browser appears. Choose Photoshop from the Format menu and navigate to the Lesson03/03Start folder.

8 Click the Save button to save the file **GarlicPoster.psd** to this location.

▶ **Tip** When you're creating any raster-based document, it's a good idea to never use a pixels-per-inch setting below 300ppi. This is considered a dense enough setting for print, but you can create smaller, derivative images from this file for screens as well. If you begin at 72ppi, and then find later you need a 300ppi document, things will be much harder for you.

Setting up the background

We'll begin building up the design of our promotional document by laying down a nice gradient background.

1 In the toolbar, choose the Gradient Tool ▢. If the Gradient Tool is not visible, click and hold the Paint Bucket Tool ⬧. to reveal other tools grouped along with it—including the Gradient Tool.

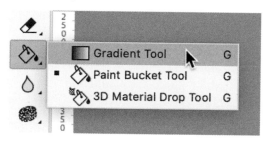

2 In the Options bar, ensure that the linear gradient option is selected, and from the gradient menu select a gradient swatch.

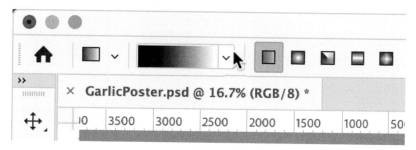

A swatch selection overlay appears.

3 Open the Greens folder and locate the Green_18 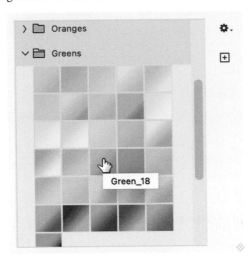 swatch. Click it to set the gradient to this swatch.

The overlay disappears and the selected swatch is now displayed in the gradient menu.

4 In the Document window, drag from the top area of the document to the bottom area.

Photoshop fills the document background with the Green_18 swatch as a linear gradient from bottom to top.

The green colors we've chosen are similar to the colors of fresh garlic sprouts.

Importing image files

We'll populate the promotional image with photographs taken of children holding garlic aloft in admiration.

1 Choose File > Place Embedded from the application menu.

2 If an overlay appears, click the On My Computer button. If it does not appear, a system-level file browser opens.

3 Select the file named Garlic_01.jpg in the Lesson03/03Start folder and click Place.

Note Whether or not the cloud versus local file decision overlay appears depends on what you chose the last time you attempted to place an image. If you have recently placed a local file, this overlay will not appear again during your Photoshop session.

Photoshop places the embedded image in the center of the document.

● **Note** A *smart object* is a layer that contains image data and that enables nondestructive editing since you are editing the container object and not the original pixels.

4 Scale the embedded image up a bit using the transform handles and reposition it so that the wrist emerges from the lower-right of the document.

Click the Commit Transform ✓ checkmark in the Options bar or double-click the image to proceed with these changes and complete the image placement.

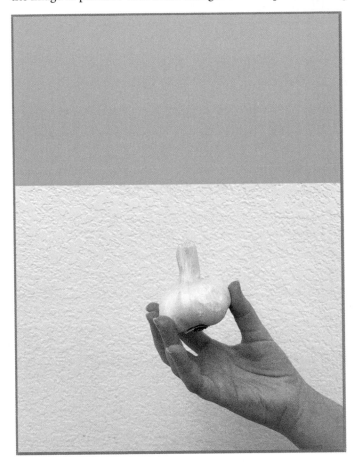

The embedded image is placed in a smart object 🗔.

5 Once more, choose File > Place Embedded from the application menu.

A system-level file browser appears.

6 Select the file named Garlic_02.jpg in the Lesson03/03Start folder and click Place.

Again, Photoshop places the embedded image in the center of the document.

7 Scale the embedded image up a bit using the transform handles if necessary and reposition it so that the wrist emerges from the center-left of the document.

Click the Commit Transform checkmark in the Options bar to proceed with these changes and complete the image placement.

You now have two similar photographs placed in the document, though the background of each image currently obscures the document background.

Masking imported content

We need to remove the pixels that make up the background of the imported photographs to better compose the promotional image. We can do this by masking out those undesirable areas.

1 Select the Garlic_02 layer and choose Layer > Rasterize > Smart Object from the application menu.

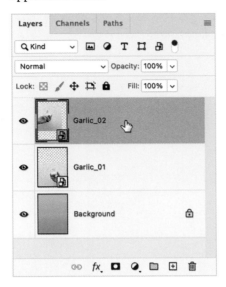

The layer is currently a smart object. Since we need to be able to interact with the original image data pixels to remove the background, we must rasterize it first.

With the layer converted to a simple pixel layer, we can now remove the background with a mask.

2 In the Properties panel, scroll down to Quick Actions and click Remove Background.

Photoshop will detect which pixels make up the image background and mask them out by applying a pixel mask to the layer.

3 Perform these same steps for the Garlic_01 layer so that both layers are rasterized with their backgrounds removed by the Remove Background Quick Action.

It's likely that the Remove Background process will make some errors in masking the content. This is expected, and we can further refine the mask to correct any imperfections in the next steps.

Adjusting a pixel mask

The Remove Background Quick Action does a good job of removing the background from the placed image, but it isn't perfect.

We'll now refine the pixel mask.

1 Click the black-and-white mask thumbnail in the Garlic_02 layer to select it.

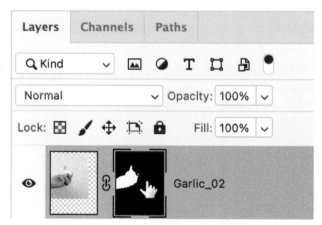

2 Choose the Brush Tool ✏. from the Tools panel and set the foreground color to white (**#FFFFFF**).

▶ **Tip** Brushing pure white across a mask will reveal content, whereas brushing with pure black will mask content. Shades of gray will mask content in accordance with how close to pure white or pure black the gray value is.

3 Brush over those portions of the image that were masked incorrectly to return those areas to a visible state.

4 Perform mask cleanup to the Garlic_01 layer mask as well, if necessary. Pay special attention to the space between fingers; you may need to zoom in and adjust the brush size to clean that space properly.

Once you've cleaned up the masks, the hands and garlic should stand out nicely against the green background.

5   Select the Move tool ✛. and use it to reposition the images so that they are closer to one another, assembled toward the bottom of the document.

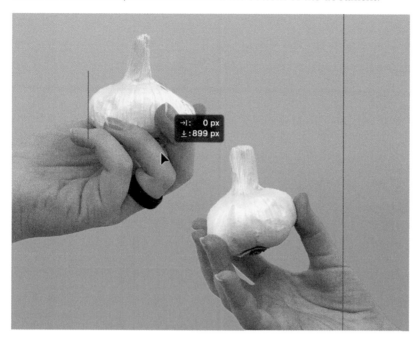

This will leave plenty of room at the top for a promotional title and additional text elements.

Adding text to your design

With our images in place and properly masked, now we'll add in some text elements to help identify and promote the garlic festival.

1   Select the Horizontal Type tool **T**. from the Tools panel and click in the upper area of the document to create a text layer.

Type **Garlic Festival** and press Esc.

Now we have a new text layer in the layer stack created as point text.

● **Note** You create *point text* by clicking and then typing your text content. The text object expands based on the amount of text in it.

▶ **Tip** Double-click the
T thumbnail in any text
layer to edit the text
easily.

2 Select the new text layer in the Layers panel. If it is not located at the top of the
layer stack, drag it into that position.

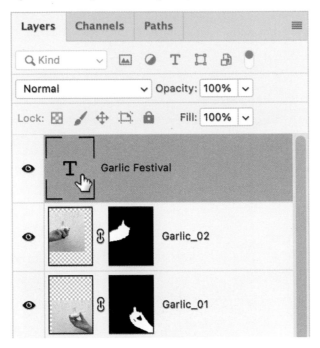

● **Note** The Strenuous
font is part of the
Adobe Fonts collection
that you can access at
https://fonts.adobe.com
as part of your Creative
Cloud subscription.

3 In the Properties panel, in the Character section, set the font to **Strenuous Cast**,
or use any other font that you find interesting. Adjust the size value to 140 pt and
set Color to **#592401**.

4 Select the Horizontal Type tool from the Tools panel and drag in the empty space below the title we previously created, making sure not to overlap any of the images.

● **Note** You can create paragraph text by dragging to establish a defined width and then typing your text content. The text object will not expand automatically but rather adheres to the predetermined width.

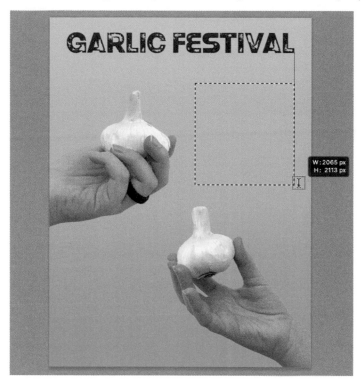

An additional text layer is created in the layer stack as paragraph text.

5 Type **Wednesday Only Join us for a celebration of everything that makes garlic... GREAT!** in the text area and press Esc.

The text takes on much of the appearance of our previous text element and does not completely fit in the text object we've created.

Modifying text properties

Unlike the title text for our promotional image, the additional informative text will take on several stylistic changes in the same text object.

1 Select all the text in the text layer you just created by double-clicking the T for that layer in the Layers panel.

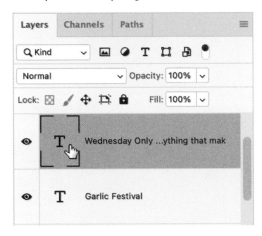

2 Set the font size to 36 pt in the Properties panel so that all the text appears in the text object and becomes manageable.

3 Click the right-align icon ≣ to right-align the text.

4   Insert a line break after "Wednesday Only" by pressing the Enter (Windows) or Return (macOS) key and insert another line break after "Join us for a celebration of everything that makes garlic..." to create three paragraphs in the text object.

These line breaks enable us to apply both character and paragraph style adjustment to each paragraph separately.

5   Drag across the text "Wednesday Only" to select it. In the Properties panel, set the font to **Europa-Bold** and set the Size value to 67 pt.

● **Note** The Europa font family is part of the Adobe Fonts collection that you can access at https://fonts.adobe.com as part of your Creative Cloud subscription.

6 Now, drag across the text "Join us for a celebration of everything that makes garlic..." to select it. Set the font to **Europa-Light** and set the Size value to 58 pt.

Set the space before 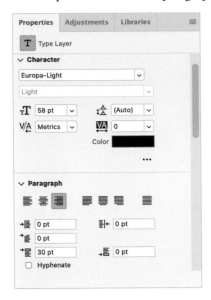 the paragraph to 30 pt.

7 Finally, drag across the final paragraph that reads "GREAT!" to select it. Set the font to **Europa-Regular** and set the Size value to 58 pt.

Set the space before the paragraph to 30 pt. You may need to adjust the size of your text object if these adjustments make your text too large for the text object you created.

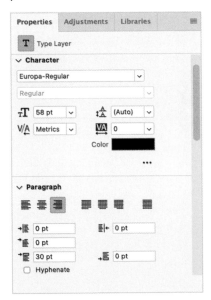

All three paragraphs of text now share certain features, but all appear slightly different from one another. Each paragraph includes enough space between to allow for them all to be easily digestible to the viewer.

Design principle: negative space

Negative space refers to the areas either between or around visual images or text objects as part of a design. It is sometimes referred to as white space.

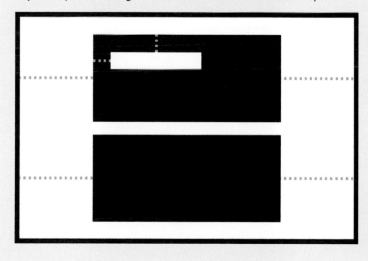

Negative space is just as important as the space populated with objects in your design. If you are careless with your use of negative space, it will have a detrimental effect on the final product. Generally, you should always include plenty of room for your design elements to exist in. Cramming elements together often makes for poor design.

In our promotional design, we have included plenty of negative space around all visual elements and have included space between paragraphs in our text layout as well.

Adding an anchoring shape

The "Garlic Festival" title is just sort of floating at the top of the design right now. We can add a shape behind the text to serve as an anchoring element, which will also increase the contrast and provide more visual weight to the title.

1 Choose the Rectangle tool ⬜. from the Tools panel and drag from the upper-left corner of the document across the width and below the title text to draw a rectangle that has the same space above the text as below it. Release the mouse button.

Photoshop creates a rectangular shape at the top of the layer stack.

2 In the Layers panel, drag the Rectangle 1 layer you just created from the top of the stack to just beneath the Garlic Festival text layer. Release the mouse button to reorder the layers.

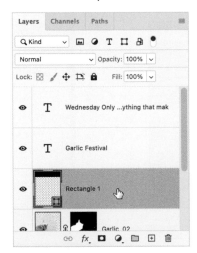

The rectangular shape now appears behind the title text.

3 Select the Rectangle 1 layer in the Layers panel and change the Fill color to white (**#FFFFFF**) in the Appearance section of the Properties panel. Ensure the Stroke color is set to None.

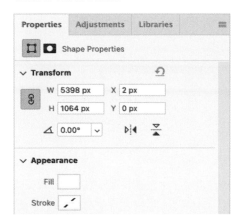

This change in color is reflected in the document.

4 With the Rectangle 1 layer still selected, use the blend mode menu at the top of the Layers panel to change the blend mode to **Soft Light**.

Adjust the Opacity slider so that the Rectangle 1 layer exhibits an opacity value of 60%.

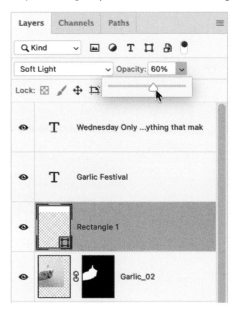

The addition of the rectangular shape successfully anchors the promotional title to the overall design. It blends nicely with the gradient background thanks to our opacity and blend mode adjustments.

Adding a decorative shape

The final asset we'll add to the promotional image is a decorative shape to balance things out in the lower-left corner.

1   Click and hold the Rectangle tool 🔲. to view other tools grouped along with it and choose the Custom Shape tool ✄..

2 In the Options bar, ensure Fill and Stroke are set to black (#000000). Open the shape selection overlay and click Shape 50 in the Flowers folder.

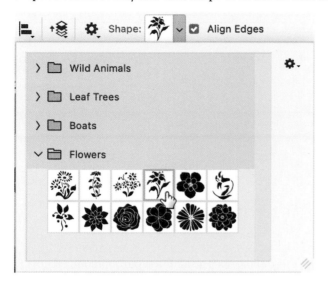

Shape 50 looks like a wild garlic plant that is flowering.

3 With the Shift key pressed, drag across the bottom-left corner of the document. Release the mouse button to create the new floral shape.

The shape is rendered in the lower corner, helping to balance out other elements of the composition.

4 Finally, to blend everything together a bit better, select the new Shape 50 1 layer in the Layers panel and set the blend mode to Overlay.

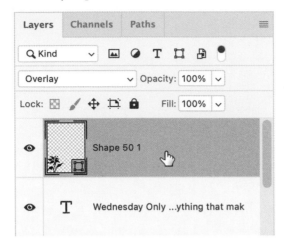

The shape blends well with the gradient background and our promotional image design is complete.

Exporting as a PNG file

We'll now export our promotional design as a PNG file for distribution across social media.

1   Choose File > Export > Export As from the application menu.

The Export As dialog box appears.

2   In the File Settings area on the right, choose PNG as the format and deselect the Transparency option, since no portion of this design is transparent (though the PNG format does allow for it, unlike the JPEG format).

3   Because we are targeting the web and various social channels, we need to resize the design on output. In the Image Size section, change the width to 2000 pixels, which shrinks the output file to **37%** of the original size.

4   Click Export.

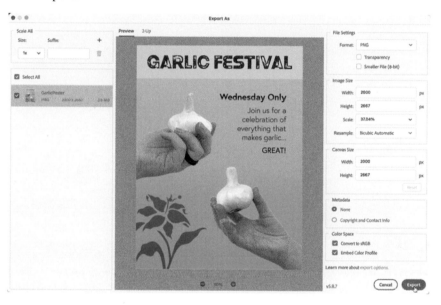

● **Note** You can produce a great variety of sizes from the original PSD file because we designed it to adhere to a large format preset and specified a high-quality 300 ppi document when we began. It is always better to create a design that is larger than you may need since it is so simple to produce smaller versions from it.

5   A file browser appears, allowing you to specify the location and name of the file before clicking Save.

Next steps with Photoshop

To further explore the creative options that Photoshop has to offer, you can make use of Adobe's help resources available at https://helpx.adobe.com/support/photoshop.html.

If you'd like to advance in your exploration of Photoshop, I encourage you to consider reading *Adobe Photoshop Classroom in a Book (2023 Release)*, also available from Peachpit and Adobe Press.

Review questions

1   What is an ideal tool for removing imperfections like dust or scratches from a photograph?

2   What are the keyboard shortcuts for changing brush sizes without having to use the user interface?

3   What do blend modes do?

4   When you're applying a mask, which color obscures the layer content—black or white?

5   When working with text layers, is it possible to create complex stylistic paragraph and character choices all in a single layer?

6   What is the minimum recommended pixels-per-inch setting that you should apply to a new Photoshop document?

Review answers

1 The Spot Healing Brush tool best serves this purpose.

2 The square bracket keys, [ ], can be used to quickly shift brush sizes up or down as you work.

3 Blend modes determine how the colors of pixels in the selected layer will interact with and influence pixels in lower layers.

4 Black obscures and white reveals.

5 Yes. When you select certain characters of your text, you can modify the attributes for only those characters or attributes for the entire paragraph that the selection is a part of.

6 300 ppi is the recommended setting.

4 DESIGNING VECTOR GRAPHICS WITH ILLUSTRATOR

Lesson overview

In this lesson, you'll learn how to do the following:

- Understand the benefits and drawbacks of working with vector graphics.

- Create a new document and manage artboards.

- Create vector shapes and modify their appearance.

- Combine shapes to form complex design elements.

- Work with text and modify type attributes.

- Reuse assets across artboards.

- Understand the design principle of repetition.

- Save and export to different formats.

 This lesson will take 1 hour to complete.

To get the files used in this lesson, download them from the web page for this book at www.adobepress.com/CreativeCloudCIB. For more information, see "Accessing the lesson files and Web Edition" in the Getting Started section at the beginning of this book.

Adobe Illustrator is a vector graphics drawing and design application that is ideal for creating logos, labels, packaging assets, or even creative vector artwork. Because everything you draw in Illustrator is vector based, it is all infinitely scalable.

Getting started

● **Note** If you have not already downloaded the project files for this lesson to your computer from your Account page, make sure to do so now. See "Getting Started" at the beginning of the book.

Start by viewing the finished project to see what you'll be creating in this lesson.

1 Browse to the Lesson04/04End folder to view the results of the project you'll complete in this lesson.

logo.pdf
PDF document - 354 KB

You will find the Illustrator authoring file here alongside PDF and PNG files generated from one of the artboards available in the AI file.

2 Open whichever file you wish.

The project is a vector logo for Bad Beans Coffee Roasters. We'll draw, assemble, and make use of many elements to design the final logo throughout this lesson.

3 Close the file.

Understanding Illustrator

While Illustrator on desktop is still the most widely used version of the software, you can also use Illustrator on the iPad. Storing documents in the cloud allows designers to easily work on the same file on both desktop and mobile devices.

Additionally, we'll examine the important differences between raster images and vector graphics.

Illustrator for desktop

One of Adobe's oldest pieces of software, Illustrator is revered as an essential application for most designers to master. Illustrator uses vector graphics to draw and edit assets with a large variety of tools and panels that have accumulated over the years.

Like nearly every Adobe desktop application, Illustrator for desktop can be installed on Windows or macOS. We'll focus on Illustrator for desktop in this lesson.

Illustrator for iPad

Still relatively new, Illustrator for iPad uses the same file format as the desktop version but allows for a much more natural way of designing vector graphics through use of a touch interface and Apple Pencil.

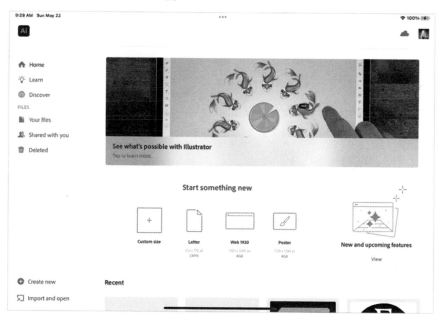

● **Note** You can view the system requirements for all versions of Illustrator by visiting https://helpx.adobe .com/illustrator/ system-requirements.html.

While Illustrator on iPad does not support every feature available in the desktop version, Adobe has thoughtfully adapted the features it does provide to a mobile interface, making good use of the iPad's capabilities and hardware.

Vector vs. raster

In the previous lesson on Adobe Photoshop, we dealt purely with raster images. Raster graphics (also commonly known as bitmap) are composed of individual pixels arranged in rectangular formation of rows and columns to create a single picture.

In fact, the term "pixel" is a shortened form of "picture element." Raster image resolution is specified by number of pixels in width and height. This image type is perfect for representing photographic content because it is capable of displaying millions of colors in a very realistic way.

One of the drawbacks to using raster images, however, is that they cannot be resized without either loss or addition of pixels. This process, called *resampling*, leads to all sorts of issues when you're performing such a procedure—especially apparent when you're enlarging an image.

Additionally, scaling up a raster image or zooming in on it will expose the illusion that it is a single picture image by revealing the individual pixels that make up the whole.

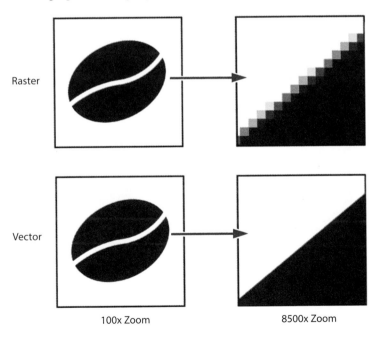

Raster

Vector

100x Zoom   8500x Zoom

Vector graphics, on the other hand, are purely mathematical in nature, composed of paths and anchor points taking up an infinite variety of possible shapes.

When you view a vector graphic, a vector graphics editor like Illustrator will visually redraw it any time you adjust its properties. This allows for infinite scalability, as zooming into or enlarging a vector graphic simply causes it to be redrawn. Rescaling preserves the sharpness of the graphic since no resampling needs to take place as with a raster image.

Because of this, vector graphics are well suited to design assets that need to be commonly represented at different sizes such as icons, logos, and really any design assets intended for multi-resolution use. Vector designs are also an excellent choice for printed material for the same reasons.

However, using vectors to represent photographic data creates incredibly complex designs that are processor-intensive to render. As explained earlier in this lesson, that type of content is best left to raster image formats as they are intended for such use and they take very little processing power to display.

First steps in Illustrator

Now that you have a basic understanding of what Illustrator can do and what vector graphics are, let's create a new document and start exploring some of what the software has to offer.

Creating a new document

We'll begin by creating a new Illustrator document and saving it as an Illustrator file that uses the .ai extension.

1   On the start screen, click the New File button.

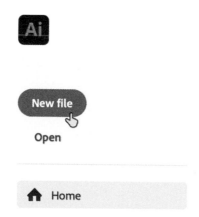

The New Document dialog box appears.

2 Click the Print category to select it and then choose Letter from the grid of presets that appears.

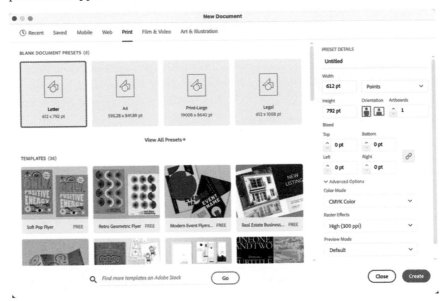

The Letter preset indicates a standard 8.5 x 11-inch page of paper.

3 Along the right side of the dialog box is the Preset Details panel. Make the following adjustments:

- Enter Branding as the document name.

- Change the units to **Inches** as this is likely more familiar to most people when dealing with print than the default unit of Points.

- Ensure the Raster Effects setting is set to **High (300 ppi)** so that any raster effects are applied to the elements we create. This ensures that they will be rendered appropriate for print purposes.

4 Click the Create button once finished.

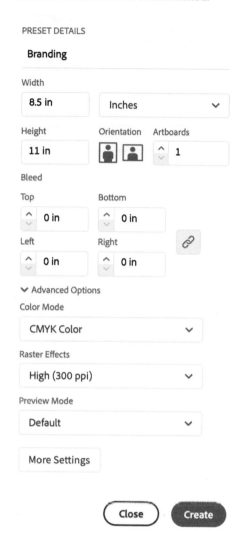

The document appears and exhibits the details you entered in the dialog box.

5 To save the new document, choose File > Save from the application menu.

A dialog box appears.

6 Click Save On Your Computer.

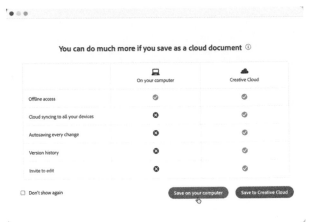

A system file browser appears.

7 The file is already named **Branding.ai** because we named the document Branding when creating it from a preset. Browse to the Lesson04/04Start folder and click Save.

The Illustrator Options dialog box appears.

8 Choose **Illustrator 2020** from the Version menu and click OK to save the file.

● **Note** The Illustrator Options dialog box lets you choose file versions going back decades. Why? Because many print shops have standardized specific versions for compatibility purposes and will require your documents to target the same version.

You are then taken back to your document in Illustrator.

Cloud-based Illustrator documents

When we saved our new file, we chose Save On Your Computer to store it as a local file. Of course, the other option is to save it as a cloud-based file.

You can tell a cloud-based file from a local one in Illustrator by looking at the document tabs at the top of the interface. A cloud-based document includes a small cloud icon in front of the document name and uses the .aic file extension.

> ✕ ☁ **Branding.aic @ 52.18 % (CMYK/Preview)**

There are many benefits to using a cloud-based document in Illustrator:

1 Document sync: The document exists on remote servers, which means you can work on it from anywhere you have access to Illustrator through your Adobe ID.

2 Autosave: The document is saved to the cloud automatically as changes are made.

3 Versioning: It saves a document version history as you work.

4 Co-editing: You can invite other Illustrator users to contribute to or comment on your document.

Whether you make use of these features on your own is completely up to you. However, if you want to edit the same documents on an iPad, you must use cloud-based documents.

The Illustrator interface

Now that we have a new document created, saved, and ready to work on, let's take a look at some of the important parts of the Illustrator UI.

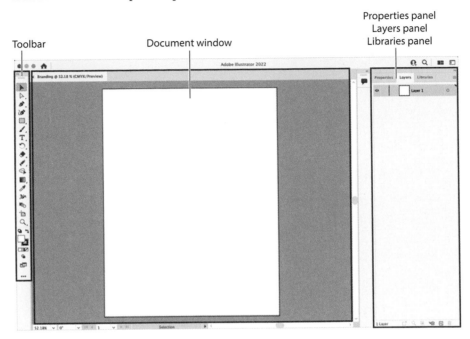

We're using the Essentials workspace since it's the default in Illustrator. If you need to switch from another workspace or reset your workspace, you can do so from the workspace switcher ⬚ in the upper-right corner of the UI.

The Essentials workspace provides you with a set of important tools in the toolbar and a number of important panels grouped along the right side of the interface.

Here are some of the important interface elements you should know:

- Document window: Your artboards exist in this window, and it serves as a canvas for your designs. Illustrator allows you to have multiple documents open at once and switch between them through a tabbed interface at the top of this window.

- Toolbar: Located along the left side of the interface, the toolbar houses many tools you can use as you design vector assets. You can access additional tools by clicking Edit Toolbar ⋯ at the bottom of the toolbar.

- Properties panel: You can adjust the properties of selected objects by accessing this extremely useful panel. If no objects are selected, you can access the document properties from here.

- Layers panel: In this panel you manage document layers and access the objects nested within each layer.

- Libraries panel: This provides access to your Creative Cloud Libraries and the design assets within.

Of course, you can access additional panels from the Window application menu at any time.

Managing artboards

In our project we currently have a document with a single artboard. During the course of this lesson, we'll create a number of design assets and organize each in different artboards.

Let's refine and duplicate our existing artboard.

1 Select the Artboard tool ⬚ from the toolbar.

The existing artboard in the Document window exhibits the artboard name and a transform rectangle that allows us to adjust the width and height.

2 To begin making precise adjustments to the artboard, switch to the Properties panel if necessary and change the width to 5 in and the height to 5 in. To rename the artboard, enter **Scratch** in the Name field.

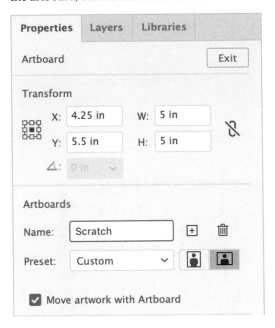

The artboard in the Document window adapts to show the changes.

3 Next, to create an additional artboard, click the New Artboard icon ⊞ in the Properties panel and change the name to **Logo**.

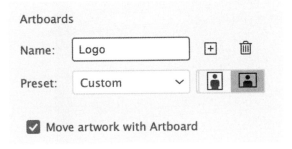

The width and height remain the same.

4 Using the Selection tool ▶, deselect the artboards.

▶ **Tip** You can easily navigate from one artboard to another by using the Artboard Navigation ◄◄ ▸ ▾ ▸▸◀ controls at the bottom of the Document window.

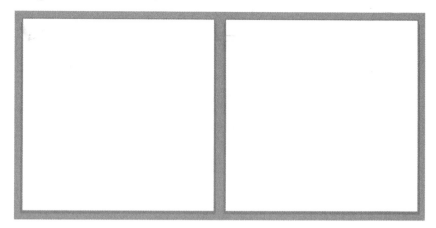

We now have two distinct artboards within the document. One will serve as a scratchpad to create rough elements, and the other we'll use for the completed logo design.

Drawing simple vector shapes

To get started, let's explore drawing a shape in the Scratch artboard, since this artboard is meant to be a playground more than anything else.

1 Click and hold the Rectangle tool ▭, in the toolbar to view the various shape tools that are available.

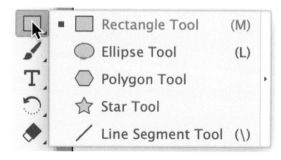

You can choose from a variety of shapes.

2 Choose Ellipse Tool ◯, from the menu.

The Ellipse tool replaces the Rectangle tool in the toolbar.

3 Using the Ellipse tool, drag in the Scratch artboard but do not release the mouse button yet.

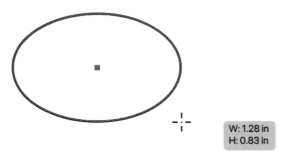

Notice that as you draw the ellipse shape, continuing to drag the mouse up, down, left, or right changes the size and shape of the ellipse.

Additionally, width and height information appears in a small overlay.

4 Hold down the Shift key as you continue dragging to lock both width and height, creating a perfect circle.

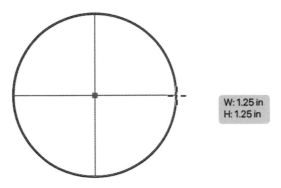

5 Release the Shift key to create the ellipse when the informational overlay reads **1.25in** in width and height.

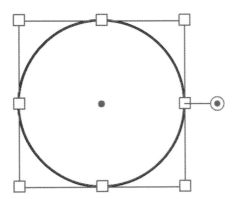

Transform handles appear on the shape. You can use these handles to modify different shape properties.

Tip Pressing the Shift key will work with the Rectangle tool as well, creating a perfect square. In fact, this works with any shape-building tool.

Placing a guide image

For our logo, we need to replicate the image of a stylized coffee bean in vector format. But all we have right now is a low-quality, pixelated raster image.

You will use this raster image as a guide as you create the vector shapes.

1 In the application menu, choose File > Place.

A file browser dialog box appears.

2 Locate the file named guide.jpg in the Lesson04/04Start folder and select it. Ensure the Link option is deselected. Click Place to continue.

 1/1

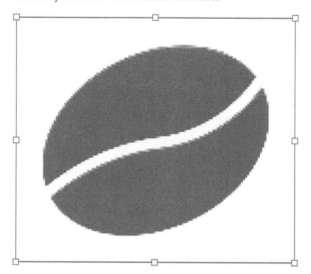

A preview of the image appears alongside the mouse cursor, indicating that you can drag it to specify a size for placement. You can also click anywhere to place the artwork at its native size.

3 Click anywhere in the Scratch artboard.

Tip You may want to use the Selection tool to adjust the image position to the artboard's vertical and horizontal center. Smart guides will appear, indicating correct placement.

Illustrator places the raster image file on the artboard at its native size.

Designing vector assets

While drawing shapes like rectangles and ellipses is a simple task, drawing more complex shapes requires the use of a more complex set of tools.

We are going to use the Pen tool to trace over the raster image of the coffee bean and create custom vector shapes. We'll then use the Direct Selection tool to refine rough shapes into a clean, vector version of the imported raster image.

Using the Pen tool

The Pen tool enables you to create custom vector shapes through the use of anchor points, anchor handles, and paths.

1 Select the Pen tool ✎ from the toolbar.

2 Position it over the bottom-right corner of the top coffee bean segment.

This will be the point where you start drawing the top of the coffee bean.

3 Click and drag toward the right of the bean so that the handles that emerge from the anchor point you are creating somewhat line up with the curve of the coffee bean.

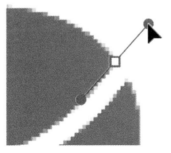

The opposing handle will extend out along with your mouse cursor. If you were to release the mouse button now, you would create a smooth anchor point.

4 Hold down the Option (Windows) or Alt (macOS) key to break the handles and allow for a change in direction. Reposition the mouse cursor to a point up and along the top of the coffee bean and release the mouse button to create an initial corner anchor point.

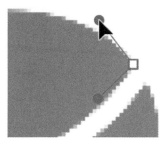

Your first anchor point is established along with directional anchor handles that will influence the curve and direction of the subsequent paths you create.

5 Move the mouse cursor to the opposite side of the coffee bean so that it rests atop the other sharp corner.

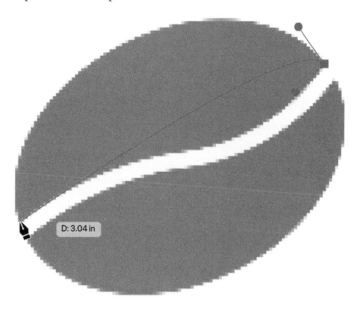

● **Note** Don't worry if the paths you are drawing don't exactly match the curve of the coffee bean—you can adjust the vector paths later. The important thing during this process is to establish a set of anchor points and get a basic direction for each of the anchor handles.

A preview path is generated, showing you what the curve of the path currently looks like.

Note Now that we have an actual path created, the fill and stroke are visible on the path as appearance settings. The default appearance is a white fill and a black stroke.

6   Drag toward the bottom of the bean so that the handles that emerge from the anchor point you are creating point roughly up and down along the side of the coffee bean. Then hold down the Option/Alt key to change direction of the bottommost handle toward the right. Release the mouse button to create a corner anchor point.

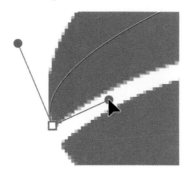

You now have two anchor points and a path between them.

7   Drag from the center of the wavy part along the bottom of the top half of the coffee bean so that opposing handles emerge from the anchor point positioned parallel to the bottom of the shape. Release the mouse button to create a smooth anchor point.

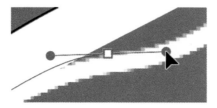

You don't need to specify a change in direction for these handles.

8   Return the mouse cursor to rest above the first anchor point and drag to pull a handle toward the left, completing a closed path.

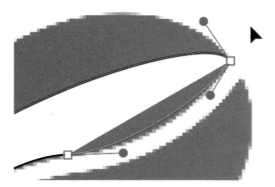

You have now completed a shape to represent the top half of the coffee bean.

The shape you just created likely looks very rough at this point, and the curves do not match the curves of the underlying guide image unless you are well practiced with this tool. No worries—we'll make it perfect in the next exercise!

Using the Pen tool

The Pen tool is one of the more complicated tools to use effectively. But once you get a feel for it and understand some of its nuances, it becomes very powerful.

Here are some things to remember:

1 Simply clicking with the Pen tool will create anchor points without handles. This is how you go about forming straight lines from one point to the next.

2 Dragging, on the other hand, will pull out handles from the anchor point that are directionally opposite from one another, creating a curve.

3 The longer a handle is, the more intense the curve will be.

4 Pressing the Option/Alt key while dragging will break the connection between opposing handles, allowing you to adjust direction to influence the curve.

5 Clicking the original anchor point will close the path.

6 Since we are creating vector paths, it's okay if things are not perfect as you create a shape. You can modify the path and make it look exactly as you intend after you complete it.

As with many things, the more you practice, the more natural the use of this tool will become.

Modifying anchor points and handles

Your shape probably looks very dissimilar to a coffee bean right now—especially if you're just getting started with the Pen tool. As mentioned earlier, that's fine! We have the anchor points and handles in place, and all it takes is some slight modifications to line up everything on the guide image.

1 Choose the Direct Selection tool ▷ from the toolbar and click the shape to view the path along with its anchor points.

▶ **Tip** Clicking an individual anchor point will select it.

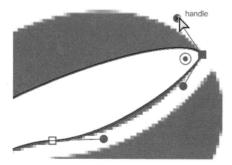
handle

2 Adjust the direction and length of each anchor point handle to make the shape better conform to the guide below it.

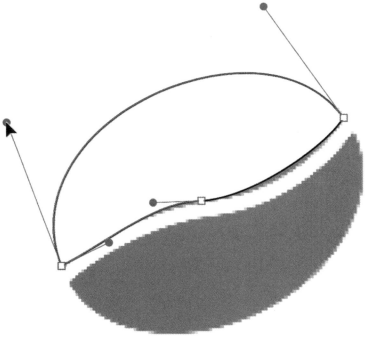

▶ **Tip** You can also drag anchor points to reposition them more accurately or select them and use the arrow keys on your keyboard to nudge them.

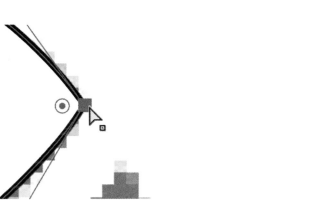

A combination of tweaking anchor point position, handle direction, and the length of each handle in this way will allow you to perfect the shape.

3 Keep tweaking the anchor points with the Direct Selection tool ▷ until everything lines up with the underlying raster guide image.

▶ **Tip** Try to use as few anchor points as possible when defining a shape. With fewer points to deal with, you'll find it much easier to adjust the overall paths than if you had more points in your shape.

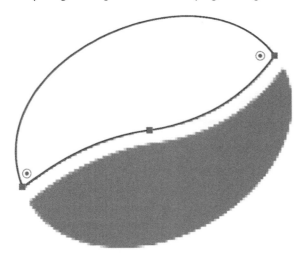

Now the top half of the coffee bean should be aligned precisely over the image guide.

Duplicating shapes

With the top portion of the coffee bean created, you'll duplicate it and use that copy for the bottom portion.

1 Using the Selection tool ▶, hold down the Option/Alt key on your keyboard and drag the shape you just created. This creates an exact copy of the object, and the mouse cursor changes to display a double cursor ▶, indicating what is happening. Release the mouse button.

▶ **Tip** You can also use copy and paste (Ctrl/ Cmd+C, Ctrl/Cmd+V) to perform this action and achieve the same result.

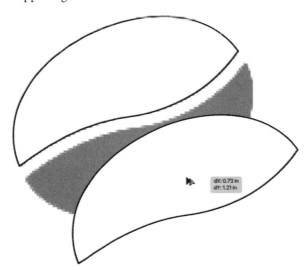

2 Click the new shape to select it and hover your mouse near any of the corners of the transform rectangle until a double-header arrow appears. Drag to rotate the shape 180 degrees.

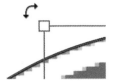

3 Drag the shape copy to position it as best you can atop the lower half of the raster image guide.

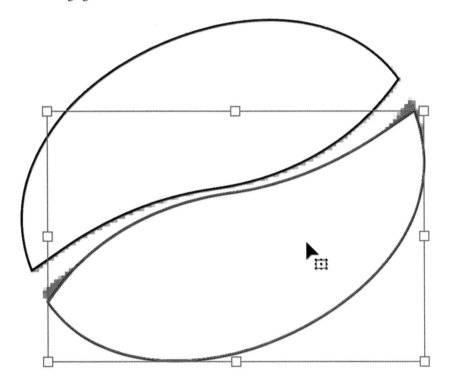

Things aren't going to match up perfectly, but as always, vectors can be easily adjusted.

4 Using the Direct Selection tool ▷ , adjust the direction and length of each anchor point handle to make the shape conform more closely to the guide below it. Modify each anchor point position if necessary.

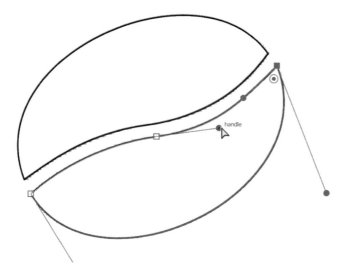

We now have both segments of the coffee bean created as unique shape elements.

Adjusting appearance

Comparing the shape objects we've drawn with the Pen tool and the original guide image, it's obvious that certain elements such as fill color and stroke need to be adjusted to complete the coffee bean.

1 Select both the shapes by holding down the Shift key and clicking one with the Selection tool ▶ , and then clicking the other shape.

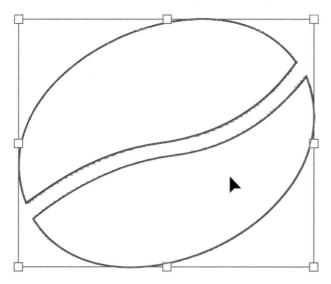

You will see a transform rectangle around both shapes, indicating that both have been selected.

2 Open the Properties panel and locate the Appearance section. Click the fill color and select the black swatch from the overlay that appears. Click the Stroke color and remove the stroke by selecting the None swatch ✎ from the color overlay.

Because you selected both shapes, both now exhibit black fills and no stroke.

3 Deselect the shapes by clicking anywhere outside the artboard.

Notice that while the appearance of the bean is much nicer, we can still see portions of the guide image beneath.

Managing layers and objects

You have now created enough objects in this document that you need to organize layers and the objects within them before things get too busy.

1 Locate the Layers panel and open it. If you cannot locate it, you can open it from the application menu by choosing Window > Layers.

2 Expand Layer 1 to view its contents by twirling down the small icon ⟩ to the left of the layer preview and name.

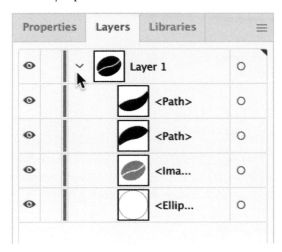

In Layer 1 you'll see all of the objects you've drawn or placed in the document.

3 You can click the small circle to the right of any layer or object to target it. Click to target one of the <Path> objects and then hold the Shift key while you click the other to target both sections of the coffee bean.

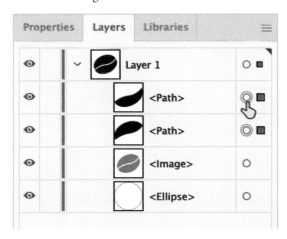

Both sections are now selected in the Document window as well.

Tip To adjust objects in a group, you can expand it just as you did with Layer 1 by clicking the small chevron.

4   Choose Object > Group from the application menu.

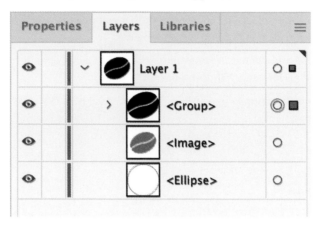

The two <Path> objects are now contained within a <Group>. This enables us to manage the entire bean as one object.

5   Below the coffee bean group is the raster image you placed earlier as a tracing guide. You no longer need this in the document. Click to target the <Image> object and then click the Delete Selection button 🗑 to delete the image.

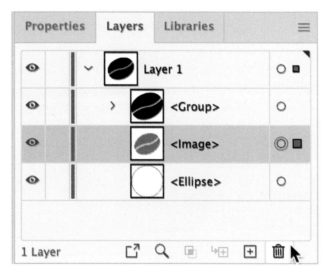

With the raster image gone, the vector coffee bean edges appear sharp and without any roughness visible from the image below.

The <Ellipse> object you originally drew on the artboard now appears, along with the coffee bean.

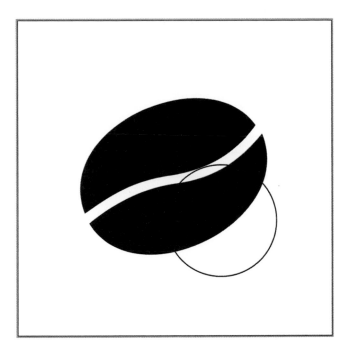

This is because it was previously at the bottom of the layer stack and was obscured by the raster image above it. Objects higher up the layer stack obscure those lower down.

6   Click the New Layer button ⊞ to add a new layer to the document.

A new layer named Layer 2 appears.

7   Drag the coffee bean <Group> onto the new layer until it turns blue and release the mouse button.

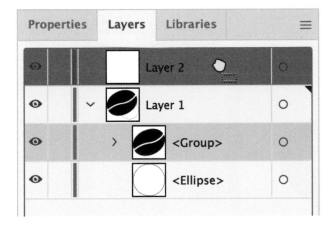

The coffee bean <Group> is now nested in Layer 2 instead of Layer 1.

8 Double-click the name Layer 2 to edit it, and rename it **Bean**. Double-click Layer 1 and change it to **Misc**.

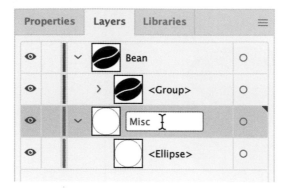

It's important to keep layers organized and named appropriately.

Assembling the logo

The completed logo will include the coffee bean asset in the center of a circular band with text matching the arc of the circle. Now that we have the coffee bean asset, we need to pull together the remaining elements.

The next step in our design process involves creating additional shape and text elements to form the complete logo and to integrate the completed coffee bean asset into our design.

Designing the enclosing circular band

We already have a circle shape in our document. In fact, it's the first object we created! Now we'll use it as we begin assembling the Bad Beans Coffee Roasters logo.

Before we do anything, recall that we have two artboards right now: Scratch and Logo.

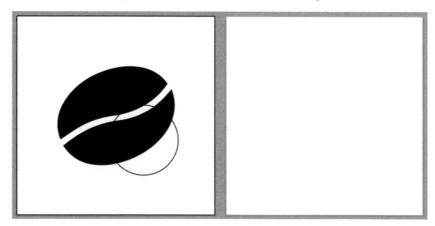

We will be working across the Scratch and Logo artboards during the next few steps as we build the full logo on the Logo artboard.

1   Using the Selection tool ▶, drag the existing circle shape from the Scratch artboard and, using the smart guides that appear, align it to the center of the Logo artboard. Release the mouse button.

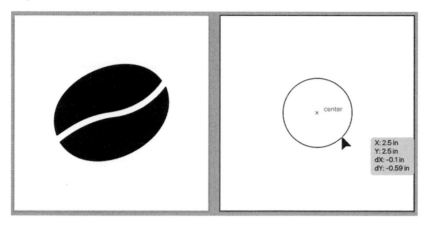

Note Even though the circle shape is on a different artboard now, the layer structure is shared across all artboards of the document and so remains exactly as we organized it previously.

The circle is placed at the center of the Logo artboard.

2   Ensuring the circle is selected, hover over any of the corner transform points until the cursor changes to a two-headed arrow, indicating scale transform is possible. Drag toward the nearest corner of the artboard with the Shift and Option/Alt keys pressed to both constrain the aspect ratio and scale from the center until the informational overlay reads a width and height of **4.5 in**. Release the mouse button.

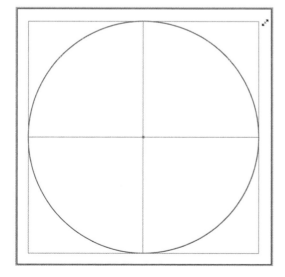

The resized circle now fills much of the artboard.

You can verify that everything is positioned and sized correctly in the Transform section of the Properties panel.

3   In the Appearance section of the Properties panel, change the fill to black and set the stroke to None.

The circle shape is now completely black, and the stroke has no appearance whatsoever.

Drawing the inner circle

If we were to place the coffee bean asset within the circle shape right now, no one would be able to distinguish between them since they are the same color.

We will create a gray inner circle shape to define the extent of the logo banding.

1   Drag the existing circle to another location while holding down the Option/Alt key in order to duplicate the shape. Release the mouse button.

There are now two circle shapes. The original remains at the original location.

2 With the new circle shape selected, use the Properties panel to change the fill to a medium gray, the X and Y position to 2.5 in, and the width and height to 3.25 in.

● **Note** Any gray will do. We simply need a color other than black to distinguish between both objects.

This will center and scale the shape while coloring it gray.

We now have two overlapping circular shapes and can clearly see the shape that will become the banding loop to encircle the coffee bean and act as a container for the logo text.

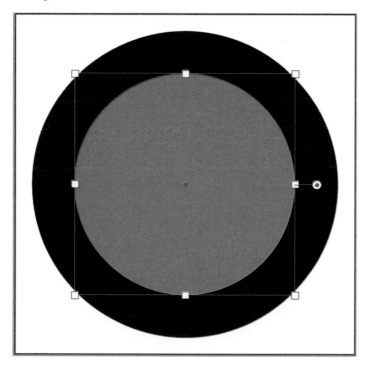

Using the Pathfinder tools

We are going to use the gray circle to punch a hole through the black circle, resulting in a circular band around the coffee bean logo.

For this task, we will make use of the Pathfinder feature.

1   Select both <Ellipse> objects by pressing the Shift key, and then select each circle using either the Selection tool or the Click To Target feature in the Layers panel.

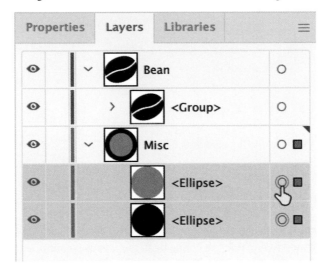

In either case, both circle shapes should be visibly selected on the artboard and in the Layers panel.

2   Locate the Pathfinder section in the Properties panel and click the Minus Front ⬚ option.

The overlay shape is used to punch a hole through the shape beneath it and is then removed. The object that remains is now a compound path since it contains multiple paths with holes appearing wherever paths overlap.

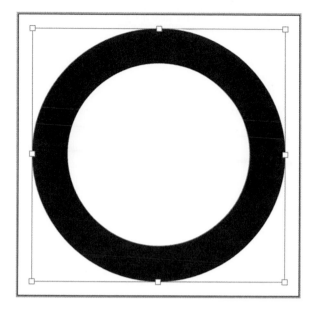

● **Note** Illustrator has many more Pathfinder options to explore. They all produce different results on the selected objects by combining, dividing, or subtracting selected elements where paths cross.

Placing the coffee bean

We'll now make a copy of the coffee bean asset and place it at the center of the Logo artboard, scaled to the compound path.

1   With the Selection tool active, select the bean asset on the Scratch artboard and then, with the Option/Alt key pressed, drag it all the way over to the Logo artboard. Release the mouse button once the bean is centered on the artboard.

▶ **Tip** If you're ever worried about making mistakes with your assets, you can always maintain a special artboard with your original objects intact while you further manipulate copies elsewhere.

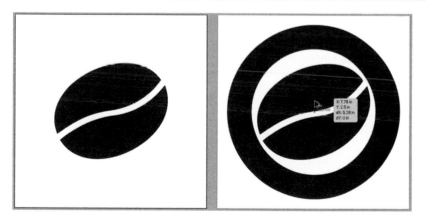

The original asset remains on the Scratch artboard and a copy is created on the Logo artboard.

The copied coffee bean asset group is too large; we need to scale it down a bit.

Tip If you do not know the proper position values to use when aligning an object, you can always use the Align panel accessible from Window > Align, or via the Align section of the Properties panel.

2   In the Properties panel, ensure that the X and Y positions are both set to **2.5 in** and adjust the width of the asset to 2.3 in with the Maintain Height And Width Proportions toggle selected.

The aspect ratio is respected when the asset is scaled down and centered on the artboard.

3   In the Layers panel, rename the Misc layer to Logo and drag the coffee bean <Group> copy into it. Release the mouse when the layer is highlighted.

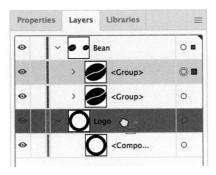

The coffee bean copy is now in the Logo layer and the original remains in the Bean layer.

4   Lock the entire Bean layer by clicking the empty Lock area between the Visibility toggle and the layer preview thumbnail. Do the same to each object in the Logo layer but do not lock the layer itself.

This ensures that only layers and objects we want to manipulate further will be selectable and those that we are done with at the moment will be locked down.

Adding type along a path

We need to add the text "Bad Beans Coffee Roasters" along the band encircling the coffee bean asset. To do so, we will employ the Type On A Path tool.

1 Click the Default Fill And Stroke button below the toolbar to set the fill to white and the stroke to black.

Changing the fill and stroke colors makes it easier to see the path itself via the default stroke.

2 Choose the Ellipse tool ⬭. and drag to create a new circle the same size as the existing one. Use the smart guides to assist you and release the mouse button when ready.

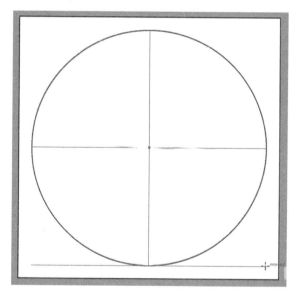

A new circle shape with the default appearance is created at the same size and position of the existing circular shape.

3 Select the Type On A Path tool 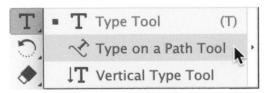 which is grouped among the Type tools **T** on the toolbar.

4 Click the top of the shape path you've created.

Text is inserted and encircles the other objects. The circle we recently created is replaced by this path type.

5 Enter Bad Beans Coffee Roasters in the selected type object.

This is the name of the company and must be prominent within the logo.

6 Choose the Selection Tool to exit type mode and then click the text object to select it. In the Appearance section of the Properties panel, change the fill color to white. In the Character section, set the font family to Abolition Soft with a size value of 44 pt and set Tracking to a value of 152. Choose **Align Center** from the Paragraph section.

7 In the application menu, choose Type > Type On A Path > Type On A Path Options to open the Type On A Path Options dialog box.

Set the Align To Path option to Ascender and select the Preview checkbox to visualize the change. Click OK.

Type on a Path Options		
Effect:	Rainbow	☐ Flip
Align to Path:	Ascender	
Spacing:	↕ Auto	⌄
☑ Preview	(Cancel)	(OK)

The text now appears across the black circular band.

● **Note** You will likely need to adjust both sides to get everything centered correctly.

8 Choose the Selection tool from the toolbar. A set of three handles appears, projecting out from the path type object. Hover the mouse over either handle line that is present at either side of the text itself until a small arrow icon appears. Drag this handle to center the text along the top of the circular band through rotation.

Center handle

Side handle

Side handle

Duplicating and modifying path type

The final step in our logo design is to add the founding year to the bottom of the circular band and adjust the band itself to fit the text more closely.

1   In the Layers panel, in the Logo layer, drag the existing type object to the New Layer icon ⊞ and release the mouse button.

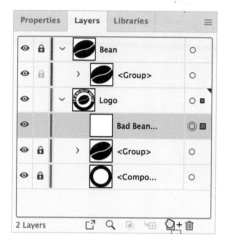

A duplicate type object is created and placed in the Logo layer.

2   Choose the Selection tool from the toolbar and triple-click the text on the artboard.

Triple-clicking selects all the text within, making it easy to change its value.

3 Type **1976** to represent the year and press the Escape key to exit from editing the text value.

The type object remains selected and we have access to the three transformation handles that accompany path type.

4 Hover over the center transform handle at the very top of the type object until the cursor changes to display a small arrow. Carefully drag around the perimeter of the type object to rotate it so that the year appears at the very bottom of the logo, and release the mouse button.

The year is now in the correct location but is upside-down.

5 In the application menu, choose Type > Type On A Path > Type On A Path Options to open the Type On A Path Options dialog box.

Set the Align To Path option to **Descender** and select the Flip checkbox. Select the Preview checkbox to visualize the change and click OK when complete.

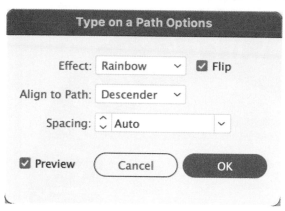

The text is placed in the black band and reads correctly.

6 Now that you have the text well positioned, you can adapt the black band to be a bit thicker, allowing the text within more room to breathe. Click the Toggle Lock icon 🔒 to unlock the <Compound Path> object.

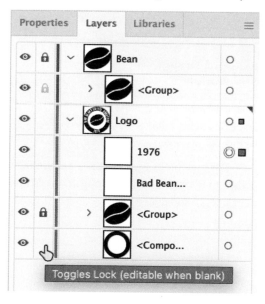

The Toggle Lock icon disappears, and the object can now be selected and adjusted.

7 Choose Object > Path > Offset Path from the application menu.

The Offset Path dialog box appears.

8 Leave everything at the default values—such as an offset of **0.1389 in**—and click OK.

The changes are applied, resulting in a thicker band encircling the coffee bean asset and giving the entire logo a heavier presence.

The logo is now complete! You can use this logo on its own or create additional artboards for assets like a label on which to integrate the logo alongside additional information—perhaps suitable for a bag of ground coffee beans.

Design principle: repetition

Repeating elements within a design or even across related design assets creates unity and consistency. The design principle of repetition is performed by reusing colors, lines, or shapes, or through similarly positioned objects across a canvas. You can apply repetition either evenly and regularly, or with an uneven and more irregular pattern in your designs.

You can even apply repetition through the use of more complex assets like logos. You can create additional artboards for labels, advertisements, flyers, and so on, all making use of the logo you designed in this lesson as a repeating element.

Exporting design assets

Illustrator features several workflows for getting assets—and even entire artboards—out of the application as different file types to be used elsewhere.

We'll look at two of these before concluding this lesson.

Saving as a PDF

PDF files are perfect for both digital distribution and sending your work to a print house as a final design. They can also be used as assets for designers to incorporate within larger works.

We will save only the Logo artboard as a PDF.

1 Choose File > Save As from the application menu.

2 A dialog appears asking if you want to save On your computer or as a cloud document. Choose On your computer.

3 In the Save As dialog box that appears, provide a name for the file and browse to the location you wish to save to.

4 From the Format menu, choose Adobe PDF (pdf). For Range, enter **2**. Click Save.

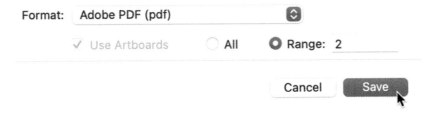

Since you chose Adobe PDF (pdf) as the file format, the Save Adobe PDF dialog box appears.

5 Here you can select from various PDF presets or make manual changes to the PDF generation options. For now, just leave the default settings and click Save PDF.

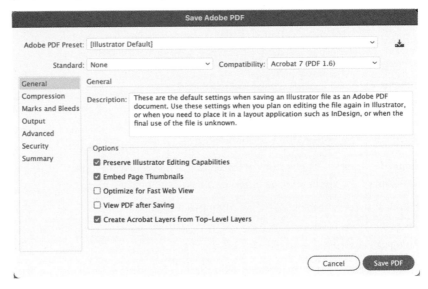

Illustrator generates a PDF file and saves it to the location you chose earlier.

6 In your system file browser, open the location you saved the file to and open it.

The PDF file consists of a single artboard and is ready to be used elsewhere.

Exporting to other file types

Illustrator has a very flexible, organized approach to generating assets through use of the Asset panel and Export For Screens workflow.

First, you'll define what assets to export, and then you'll configure how you want to export them.

1 Choose Window > Asset Export from the application menu.

The Asset Export panel appears and is currently empty. You need to define some assets to work on.

2 In the Layers panel, unlock all objects in the Logo layer.

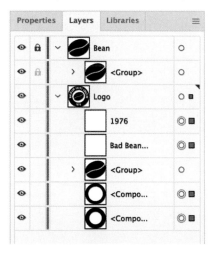

Defining assets in the Assets panel relies on selections, so you must be able to select all aspects of the logo.

3 Using the Selection tool or the Layers panel, select every object that is part of the Logo layer.

4 In the Asset Export panel, click the "Generate a single asset from the selection" button ⊞ located alongside the Export Settings section heading.

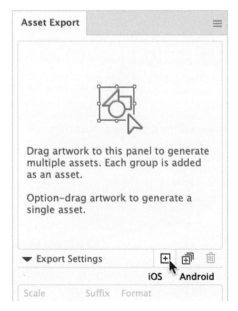

The entire selection is added as a single asset for export.

Note It's important to name your assets just like naming layers and objects for clarity and organizational purposes.

5   Double-click the name, Asset 1, and enter Logo as the new asset name.

6   In the Export Settings section, choose **300 ppi** for Scale, **None** for Suffix, and **PNG** for Format.

7   Click the Export For Screens button ⊞ at the bottom of the panel.

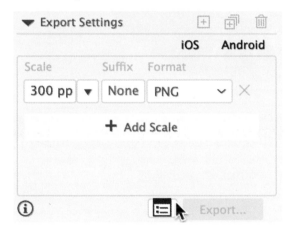

The Export For Screens dialog box appears.

8   Ensuring the Logo asset is selected, deselect Create Sub-folders and set the location for export using the Export To Folder browser.

9 Click the "Advanced settings for exported file types" icon ✿ when ready.

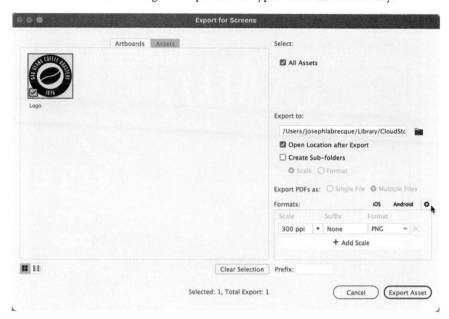

The Format Settings dialog box appears.

10 In this dialog box, you want to ensure that Background Color is set to Transparent for your PNG options. Change it if necessary and click Save Settings.

Illustrator returns you to the Export For Screens dialog box.

▶ Tip The Asset Export panel saves your asset selections and export options for a document—even when you quit Illustrator.

11 Finally, click the Export Asset button to generate the file.

Illustrator generates a PNG file of the logo asset with a transparent background at the location you chose.

Next steps with Illustrator

To further explore the creative options that Illustrator has to offer, you can use Adobe's help resources available at https://helpx.adobe.com/support/illustrator.html.

If you'd like to advance your exploration of Illustrator in greater depth, I encourage you to consider reading *Adobe Illustrator Classroom in a Book (2023 Release)*, also available from Peachpit and Adobe Press.

Review questions

1 What is the benefit of designing with vectors over a raster image?

2 What are vector graphics composed of?

3 What are artboards used for in Illustrator?

4 When using the Pen tool, how can you ensure that you're creating a smooth curve with your anchor point?

5 How do Pathfinder tools modify selected objects?

6 When saving a multi-artboard document as a PDF, how can you ensure only a single artboard is used?

Review answers

1 Vectors can be infinitely scaled with no loss in quality.

2 Vector graphics are composed of anchor points and paths.

3 Artboards are generally used to organize different designs within a single document.

4 When creating a new anchor point, be sure to drag before releasing the mouse button and not simply click and release.

5 Pathfinders will combine, divide, or subtract selected elements where paths cross, depending on the Pathfinder tool chosen.

6 In the Save dialog box, be sure to specify the artboard number you want to export.

5 MANAGING PAGE LAYOUT WITH INDESIGN

Lesson overview

In this lesson, you'll learn how to do the following:

- Create and configure InDesign documents.

- Work across pages and parent pages.

- Manage text and text frames.

- Adjust text properties and create reusable styles.

- Gain an understanding of the design principle of hierarchy.

- Import and manipulate visual graphics.

- Work with shape tools and associated text elements.

- Export and share your document.

This lesson will take less than 1 hour to complete.

To get the files used in this lesson, download them from the web page for this book at www.adobepress.com/CreativeCloudCIB. For more information, see "Accessing the lesson files and Web Edition" in the Getting Started section at the beginning of this book.

Adobe InDesign enables designers to create complex layouts involving rich text constructs and integrated graphical elements across pages and spreads to produce professional publications in print and digital media.

Getting started

● **Note** If you have not already downloaded the project files for this lesson to your computer from your Account page, make sure to do so now. See "Getting Started" at the beginning of the book.

Start by viewing the finished project to see what you'll be creating in this lesson.

1 Open the 05End.pdf file in the Lesson05/05End folder to view the final project.

The project is a two-page magazine spread with information about growing and harvesting rhubarb. It includes somewhat serious narrative textual content alongside some illustrations of rhubarb painted with Adobe Fresco.

2 Close the file.

Introducing InDesign

Adobe InDesign is page layout software that enables you to create multiple project types across print and digital spaces. You can design posters, magazines, flyers, brochures, CD booklets, books, and more.

InDesign comes loaded with presets and gives you full control over the typographic elements of your design and the precise layout for imported graphical assets.

When launching InDesign, you'll be presented with a familiar start workspace with presets, recent files, a Learn space, and the ability to create a new file from scratch.

We'll examine the main InDesign interface once we have created a new document and begun working directly within the software.

Getting started with a new document

The first step to any InDesign project is to create your document and set up your pages in a way that works best for the chosen document type.

A magazine spread is something encountered in all types of magazines. Spreads provide additional opportunities for layout and design across two pages instead of just one.

Creating a new InDesign document

Let's use one of InDesign's many presets to create a new document for our magazine spread project.

1 From the start workspace, click the New File button.

The New Document dialog box appears and displays any recent document settings you may have used in the past.

2　Click the Print tab the top of the New Document dialog box to reveal a set of print-focused presets and templates.

Presets are blank documents that conform to certain paper and project specifications, whereas templates are preconfigured with design assets, typographic styles, and more.

3　Choose the Letter preset if it isn't already selected.

4 In the Preset Details column, give your document the name Rhubarb, and choose Inches from the Units menu.

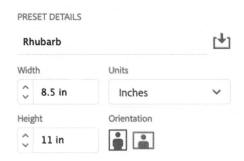

Inches are the unit value we will be using in this lesson. If you do not switch to inches in this step, any values detailed (in inches) in the lesson will not make any sense!

5 This part is really important: Enter **2** in the Pages field and **2** in the Start # field. Select Facing Pages.

Specifying these Pages settings ensures that our magazine spread will be 2 pages.

Because it is a spread, we should use facing pages. And if we start our document at page number 1, our two pages will not form a spread since page 1 is an odd-numbered page. All odd pages display as the right page of a spread and each even-numbered page displays at the left side of a spread.

6 With these adjustments to the preset completed, click Create in the lower right of the dialog box.

InDesign creates a new document per your specifications and opens it.

7 Choose File > Save from the application menu.

A save dialog box appears and the file is given the default name of Rhubarb.indd, reflecting the name we gave the document when we created it, plus the "indd" InDesign project file extension.

8 Choose the Lesson05/05Start folder for the location and click Save.

The document file is now saved. Be sure to save often as you work through any project.

Columns, margins, bleed, and slug

You likely noticed several additional properties that we could have adjusted within the preset details. Most of these items are guides.

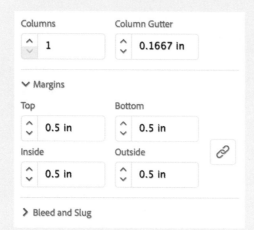

We have left these guide settings at their defaults for this project, but it is good to know what each one represents.

- **Columns/Column Gutter:** These settings determine a set of guides across the page to assist with columnar layout. The gutter is the space between columns.

- **Margins:** This setting creates a guide across the page to ensure negative space and a bit of breathing room against the edges of your document.

- **Bleed and Slug:** This setting will create an additional set of guides for assistance with each of these concepts. **Bleed** refers to the act of extending content a bit past the document edges to ensure that uneven trims will still look okay. **Slug** is the space outside both the bleed and printable area and is often used to place printers' marks.

The InDesign interface

Now that we have a new document created, we can get a better look at the InDesign interface.

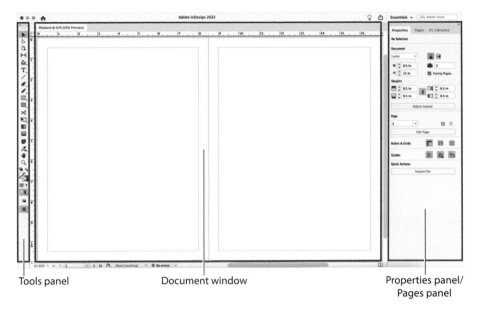

Tools panel   Document window   Properties panel/
Pages panel

In the Document window, we can see our two-page spread nicely aligned in the center since we selected Facing Pages.

If your pages do not appear in this way, you can fix the page setup by choosing File > Document Setup from the application menu and selecting the Facing Pages checkbox.

You can even select the Preview checkbox to see the effects of changes before committing them.

Along the left side of the interface is your Tools panel, and the right side includes a group of panels—most importantly, the Properties panel and the Pages panel.

Directly above this area you can find the workspace switcher, where you switch to different arrangements of panels and interface options.

The default workspace is Essentials. That is the workspace we'll be using in this lesson.

Making use of parent pages

To begin designing our magazine spread, we'll start by including any assets that are meant to exist across all spreads within what is known as a *parent page* in InDesign.

1 Click the Pages tab in the column to the right of the Document window to switch to the Pages panel.

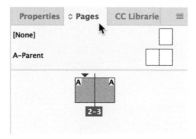

If you observe pages 2–3, you'll see a small A in the top-right and top-left corners. This indicates that the A-Parent page spread has been applied and that any content you add to A-Parent will also appear on these pages.

2 Double-click the space between A-Parent at the left and the visual representation of that parent to the right.

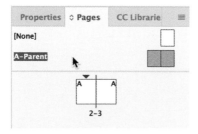

A-Parent becomes selected and is now represented in the Document window. Notice that the selected pages are always indicated with a blue highlight.

3 Choose File > Place from the application menu to select a visual asset to place within the parent page spread.

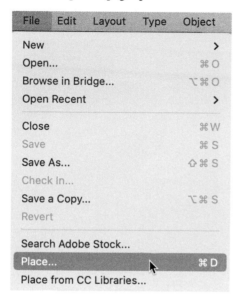

A file browser appears.

4 Navigate to the Lesson05/05Start folder, select the file named Sky_Photo.jpg, and click Open.

The cursor changes to a placement cursor and a preview of the image file appears as part of the cursor. Placing a file in this way gives you greater control over how InDesign scales and positions it as part of your layout.

5 Drag the image from the upper-left corner of the spread to the bottom-right corner and release the mouse button. Ensure that this file covers the entire spread. It's okay to go past the spread bounds.

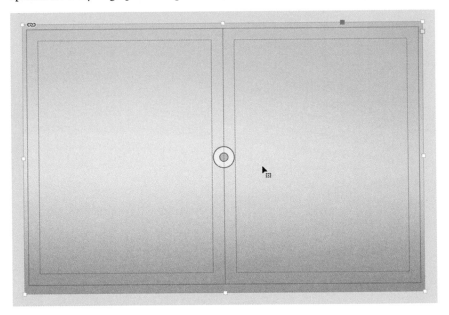

The image is placed across the spread within the A-Parent parent page. We are finished with parent pages.

6 Locate the page switcher in the lower-left corner of the interface. Open it and choose page 2.

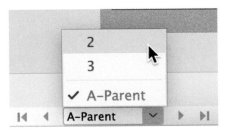

► **Tip** You can always switch to any page by double-clicking its icon in the Pages panel.

You are no longer editing the parent pages or viewing the document pages with the parent pages applied.

Working with text elements

With our parent pages set up and propagating onto the existing spread, it's now time to lay out the content for our document.

We will begin by creating text frames and adding precomposed text copy to our project.

Creating text frames

We need to establish text frames for both the title of our magazine article on rhubarb and the body content across both pages of the spread.

Text frames in InDesign are layout containers for text-based content that have a number of additional properties beyond simple text box–like column arrangements, which we will see a bit later.

1 To create a text frame for the title, select the Type tool **T.** from the Tools panel and drag a frame from the left margin guide at the top of page 2 across to the right margin guide. The text frame should measure about 2.25 inches in height. A small information box will appear letting you know the dimensions of the frame. Release the mouse button.

2 Now that you've created the text frame, you can begin typing in content using the keyboard. Enter **Glorious Rhubarb**, which will serve as the article title.

Note The text looks a bit small and plain right now. We'll stylize it after we've placed all of it in the appropriate frames.

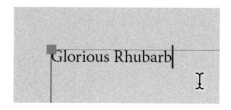

3 Now you'll prepare a text frame for the article body. With the Type tool still selected, begin at the left margin guide a bit beneath the title frame and drag across to the bottom-right corner, aligning with the margin guides until you've created a text frame measuring about 7 inches in height. Release the mouse button.

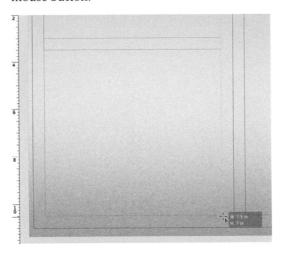

4 Turn your attention to the facing page, page 3. With the Type tool selected, begin at the left margin guide about 1.5 inches from the top and drag across to the bottom-right corner, aligning with the margin guides until you've created a text frame measuring about 9 inches in height. Release the mouse button.

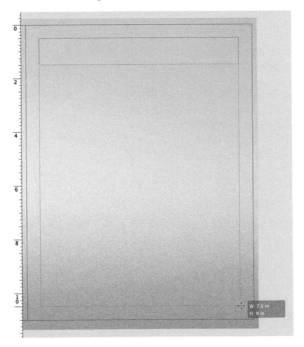

We now have three text frames as part of our document: two on page 2 and one on page 3. The only text frame with text in it at this moment is the initial frame we created on page 2 to hold the article title.

Adding body content

As we saw earlier, you can simply begin writing text within a text frame to add it to the document. But what if you have a lot of prewritten body text for an article?

It's simple to add prewritten copy to a text frame. You'll do that now.

1 Using the Selection tool ▶, click the empty text frame on page 2 to select it.

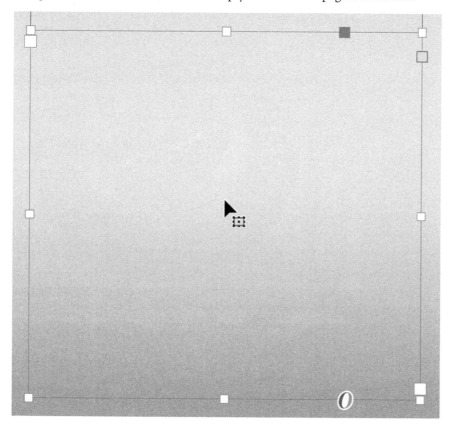

Transform handles and additional icons appear around the selected text frame.

2 Choose File > Place from the application menu to open the Place dialog box; then locate and select the file Rhubarb_Copy.rtf from the Lesson05/05Start folder.

The Rhubarb_Copy.rtf file contains all of the prewritten text about rhubarb that we will use for this magazine spread.

3 Click Open in the Place dialog box.

InDesign places the content of the Rhubarb_Copy.rtf file in the selected text frame.

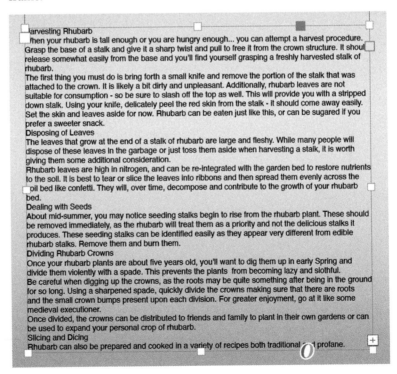

The text is mostly unformatted and contains only line breaks right now. That's okay.

Dealing with overset text

Have you noticed that the text cuts off abruptly at the end of the text frame? That's because there is too much text for the size of the frame and so the remainder gets cut off.

This is known as *overset text* in InDesign. Let's use the built-in tools to fix this.

1   With the text frame with placed text still selected, in the lower-right corner you'll see a small icon of a white box with a red cross along the edge. Click this icon to begin the process of directing InDesign where to flow the overset text.

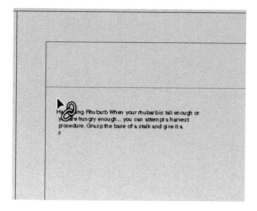

The overset text will appear as though attached to the cursor when hovering over other text frames.

2   Click the empty text frame on the opposing page to instruct InDesign to send any overflow text from the text frame on page 2 across to the text frame on page 3.

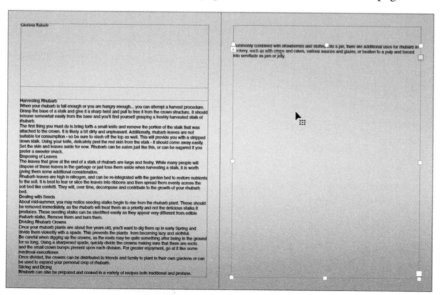

With this connection established, both text frames work as though they are one larger text frame, and the text will flow between the two as properties are adjusted or text is edited. In InDesign, this is called a *threaded text frame*.

Using the Preflight panel

When you placed the text into the text frame on page 2, you may have noticed an error indicator appear at the bottom of the InDesign interface. This error indicator works in tandem with the Preflight panel that can be activated by choosing Window > Preflight from the application menu.

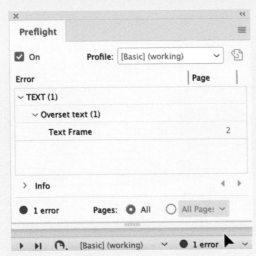

You will find the Preflight panel very useful. It lets you know when errors occur so that you can immediately address them.

With overset text present, we get a distinct warning about the problem, and InDesign even details which object is causing the issue, making it easier to address.

Defining text columns

By default, any text frame will behave as though it consists of a single column. With publications like a magazine or newspaper, having to read text that runs across the entire page width can wear on the eyes.

A solution for this is to have the text frames render text across several narrower columns instead.

1 Select the text frame on page 2. In the Properties panel Text Frame section, note that we currently have a column count of 1.

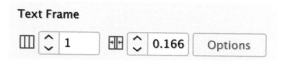

2 Making sure that you are still calculating units in inches, change the column count to **2** and the Gutter to **0.333**.

3 Do the same for the text frame on page 3 to make the text frame properties identical between the two.

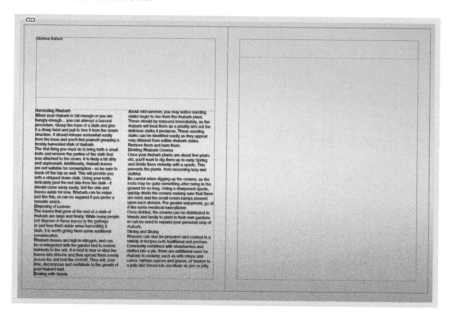

The text content within the threaded text frames shifts accordingly.

Adjusting title properties

Now we have all of our text frames configured how we want them, but the text content itself still retains the default styling and isn't great to look at.

Let's adjust the properties of our title text to make it all much nicer-looking.

1 With the Selection tool chosen, triple-click the first text frame on page 2 that reads "Glorious Rhubarb."

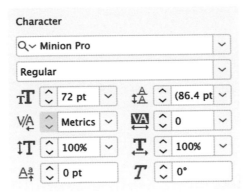

The Properties panel displays the Character properties section and additional Paragraph properties beneath it.

● **Note** The Charcuterie Deco font is part of the Adobe Fonts collection that you can access at https://fonts.adobe.com as part of your Creative Cloud subscription.

2 Select a decorative typeface for the article title. I suggest using Charcuterie Deco for the font at a Font Size value of 72pt.

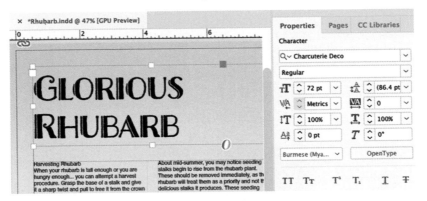

3 Double-click the text frame to edit the text directly and drag across the type to select all characters.

4 In the Appearance section of the Properties panel, click the Fill property and select the red color chip 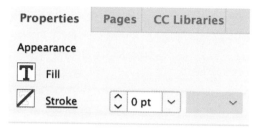 (C=15, M=100, Y=100, K=0) from those presented to you.

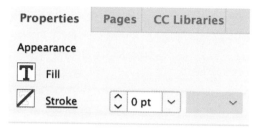

The "Glorious Rhubarb" title text turns red.

Adjusting paragraph properties

With the title text properties set, let's turn our attention toward the main body paragraph text.

1 Select all the text within the large text frame on page 2 that includes the body text we placed there earlier.

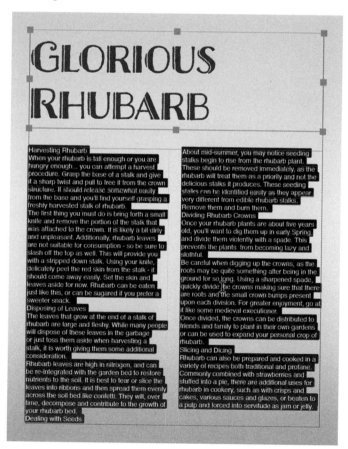

Note The Agenda font is also part of the Adobe Fonts collection that can be accessed at https://fonts.adobe.com as part of your Creative Cloud subscription.

2 In the Character section of the Properties panel, switch to a clean font such as Agenda. Set Font Size to 15pt and Leading to 21pt.

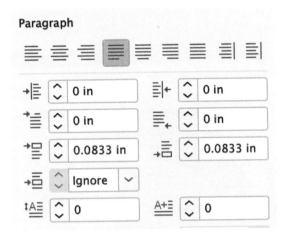

Note Leading refers to the space between lines of text. Kerning is the space between individual characters.

Increasing the leading in this way will give the text more room to breathe between each line and can make it easier to read when applied properly.

Note Again, the units that appear here will depend on what units you selected upon document creation.

3 In the Paragraph section of the Properties panel, switch the alignment to Justify with the last line aligned left, and set both Space Before and Space After to a value of 0.0833in.

The properties Space Before and Space After define how much space is present between paragraphs that follow one another. The value we've used will give good visual separation between text paragraphs.

4 Deselect all the text by choosing the Selection tool and clicking any of the empty space outside the document bounds.

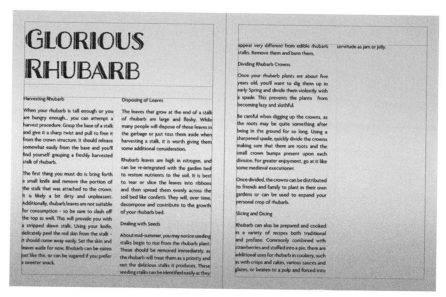

We can now see the effect that these changes have had on the body text, and we can easily distinguish the article headings as well.

Adjusting heading properties

With the text that will become our headings now standing out much more distinctly, it's time to give those headings some much needed style.

1 Select the entire first heading that reads "Harvesting Rhubarb" in the second text frame of page 2.

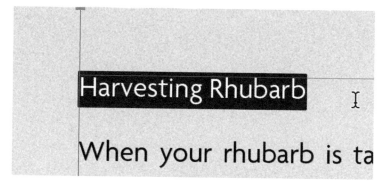

2 In the Character section of the Properties panel, choose Charcuterie Etched as the typeface, and set Font Size to 28pt and Leading to 24pt.

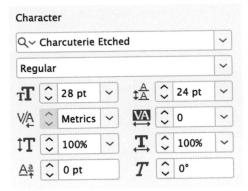

This choice of font is very similar to the font used in the article title but with some subtle variance. This creates harmony between the title and headings while contrasting with the body text.

3 In the Paragraph section of the Properties panel, switch the alignment to Align Left and set the Space Before property to a value of 0.2361 in.

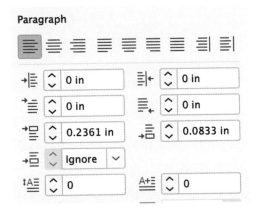

4 In the Appearance section of the Properties panel, click the Fill property and select the green color chip ▇ (C=75, M=5, Y=100, K=0) from those presented to you.

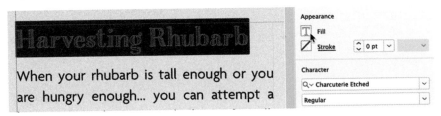

Rhubarb exhibits colors of red and green, so we'll use a basic green for the headings since we used red for the title.

Look at how nicely the title and heading now work together in the document!

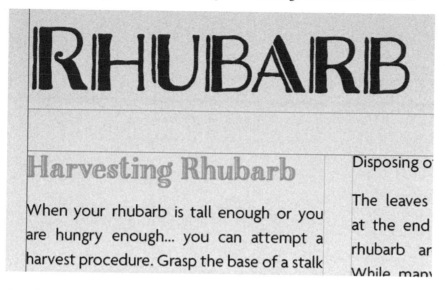

Our choices speak to the subject at hand but also make the content easily digestible.

Creating text styles

While we keep using terms like "title," "heading," and "body," these things have not yet been formally defined as document styles.

Let's create distinct styles to be applied consistently across the document.

1   If your styled heading text "Harvesting Rhubarb" is no longer selected, go ahead and select it now.

2   In the Text Style section of the Properties panel, click the New Paragraph Style icon ⊞ to create a new paragraph style from the attributes you've applied to this selection of text.

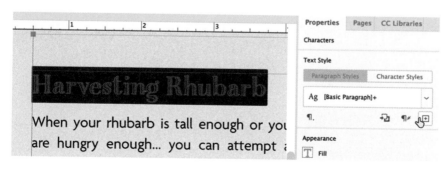

● **Note** Notice how the unsaved style is called [Basic Paragraph]+? The little plus sign indicates that style overrides have been applied and the [Basic Paragraph] style is exactly what you would think it is—the default paragraph styles used in a new document.

3 InDesign prompts you to give the new paragraph style a name. Type **Heading** and press Enter/Return to commit the changes.

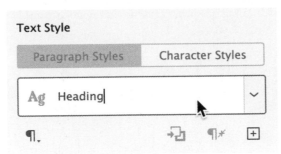

4 We'll do the same for the body text. Select a word of regular paragraph text beneath your heading in the same text frame and click the New Paragraph Style icon ⊞. When prompted, name it **Body**.

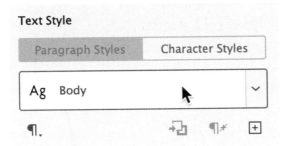

5 Select the title text in the appropriate text frame and click the New Paragraph Style icon ⊞. When prompted, name it **Title**.

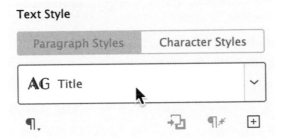

We now have three distinct, reusable paragraph styles within our document. We can much more effectively apply, modify, and reuse specific styles when we've established them in this way.

Paragraph styles vs. character styles

You may notice as we create these different paragraph styles in our document that we can alternatively create character styles as well by toggling between each button in the Text Style section of the Properties panel.

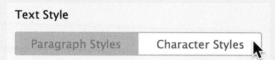

Even though we are using only paragraph styles for our document, both types of styles have their uses. Here are the fundamental differences between the two.

Paragraph style: Preserves both character and paragraph styles and is applied to a paragraph.

Character style: Preserves only character styles and is applied to spans of text within a paragraph instead of the entire paragraph.

Paragraph content may contain multiple character styles but only a single paragraph style.

Applying text styles

We need to apply the newly created Heading paragraph style to the remainder of our actual headings. This is our last step in dealing with text in this document before moving on to add illustrative, graphical elements.

Let's finish this up!

1   In the article text frame on page 2, select any of the text from the heading that reads "Disposing of Leaves."

● **Note** I've selected a word just by double-clicking it, but you can select the entire thing if you wish or even just position the cursor in that block of text. Since we are using paragraph styles, it really doesn't matter!

2 In the Text Style section of the Properties panel, choose Heading from the style menu.

The Heading style we created earlier is applied to the chosen block of text.

▶ **Tip** If you ever need to modify a paragraph style after it's already been defined, make the style modifications on some text and then click the Redefine Style button ⬚ below the style chooser in the Text Style section of the Properties panel. Any paragraph that uses that style will automatically be updated to reflect the change.

3 Perform the same process of selecting heading text and applying the Heading style to the remainder of the heading text blocks that read "Dealing with Seeds," "Dividing Rhubarb Crowns," and "Slicing and Dicing."

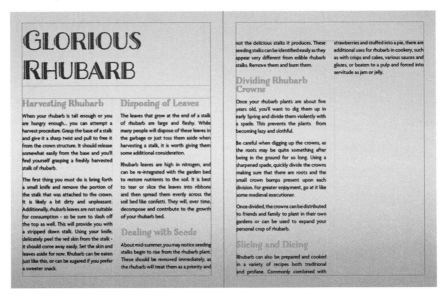

The text elements of our document are now completely stylized.

Design principle: hierarchy

The principle of hierarchy doesn't always apply to text but is of the utmost importance when you're styling and laying out text-based elements within a document.

In our document, we have made the hierarchy of elements very obvious. The title is large and set aside from the rest of the document, the section headings stand out with both visual weight and spacing, and the body paragraphs are easy to distinguish from one another.

You can apply hierarchy to nontext visual elements as well. Making certain elements more pronounced by increasing scale, contrast, or negative space can give those elements greater visual weight than others, establishing an understandable scale of importance.

Working with graphic elements

Aside from the text of our article, we have also prepared several illustrations we want to include. These not only serve as design elements that make the document more attractive, but also inform the reader because they illustrate concepts discussed in the article.

Placing imported graphics

Just as we placed text from a file, we can also place image files within our layout using the same process.

1   Choose File > Place from the application menu and browse to the Lesson05/05Start folder.

2 Select both Rhubarb_Stalk.png and Rhubarb_Bits.png files by holding the Ctrl/ Command key and clicking Open.

● **Note** Both of these illustrated elements were created in Adobe Fresco. You learned a bit about Fresco in Lesson 3, "Raster Image Compositing with Photoshop."

Both images are loaded into the cursor, ready to be placed into the document one after the other.

3 Drag the first image of the rhubarb stalk across the upper-center portion of the document to place it there. Place the second image of the rhubarb bits in the lower-right corner.

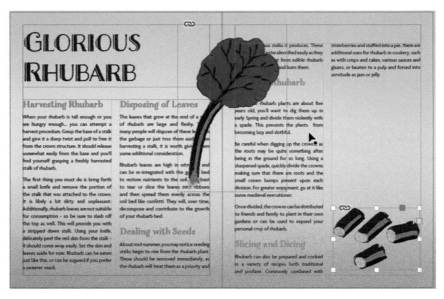

We'll adjust the position, scale, and rotation of these images later on.

Adjusting image properties

You can make adjustments to image width, height, position, and rotation through use of the transform handles that appear around the image when selected, or by manipulating values in the Properties panel.

Let's modify our set of images by using both methods.

1 Using the Selection tool, select the rhubarb stalk image.

2 In the Transform section of the Properties panel, be sure the Constrain Proportions icon between width and height is enabled and enter **8.25 in** for the height. Set the rotation value to **33** degrees.

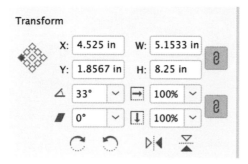

3 Use the Selection tool to reposition the rhubarb stalk image so that it sits somewhere across the center of the spread.

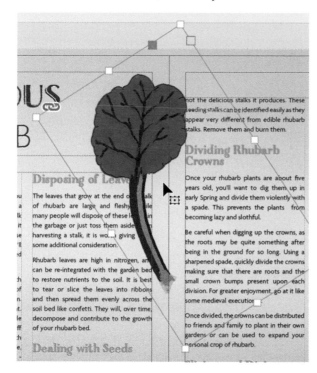

You can also type values into the Transform properties if you prefer to continue working in that way.

4   Select the illustration of rhubarb bits and align the bottom-right edges of the selection rectangle with the bottom-right margins of the spread.

5   Hover over the upper-right transform handle and drag until the frame is aligned with the column gutter. Release the mouse button.

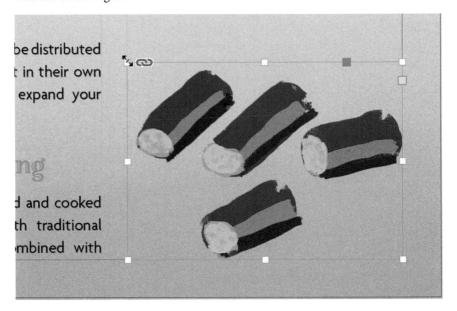

While the rhubarb stalk illustration sits across the entire spread, the rhubarb bits simply settle into the column structure we established when modifying our text frames.

Adjusting image frame fitting

Most likely, you have noticed that when you resize the width or height of the placed image files, the frame is transformed as expected but the image content remains at its original size. This is due to the fact that, just as text resides in frames, so do images.

To remedy this, we will adjust the frame fitting of our placed images so that they fill their frames nicely.

1   Select the rhubarb stalk image frame and view the Frame Fitting section of the Properties panel. Choose the first option: Fill Frame Proportionally.

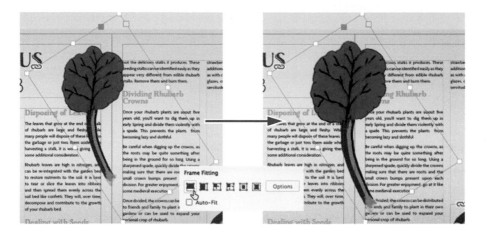

The illustration is scaled up within the frame to fill it in such a way that there is no change in aspect ratio.

2   Now select the rhubarb stalk image frame and view the Frame Fitting section again. Choose Fill Frame Proportionally and select the Auto-Fit option.

Selecting Auto-Fit ensures that whenever we change the frame size in the future, the content within will automatically adapt to those changes, filling the frame.

Adding a callout shape

You can add shape content natively within InDesign and even use those shapes as text frames.

We'll create a callout, warning readers to be sure they do not attempt to eat rhubarb leaves.

1   Choose the Ellipse tool ◯ from the Tools panel.

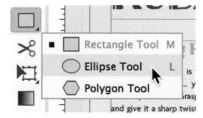

The Ellipse tool is grouped beneath the Rectangle tool.

2 Drag from the upper-right margin of the spread on page 3 and toward the left edge of the column that resides there, holding down the Shift key to ensure a circle is created. Release the mouse button.

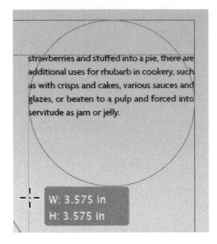

A circular shape is created, filling the column.

3 Select the shape and look at the Appearance section of the Properties panel. Choose the same red color used for the title text as the fill color and disable the stroke by setting its Size value to 0 pt.

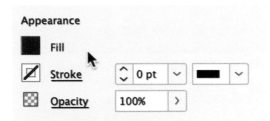

4 Choose the Type tool **T.** from the Tools panel and hover over the shape.

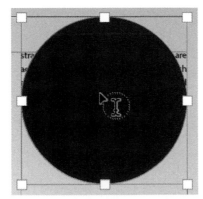

Notice the cursor changes to indicate that clicking here will transform the ellipse shape into a text frame.

5 Click the shape and type **Don't Eat the Leaves!** into the new frame. You may want to include a line break so that the text takes up more than a single line. Adjust as desired.

6 Ensure that your text is selected within the frame and, in the Properties panel, apply the Heading paragraph style. Change the fill color to white, the size to 35 pt, the alignment to Center Align, Space Before to 0.3125 in, and Space After to 0 in.

Notice the Paragraph Styles menu now displays Heading+, indicating that we have overridden certain properties of the Heading style.

7 In the Transform section of the Properties panel, select the text frame and change the rotation to −15 degrees.

We now have a large, eye-catching warning sure to draw the reader's attention.

Adding a horizontal divider

One last element to add is a visual separator between the title and the body of our article in the spread.

We'll create a simple line to accomplish this but with properties to somewhat match the design of our title text.

1 Choose the Line tool ╱ from the Tools panel, and somewhere between the two text frames on page 2, click-drag from the left margin across toward the right and release the mouse button when the tooltip reads about *5.25 in* in line width.

A thin line is produced.

2   In the Appearance section of the Properties panel, set the stroke color to the very same red as the title and set the stroke size to 10 pt and the stroke type to Thick – Thin. Fill should be set to None.

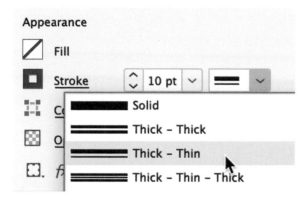

This produces a red divider with an appearance similar to the title text font.

3   Use either the mouse or the arrow keys on the keyboard to adjust the positioning of your dividing line if need be.

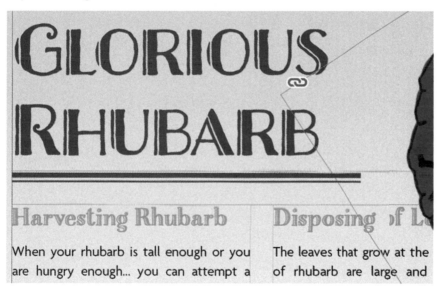

The divider should appear somewhere between the title and body of the article.

Text wrap options

The last thing we need to do is make sure all text is visible within our magazine spread layout. Right now, the images we've added are overlaying the text, making it impossible to read.

We can fix this by specifying specific text wrap options on each image or overlaying text frame.

1 First, select the rhubarb stalk image with the Selection tool.

2 You'll find a set of text wrap options in the Properties panel, but they're very limited. Choose Window > Text Wrap from the application menu to open the dedicated Text Wrap panel.

The Text Wrap panel appears with no text wrap selected as the default option.

3 Choose the third option, Wrap Around Object Shape  and set the offset value to 0.5 in for all sides. For the Type option, if it's not already chosen, choose Select Subject.

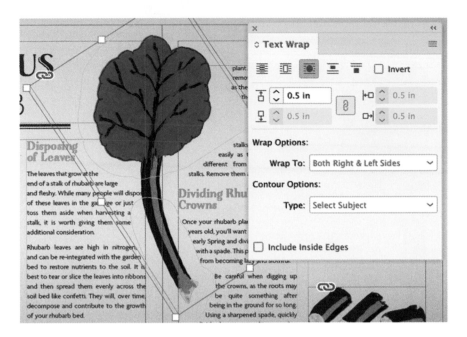

Select Subject makes use of Adobe Sensei to determine the subject contours and automatically create a path to serve as the wrapping element based on the shape.

4   In some cases, the Sensei AI will perhaps make some errors. In this case, there is a gap in the path generated along the stalk. Select the Direct Selection tool located directly beneath the Selection tool and modify the anchor points to provide the offset coverage necessary to remedy any issues you may identify.

● **Note** Adobe Sensei is Adobe's artificial intelligence (AI) service that is accessible across just about every application in some way or another. It takes various forms depending on the software being used.

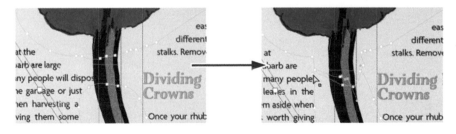

Portions of the path may be generated too close to the illustration or too far from it. Make corrections as necessary in order to balance out the space.

5 Switch to the Selection tool and click the "Don't Eat the Leaves!" callout to select it. Set the text wrap options to Wrap Around Bounding Box.

All right! We've completed our magazine spread. All we need to do now is publish it and share it with the wider world.

Publishing your document

There are a number of ways to share your completed InDesign document for publication, for review, or for online consumption.

We'll go over two of the most common here.

Saving the document as a PDF

If you are going to print your magazine spread, you'll need to generate a PDF document to send to the printer.

Here's how to do it.

1   Choose File > Export from the application menu and make sure Adobe PDF (Print) is selected in the Format menu. Click Save.

2   The Export Adobe PDF dialog box appears. The default settings should be fine for your print needs, unless your print shop has explicitly informed you otherwise. Click Export.

Your document is saved to a PDF file and is ready to be sent off to a printer or distributed electronically.

Publish and share online

InDesign makes sharing your publication online a very simple task.

1 Open the Share menu  from the upper-right portion of the InDesign interface and choose Publish Online.

2 In the dialog box that appears, provide a document title, and be sure to select Spread as the Export As choice in the General properties.

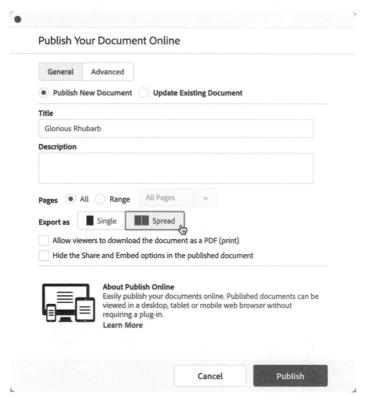

3 Click the Advanced properties and change any settings you think are appropriate for exporting your document online in the best way possible. Click Publish.

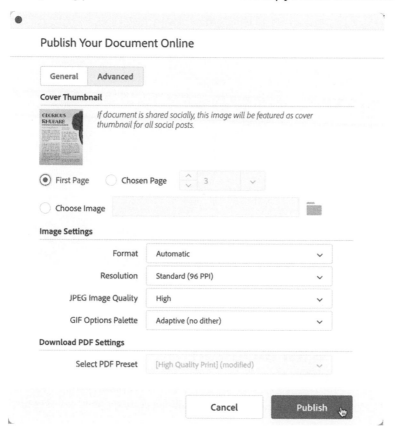

4 The document will be uploaded and published to Adobe's servers. Click View Document to open the magazine spread in your web browser.

Publish Online

GLORIOUS
RHUBARB

Glorious Rhubarb

Feedback

Your document was successfully uploaded.

View Document

COPY THIS URL TO SHARE:

https://indd.adobe.com/view/d1a145cf-4a   Copy

SHARE ON SOCIAL NETWORKS:

To manage your published documents, visit the *Publish Online Dashboard*.

Close

5 Explore the published document in your web browser. It should be identical to the layout created in InDesign.

Your published document can be shared via link or embedded within other systems.

Next steps with InDesign

To further explore the creative options that InDesign has to offer, you can make use of Adobe's help resources available at https://helpx.adobe.com/support/indesign.html.

If you'd like to advance in your exploration of InDesign in greater depth, I encourage you to consider reading *Adobe InDesign Classroom in a Book (2023 Release)*, also available from Peachpit and Adobe Press.

Review Questions

1 What is the function of a parent page?

2 What is overset text?

3 How do paragraph styles differ from character styles?

4 What is the importance of hierarchy in typography?

Review Answers

1 Any elements present within a parent page will be present within pages that are derived from the assigned parent page.

2 Overset text is text content that does not fit within an assigned text frame.

3 Paragraph styles apply to the entire paragraph text block and cannot be applied exclusively to a span of words or characters.

4 Typographic hierarchy informs the reader or viewer of the importance of different typographic constructs such as titles or headings based upon size, contrast, and space.

6 PROTOTYPING FOR SCREENS WITH ADOBE XD

Lesson overview

In this lesson, you'll learn how to do the following:

- Create and manage Adobe XD documents.

- Manage multiple artboards in a document.

- Design mobile experience screen layouts.

- Build a set of interactive components.

- Understand the design principle of balance.

- Prototype interactions between screens.

- Work with time triggers and screen transitions.

- Publish and share your prototypes.

 This lesson will take less than 2 hours to complete.

To get the files used in this lesson, download them from the web page for this book at www.adobepress.com/CreativeCloudCIB. For more information, see "Accessing the lesson files and Web Edition" in the Getting Started section at the beginning of this book.

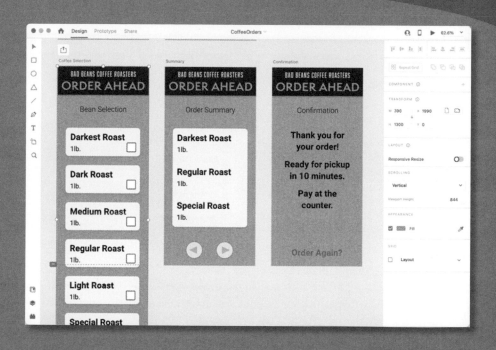

Adobe XD is a rapid user experience, user interface design, and prototyping application that is focused on screen-based layout and interactions. Leverage XD to design for mobile, web, desktop, or any other screen you can think of.

Getting started

● **Note** If you have not already downloaded the project files for this lesson to your computer from your Account page, make sure to do so now. See "Getting Started" at the beginning of the book.

Start by viewing the finished project to see what you'll be creating in this lesson.

1 Open the 06End.xd file in the Lesson06/06End folder to view the final project in XD.

The project is an order-ahead convenience application prototype for Bad Beans Coffee Roasters. It enables mobile users to make coffee bean selections that they can pick up easily at the business location.

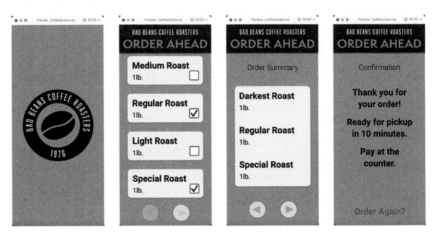

2 Click the Desktop Preview button ▶ in the upper right of the XD interface to open a preview window on your computer where you can click through the experience.

3 Close the preview window and the XD file.

First steps with Adobe XD

Let's step through some of the basics when using XD in Design mode. We'll create a new document, work with artboards, and perform some initial design work to be shared across screens.

Navigating the home screen

The first time you launch Adobe XD, you'll see the home screen. Here you can create new files, access recent files, retrieve cloud-based XD documents that you own or that have been shared with you, and even manage links you've created in the past.

● **Note** Creating a new file from a preset only determines the size of your initial artboard. You can create multiple artboards of varying dimensions in the same XD document.

Prominently, there are a set of presets that you can use to start a new document with a specific artboard size. Most presets target certain devices or social platforms. You can create new documents using these presets or by clicking the New File button in the upper-left corner of the home screen.

Creating a new document

The first step of just about any project is to create a document and save it as a new file.

Let's perform these steps from the home screen.

1 Locate the New File button in the upper-left corner of the home screen. Click it.

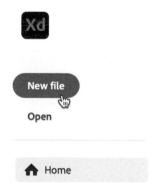

A new document is created with a single artboard and Design mode is activated.

2 Choose File > Save As Local Document from the application menu. When the confirmation dialog appears, click Continue.

A system-level file browser will appear.

3 Give your file the name **CoffeeOrders.xd** and browse to the Lesson06/06Start folder. Click Save.

CoffeeOrders.xd
Adobe XD document · 91 KB

The file is saved as a local XD file and you are returned to Design mode.

Working in the cloud

By default, when you choose to save a new file, XD will save it to the cloud as a cloud-based XD document. You can also convert a local XD file to a cloud version at any time by choosing File > Save As from the application menu.

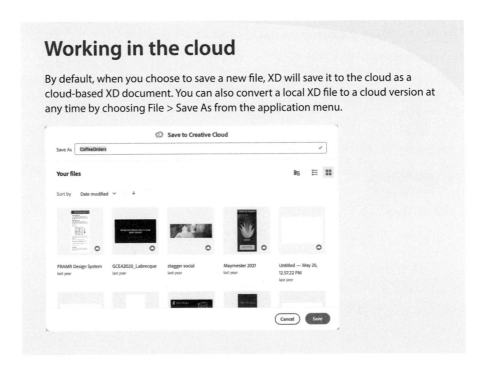

There are many benefits to using cloud-based documents:

1 Document versioning: As you make changes to your document, XD will automatically version these changes by date and time. Versions expire in 30 days, but Marked Versions never expire. You can manage versioning by clicking the name of the document in the top center of the interface.

2 Co-editing and sharing: The owner of a cloud document can invite others to co-edit based on their Adobe ID. Cloud documents can also be shared as a Creative Cloud Library.

3 File autosave: XD will save changes to your document automatically as you modify your design and layout.

4 Linked assets: Design assets shared from one cloud document can be used in other documents, and any changes made to the original assets can sync across to documents that make use of them. This approach is ideal for creating and distributing design systems and branding assets.

5 Cross-device access: Open your XD project from any computer using your Adobe ID. Additionally, use the XD mobile application to open and test your designs on real hardware.

We are working with local documents in this book to ensure you have access to all the files, since cloud-based documents are tied to the owner's Adobe ID, even when shared.

The XD interface

With our document saved and ready to go, let's take a look at the overall interface and identify some of the important features of the software.

There are three interface modes you can switch among when working in XD. They are listed as tabs along the top left of the interface.

These modes target different aspects of user interface design and prototyping:

- **Design:** This is the primary working mode and the most complex. You'll use Design mode to manage artboards, assets, color, layout, and any design properties of such assets. All of your design and layout work happens here.

- **Prototype:** Once you have a set of artboards designed and populated with assets, you can switch to Prototype mode to wire up interactions across artboards, in components, and through the use of more advanced transitions and animations. All of your interactive work occurs in Prototype mode.

- **Share:** The least complicated mode, Share enables you to create links to share your project on the web for design review, presentation, user testing, or even for developer handoff.

We will be working primarily in Design mode for most of this lesson, and so we'll emphasize the way the interface is arranged when using this mode.

Toolbar

Property Inspector

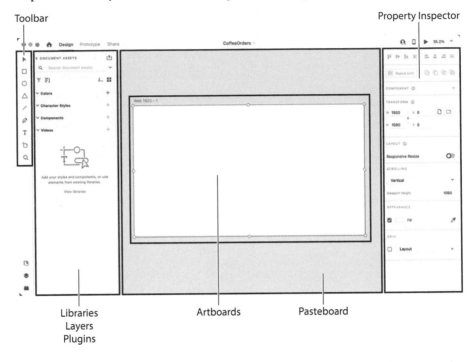

Libraries
Layers
Plugins

Artboards

Pasteboard

These are some of the major interface elements we'll be interacting with as we work in our XD document:

- **Toolbar:** XD includes a small number of tools for selections, the drawing of assets, and artboard management. If you need additional tools, you can always create content in Adobe Illustrator or Adobe Photoshop and import it.

- **Libraries:** When Libraries ⬚ is selected, the left-side column will give you access to document assets such as colors, character styles, and components, as well as your Creative Cloud Libraries.

- **Layers:** As in the Layers panel in other Creative Cloud applications, you can explore and manage artboards, object groups, components, and other assets through the left-side column when Layers ⬙ is active.

- **Plugins:** Activating the Plugins ⬛ option provides access to all your installed XD extensions in the left column. You will also find direct access to the Creative Cloud Desktop application where you can locate and install more extensions.

- **Artboards:** In XD, artboards are basically screens. You can include as many artboards as you like in a document, along with prototype interactions between them to create compelling user experiences.

- **Pasteboard:** The pasteboard is the darker-gray design surface that all artboards exist in. You can include design assets in artboards or they can exist on the pasteboard, apart from any artboard. Assets on the pasteboard will not appear in any shared content.

- **Property Inspector:** In the right-hand column of the XD interface, you will find the Property Inspector. The properties here will adapt depending on the currently selected objects. When in Prototype mode, the inspector changes to display Interaction properties. When Share mode is active, Link Settings are displayed.

With a basic understanding of the XD interface in mind, it's time to start designing.

Working with artboards

Whenever you create a new document in XD, it will always include a single artboard. Since we didn't create our document from a preset, the artboard that XD created is targeting the web and measures 1920 x 1080 pixels. This is much too large for a mobile experience.

We need to establish a new artboard targeting mobile devices and remove the existing Web 1920 artboard.

1 Choose the Artboard tool 🗂 from the toolbar. Go to the Property Inspector and scroll down until you locate the Mobile artboard presets.

MOBILE

iPhone 13, 12 Pro Max	428 × 926
iPhone 13, 12 Pro	390 × 844
iPhone 13 mini	375 × 812
iPhone 13, 12	390 × 844
iPhone X, XS, 11 Pro	375 × 812

You'll find many more presets here than you saw on the home screen.

2 Click the preset named iPhone 13, 12. A new artboard measuring 390 x 844 pixels appears directly to the right of the existing artboard.

The new artboard is now selected as well.

▶ **Tip** Clicking an empty artboard like this will select it easily, but if your artboard contains several assets, you can click the artboard name to select it instead.

3 Choose the Selection tool ▶, and click the original Web 1920 – 1 artboard to select it. Press the Delete key on your keyboard.

The artboard is removed. Only the iPhone 13, 12 – 1 artboard remains.

4 Double-click the iPhone 13, 12 – 1 artboard name to make the text editable. Enter **Coffee Selection** for a new artboard title and press the Enter (Windows) or Return (macOS) key to commit the change.

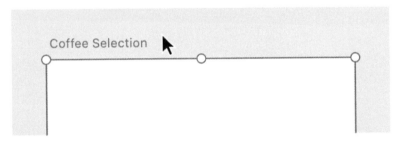

You now have a new artboard suitable for your mobile application design.

5 With the artboard still selected, in the Appearance section of the Property Inspector, click the Fill color swatch and in the overlay that appears, change the color value to **#ED9E43**. Click outside of the overlay to commit the change.

The artboard background now exhibits the chosen color.

Designing the application header

Many mobile applications make use of a header element. The header helps frame the experience and also provides a branding opportunity.

Let's create a header for this mobile design.

1 Choose the Rectangle tool ▢ from the toolbar and drag from the upper-left corner of the artboard to create a shape that measures **390 x 120** pixels.

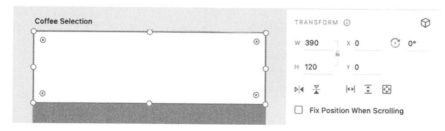

You can make necessary adjustments from the Transform section of the Property Inspector.

2 Locate the Appearance section of the Property Inspector and deselect the Border checkbox to remove the border. Click the Fill color and set the Hex value to **#000000** with an opacity of **75%**.

3 In the Effects section, select the Drop Shadow checkbox. Click the color chip and adjust the opacity to **50%**.

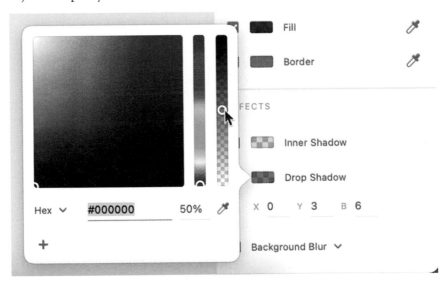

The header background shape is now complete and ready for us to add text.

4 Choose the Text tool T from the toolbar and click the artboard to create a text object. Type **BAD BEANS COFFEE ROASTERS**.

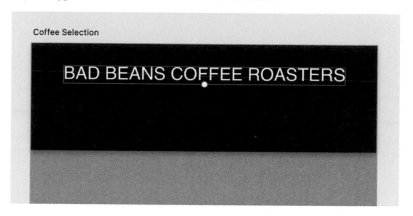

This is the branding element we will use in the header.

5 Switch to the Selection tool so that the text element is selected. To match the company typeface used in their logo, turn your attention to the Text section of the Property Inspector. Choose **Abolition Soft** as the font and set the Size value to **30**. Change the Character Spacing value to **72**. In the Appearance section, change the Fill color to **#FFEDD8**. Ensure that the center alignment option is selected.

● **Note** The Abolition font family is part of the Adobe Fonts collection that you can access at https://fonts.adobe.com as part of your Creative Cloud subscription.

6 With the Text tool T still selected, create a new text object and type **ORDER AHEAD** for the value.

Notice how the new text takes on the same appearance as the previous text object.

7 With the new text object selected, in the Appearance section of the Property Inspector, use the eyedropper to select the text Fill color from the artboard background.

8 Switch to the Selection tool so that the text element is selected. Choose **Semplicita Pro** as the font and increase the Size value to **47**. Change the Character Spacing value to **13**.

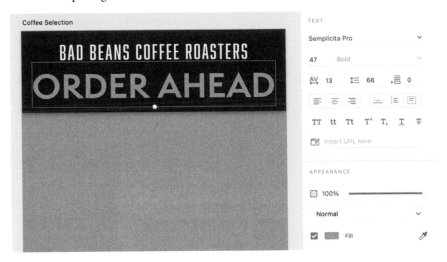

9 In the Effects section, select the Inner Shadow checkbox. Set the X and Y values to 1 and the B value to 2. Click the color chip and set the opacity to **35%**.

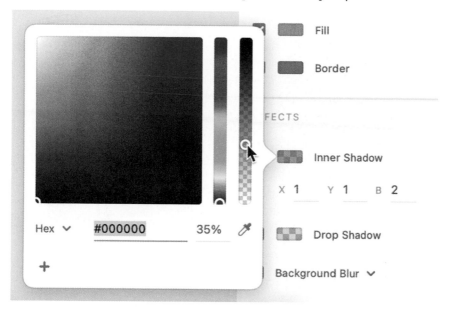

10 Using the Selection tool ▶., adjust both text objects so that they are vertically centered on the artboard according to the smart guides that appear. Ensure that the text objects are spaced out horizontally in a way that looks appropriate against the header background.

Our application header design is now complete.

Creating a component

Since we will use the application header design across multiple screens, let's make it a reusable component.

1 Using the Selection tool ▶., drag a selection rectangle around all objects that make up the application header: the background and both text elements.

A transform rectangle appears across all selected elements.

2 With all three elements selected, in the Component section of the Property Inspector, click the Make Component button +.

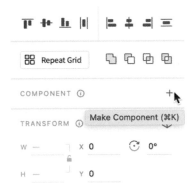

XD transforms the selected elements into a Main component.

3 Drag the Main component from the artboard and onto the pasteboard. Release the mouse button.

▶ **Tip** It is a good idea to keep any Main component in a special place, either in a dedicated artboard or simply on the pasteboard of your document.

4 Ensure that Libraries ▣ is selected so that the document assets are visible in the left-column sidebar. You will see the component has been added here with a default name. Double-click the component name and enter **Header** as its new name. Press Enter/Return to commit the change.

▶ **Tip** It is important to provide meaningful names for components—similar to naming layers.

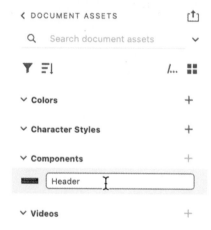

5 Drag the Header component from the Document Assets panel and place it in the Coffee Selection artboard, aligning it to the top center. Release the mouse button.

XD creates a component instance on the artboard.

Understanding components

Components serve a number of purposes in an XD document. A Main component can be used as a sort of design blueprint that can be replicated as multiple instances throughout a project. A component can also exhibit multiple states, as you'll see later.

If you edit the Main component, all component instances will update to reflect those changes. Component instances can also have their properties overridden without affecting the Main component or any other component instances in use.

There is a small diamond in the top-left corner of any selected component that will inform you as to which type of component it is:

1 A Main component is indicated by a diamond that is filled with green 🔹 If a Main component is edited, all component instances are updated to reflect the changes.

2 A component instance is indicated by a diamond filled with white 🔹 These are copies of the Main component. Changing properties of the Main component will be reflected in each instance being used.

3 A component instance can also have its properties overridden. These instances exhibit a diamond that is filled with white but includes a small green dot as well 🔹 Overridden properties do not reflect the properties present in the Main component.

Since the Main component controls so much, it's a good idea to only use component instances in artboards and then change the Main component only when necessary. Changes to the Main component will then cascade across the entire project, which makes adjustments easy to execute.

Designing the mobile experience

At this point, we've established our document with a single artboard. The artboard has been given a rich background color, and we've designed a nice Header component that can be used across many artboards.

Creating additional artboards

We need more screens for the mobile experience, and we'll create them by duplicating the existing artboard.

1 Using the Selection tool ▶., click the name of the Coffee Selection artboard to select it.

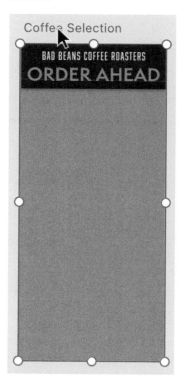

2 Choose Edit > Copy from the application menu or press Ctrl+C (Windows) or Command+C (macOS) to copy the artboard.

3 Choose Edit > Paste from the application menu or press Ctrl+V (Windows) or Command+V (macOS) to paste a duplicate of the copied artboard next to the existing one.

4 Paste three additional artboards and rename them according to the functions each will serve: **Summary**, **Confirmation**, **Splash Begin**, and **Splash End**.

You can rearrange your artboards across the pasteboard by dragging the names to better organize the document.

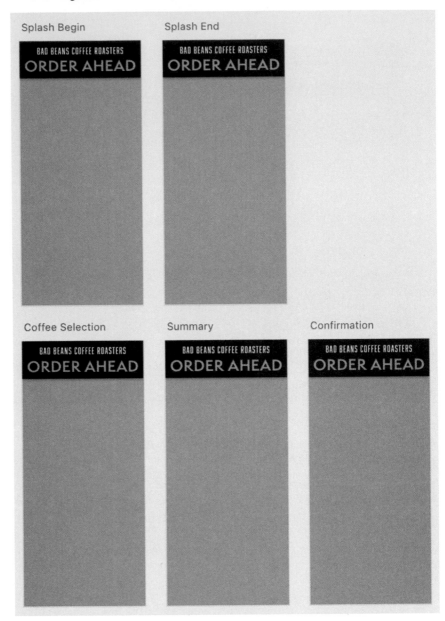

Each artboard is identical. All include Header component instances and exhibit the same background color.

5 Click the Header component instances in both Splash Begin and Splash End to select them. Press the Delete key to remove these instances, since splash screens do not include application interface elements.

The artboards that will serve as our splash screen are now empty of any content.

The artboards we've established will serve the following purposes as part of the mobile experience we are designing:

- **Splash Begin:** Later, we will design our splash screen experience across two artboards. This is the beginning state of that experience.

- **Splash End:** This is the ending state of our splash screen experience.

- **Coffee Selection:** This is our original artboard. It is the primary application screen where users can select coffee bean varieties for pickup.

- **Summary:** This screen follows the coffee bean selection, presenting a summary of what the user chose for pickup.

- **Confirmation:** This confirmation screen lets the user know their request has been completed and they can pick up their order soon.

Importing additional content

In the previous section we created shapes, text, and components. To save time, we've included a prebuilt set of assets for use in completing the design and layout of each screen.

We'll copy this content from the external document into our working document pasteboard.

1 Choose File > Open from the application menu and a dialog box opens that gives you access to cloud-based documents. At the bottom left of this dialog box is the On Your Computer button. Click this button.

A file browser dialog box appears.

2 Locate the file named assets.xd in the Lesson06/06Start folder and select it. Click Open.

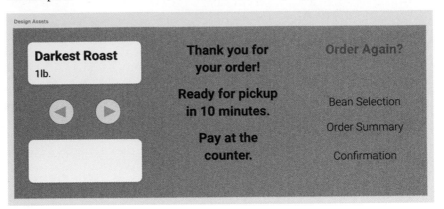

A simple XD document opens and includes a single artboard named Design Assets. Across this artboard are various assets for you to use.

3 Drag a selection rectangle across the entire artboard to select these assets and choose Edit > Copy from the application menu or press Ctrl+C/Command+C to copy the assets. You can either close assets.xd or simply ignore it from here on.

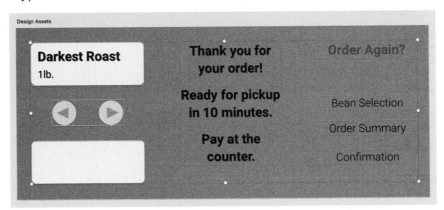

4 Back in our working document, CoffeeOrders.xd, deselect any artboards that are currently selected. Then choose Edit > Paste from the application menu or press Ctrl+V/Command+V to paste copies of the assets into the document pasteboard.

● **Note** In addition to components, we can define colors and character styles in document assets. With any asset selected, click the small plus button to add selected colors and character styles available in the selection. This is a smart way to work when dealing with larger projects because any changes to a defined color or character style will propagate across those assets in the documents that use them.

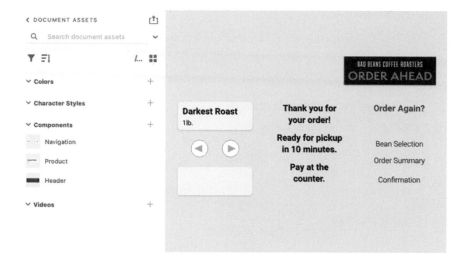

Simpler assets such as text and shapes exist only on the pasteboard. Components, however, will also appear in our document assets just like the one we created earlier. Because these components are copied from another document, they take the form of component instances on the pasteboard.

Placing imported content

With our artboards ready and additional assets copied over into our project, we can begin populating the various screens with content.

We have three identically styled text objects on the pasteboard. Each is the text heading for three of our artboards, letting the user know where they are in the experience.

1 Drag each heading onto the appropriate artboard and release the mouse button, using the guides to align to vertical center and at a Y position of **160** across each artboard.

The three headings are no longer part of the pasteboard but can be located in each individual artboard. They are all uniform and balanced.

2 In the Confirmation artboard, locate the "thank you" text message on the pasteboard. Move it into the Confirmation artboard, aligning to the vertical center. Set the Y position to **260**.

3 Additionally, locate the text object that reads "Order Again?" and move it to the bottom center of the same artboard at a Y position of **760**.

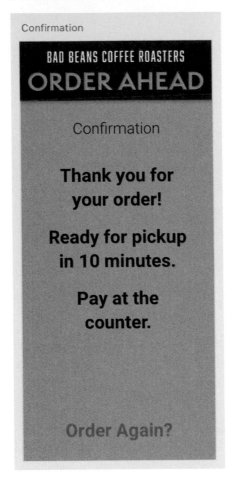

We are finished with the Confirmation artboard for the time being.

4 Moving on to the Summary artboard, locate the rounded rectangle shape and move it from the pasteboard into this artboard. The shape should be vertically centered with a Y position of **260**.

5 In the Transform section of the Property Inspector, set the shape height to **420**.

We'll leave some room at the bottom of the artboard for our navigation.

6 Locate the Product component on the pasteboard and double-click to edit its contents. Select only the text object and copy it using Ctrl+C/Command+C.

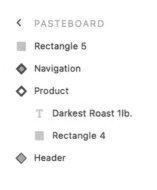

7 With the Summary artboard selected, paste the copied text by using Ctrl+V/ Command+V.

With the text pasted, move it so that it is centered vertically at a Y position of **274**.

8 Locate the Product component once more, and this time move the entire component onto the Coffee Selection artboard. It should be vertically centered at a Y position of **260** like nearly all other objects.

Having a set of objects across each screen that are similarly placed at identical spacing will establish uniformity and balance for the user.

Designing checkboxes

In our Coffee Selection artboard, we have a single selection card component instance. You'll notice that there is no way to actually make a selection from this card.

Let's design a checkbox toggle component and add it to the card.

● **Note** Whenever a Main component does not exist in your document, you can always generate one in this manner.

Since we copied the Product component from another document, it appears as an instance on the artboard. We need to edit the Main component itself.

1   Locate the Product component in the Libraries ▣ sidebar Document Assets area and right-click it. From the menu that appears, choose Edit Main Component.

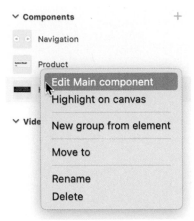

A Main component appears on the pasteboard, ready to edit.

2   Double-click the Main component on the pasteboard to edit its contents.

Switching to your Layers ⬙ panel will help you to navigate.

3   Hover over the text and rectangle objects in the Product component as displayed in the Layers panel and select the Lock 🔒 icon for each.

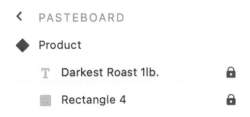

This will make it easier to draw additional content in the component by preventing you from accidentally moving the items in the locked layers.

4   Choose the Rectangle tool ▢ from the toolbar and drag from the lower right of the component with the Shift key pressed to create a square that measures **40 x 40**.

You can adjust the size in the Transform section of the Property Inspector.

5   In the Appearance section of the Property Inspector, change the border color to **#3E1800** and set the border size to **2**. The fill color should be **#FFFFFF**. Set the corner radius to a value of **4**.

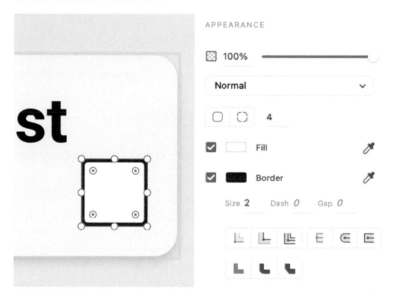

6   Click to deselect the Lock 🔒 icon for the text and rectangle objects from the Layers ◆ panel in order to unlock them both once more.

This will make them editable later on, when we will need to change text values for the Product component instances.

Note Adobe advises against ever nesting a Main component in another component. Because of this, the component we just designed is created as a component instance because we are working in the Product component. If we were to create a component outside of another component, it would be created as a Main component instead.

7 Choose Object > Make Component from the application menu and rename the component **Checkbox** in the Document Assets panel.

A component instance is created in the Product component while the new component itself is added to our document assets.

Establishing component states

Components are very powerful objects in XD. Not only can we take advantage of change propagation and property overrides, but components can also include multiple states that can be switched back and forth as the user interacts with your design.

Let's establish a toggle state for the Checkbox component.

1 Locate the Checkbox component in the Libraries ▢ sidebar Document Assets area and right-click it. In the menu that appears, choose Edit Main Component.

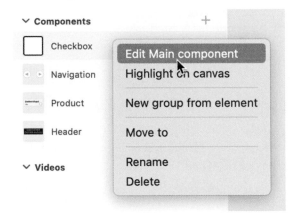

The Checkbox Main component is added to the pasteboard so that it can be edited.

2 In the Property Inspector, click the Add State + icon in the Component (Main) section.

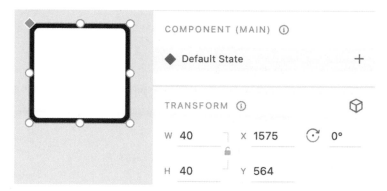

A selection overlay appears.

3 A checkbox normally behaves as a toggle. Choose Toggle State to create a new state of that kind.

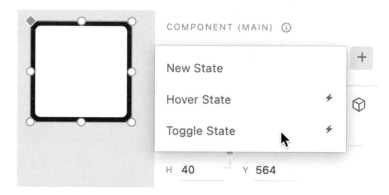

It is fine to retain the default name of **Toggle State**.

4 Be sure Toggle State is selected and double-click the component on the pasteboard to enter it.

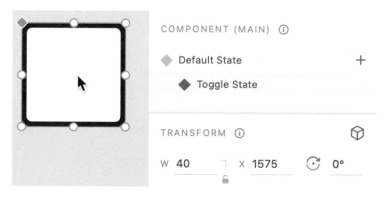

● **Note** When you create a new toggle state or hover state, XD will autowire ⚡ interactions for that component to switch states on hover or tap. Creating a New State that is not of those kinds will not autowire any interactions. You must do that yourself.

We'll be editing the Toggle State only. The Default State will remain unaffected by our changes.

5   In the Toggle State, select the Pen tool ✐ from the toolbar and use it to draw a simple checkmark within the bounds of the Checkbox component background. Only three anchor points are needed.

6   Press the Escape key to end your path when the checkmark is complete.

● **Note** Your checkmark lines may look like the ones in the figure, but they can appear different as well. The important thing is that a visible checkmark exists to distinguish the toggle state from the default state.

7   With the checkmark selected, in the Appearance section of the Property Inspector, change Border Color to **#3E1800** and the border size to **5,** and select Round Join ⌐ for the join option and Round Cap ⊂ for the cap option.

The checkmark now better matches the checkbox and is nice and large.

8   Press the Esc key to exit the component and switch back to the Default State.

9 Select the Coffee Selection artboard by clicking its name, and click Desktop Preview ▶ in the upper right of the XD interface.

Desktop Preview runs and displays the selected artboard.

10 Click the Checkbox component to toggle it from the Default State to the Toggle State and back again.

Using repeat grid

The Coffee Selection and Summary artboards have limited content in them. We want them to be filled with coffee bean choices and the resulting selections made by the user.

We could, of course, simply copy and paste elements to make duplicates but XD has a more elegant way of approaching this task.

1 In the Coffee Selection artboard, click the Product component instance to select it.

Recall that this component now includes the checkbox.

2 In the Property Inspector, activate the Repeat Grid  option to transform the selection into a Repeat Grid object.

Repeat Grid handles appear along the right and bottom edges.

3 Drag the bottom handle downward until a set of five additional repetitions are produced, making six cards in total.

The last few cards will run off the artboard.

4   Select the Coffee Selection artboard and adjust the height to **1300**.

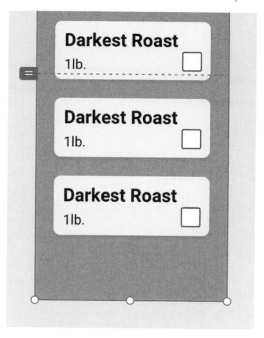

Note When the viewport indicator becomes visible, this indicates the height of the physical screen, enabling vertical scrolling in your prototype.

The artboard is now taller, and the viewport indicator becomes visible at the previous height.

Items in a Repeat Grid can have their properties adjusted after the grid is formed.

5   Adjust the names of each product by double-clicking to enter each grid repetition until you can edit the text object in each Product component instance. The product names should read as follows: **Darkest Roast**, **Dark Roast**, **Medium Roast**, **Regular Roast**, **Light Roast**, and **Special Roast**.

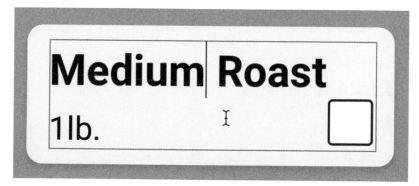

You can use the Layers panel to make this task easier.

6 Click away from the Repeat Grid to an empty area of the pasteboard and turn your attention to the Summary artboard.

7 Select the text object that reads "Darkest Roast 1lb." and activate the Repeat Grid option here as well.

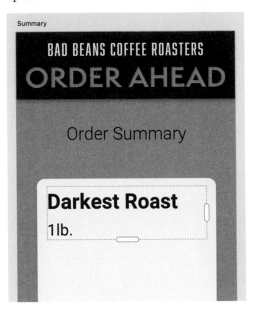

8 Drag the bottom handle downward to produce a set of two additional text elements.

9 Hover your mouse between any two text objects until the Repeat Grid margins become highlighted. Drag to increase the margins between text objects until they are all positioned more evenly across the background object with a margin of **50**.

10 Edit the value of each text object repetition to change the names, reflecting a set of selected products: **Darkest Roast**, **Regular Roast**, and **Special Roast**.

▶ **Tip** To convert a Repeat Grid into individual objects, select the Repeat Grid object and click the Ungroup Grid  button in the Property Inspector.

By using the Repeat Grid feature in this way, we have quickly populated our design with content—and even customized it.

Adding navigation elements

We've now populated all the functional screens of the application. The user needs to be able to proceed through the experience from one screen to the next.

To facilitate this, we'll place navigation elements at the bottom of each artboard.

1 Navigate to the Document Assets in the Libraries ▢ sidebar and locate the Navigation component there.

This is one of the components that was copied over from our assets.xd file previously. It includes design elements for both a back button and a next button and various states to enable or disable each button visually.

2 Drag an instance of the Navigation component onto the bottommost area of the Coffee Selection artboard. Reposition the navigation so that it is vertically centered and 30 pixels from the bottom using smart guides.

3 With the Navigation component instance still selected, change its state in the Property Inspector from the Default State to the Next Only State.

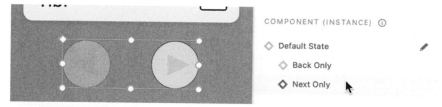

This visually indicates to the user that they can only move forward.

4 You need to adjust the position of the Header component in the layer stack so that content does not scroll over it.

In the Layers 🔻 panel, drag Header from the bottom of the layer stack to the very top.

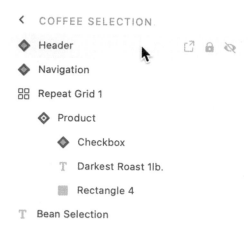

Header will appear above all over content now.

5 Recall that this artboard is taller than its viewport, allowing content to scroll. We want to be sure the application header stays in place and is unscrollable.

With Header still selected, in the Transform section of the Property Inspector, select the checkbox that reads Fix Position When Scrolling.

This will pin the header to the top of the viewport—even while scrolling.

6   Drag another instance for the Navigation component onto the bottommost area of the Summary artboard. Reposition the navigation so that it is vertically centered and **30** pixels from the bottom using the smart guides that appear.

7   With the Navigation component instance still selected, verify its state in the Property Inspector, ensuring the Default State is active.

This visually indicates to the user that they can move backward or forward from this screen.

Design principle: balance

Balance in a design or layout will provide some measure of visual equilibrium between elements that make up the composition. This is often achieved through the arrangement of objects across a design.

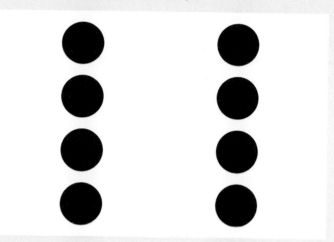

In this lesson, we've seen a number of examples of balance through the placement of different elements and even the composition of various components.

The Navigation component, in its default state, is a good representation of balance as each button has the same visual weight. This sense of balance is disturbed when either of the other states are activated, diminishing one of the two buttons and giving more weight to the other.

Completing the splash screen

The functional screens of our Order Ahead application are now complete. We still need to add some branding elements to the artboards that will make up the splash screen.

The splash screen will consist of the Bad Beans Coffee Roasters logo that holds for a moment, and then decreases in size before the application loads.

Let's set up the logo across each splash screen artboard.

1 Select the Splash Begin artboard. Choose File > Import and navigate to the Lesson06/06Start folder. Select the file named Logo.png and click Import.

The logo is too big to fit in the constraints of the artboard.

2 With the Logo image still selected, go to the Property Inspector. Ensure that the width and height are locked 🔒 and change the width to **300**. Use the Selection tool ▸. to adjust the placement of the logo until it is vertically and horizontally centered on the artboard.

3 Copy the logo by using Ctrl+C/Command+C. Select the Splash End artboard and paste a copy of the logo with Ctrl+V/Command+V. Change the width to **80** in the Property Inspector.

Note It is very important to name the logo image identically across both artboards to ensure that the intended animation works correctly. By copying and pasting the Logo object from one artboard to another, the name "Logo" should remain identical across both.

4 Use the Selection tool ▸ to adjust the placement of the logo until it is vertically and horizontally centered on the artboard.

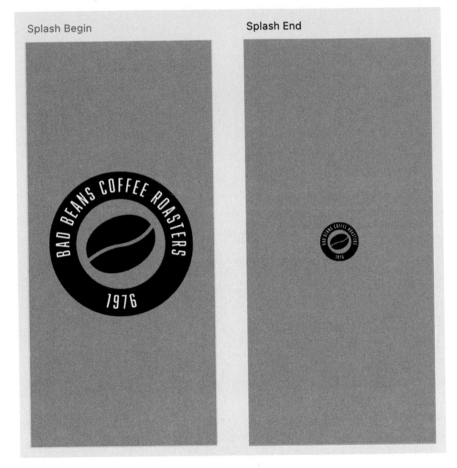

Splash Begin

Splash End

The set of splash artboards includes one with the logo filling the width of the screen and another where it is much smaller.

Prototyping and sharing

So far, we've spent this lesson in the Design interface mode. We'll wrap up our mobile prototype by briefly exploring both Prototype and Share modes.

Adding tap triggers

We'll now add interactions to specific design elements that will allow the user to navigate the application.

1 Switch to the Prototype interface mode by clicking the Prototype tab along the top left of the XD interface.

Much of the interface will appear the same in this mode, but you will no longer have access to design tools in the toolbar. The Property Inspector will change to display properties for your prototype interactions.

2 Double-click the Navigation instance at the bottom of the Coffee Selection artboard and select the Next object within it.

The object is highlighted in blue. A small circular blue icon appears to the right.

Note You will also notice that there is a wire already created for each of the Checkbox components in our Repeat Grid. These indicate the autowired toggle interactions that were created automatically along with the Checkbox Toggle State.

3 Drag the blue circular icon to the right of the Next group to pull out a wire. Continue dragging upward and to the right until the wire comes in contact with the Summary artboard. Release the mouse button to create a new interaction.

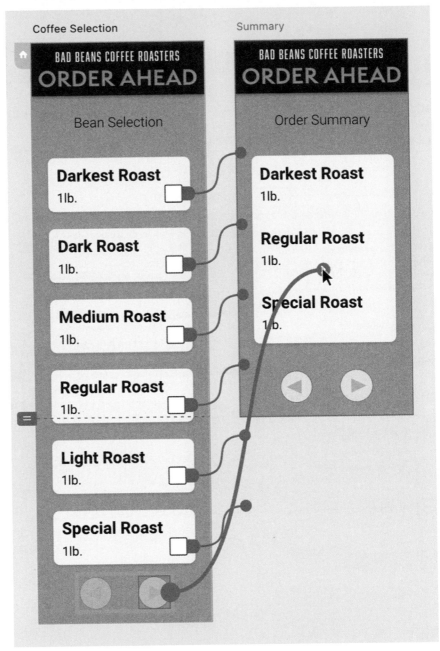

A wire appears connecting the Next object to the Summary artboard.

4 In the Property Inspector, ensure that Trigger is set to **Tap**, Type to **Transition**, and Animation to **Dissolve**. Change Easing to **Snap** and Duration to **0.4 s**.

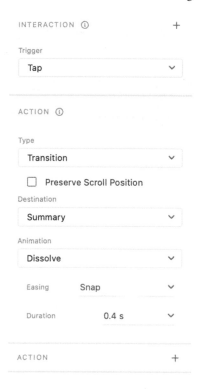

These settings will ensure a snappy transition to the next screen when the user taps the Next object.

5 Select the Back object in the Navigation component instance at the bottom of the Summary artboard. Drag a wire back onto the Coffee Selection artboard and release the mouse button.

Note XD will remember your last interaction settings and apply those to new interactions you establish. Because of this, there is no need to adjust the Tap Trigger settings.

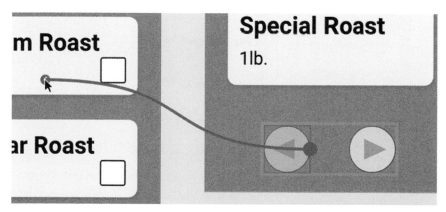

This allows the user to go back and change their coffee selections.

6 Select the Next object in the Navigation component instance at the bottom of the Summary artboard. Drag a wire onto the Confirmation artboard and release the mouse button.

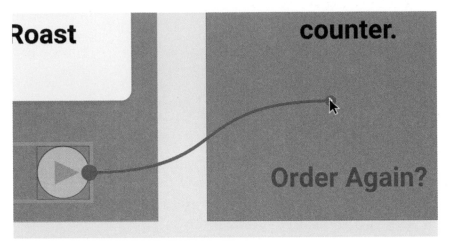

This interaction will take the user to the last step of the experience.

7 Lastly, select the Order Again? text object at the bottom of the Confirmation artboard. Drag a wire onto the Coffee Selection artboard and release the mouse button.

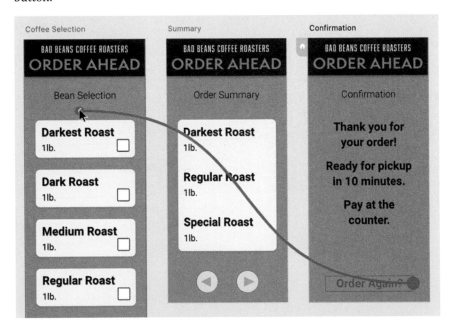

The user can now easily return to place another pickup order following order confirmation.

Animating the splash screen with time triggers

● **Note** Time triggers are available only when an entire artboard is selected.

We've designed a set of artboards that together will make up the application splash screen. We'll need to wire these up as well.

1 Select the Splash Begin artboard.

The entire artboard becomes highlighted, and a small circular blue icon appears to the right.

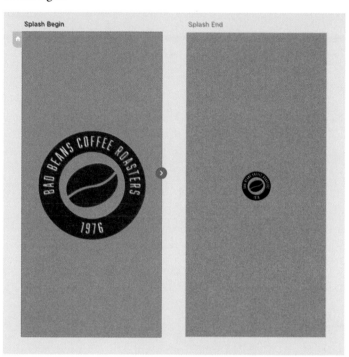

2 Drag the blue circular icon toward the Splash End artboard to create a new wire. When it is hovering well across the Splash End artboard, release the mouse button.

Note Auto-Animate works by comparing objects across two artboards that are of the same type and exhibit the same name. Any properties such as scale, position, or opacity that differ from one artboard to another are animated.

3 In the Property Inspector, change Trigger to **Time** and give it a delay of **1 s**. Set Type to **Auto-Animate**, Easing to **Wind Up**, and Duration to **0.3 s**.

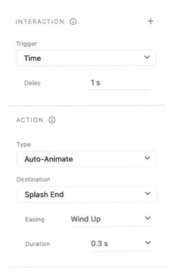

▶ **Tip** Instead of using the menu for Delay and Duration values, you can always simply enter your own.

A Time trigger will activate without any user interaction. This is perfect for something like a splash screen.

4 Select the Splash End artboard and drag the blue circular icon toward the Coffee Selection artboard to connect the two with a blue wire. Release the mouse button.

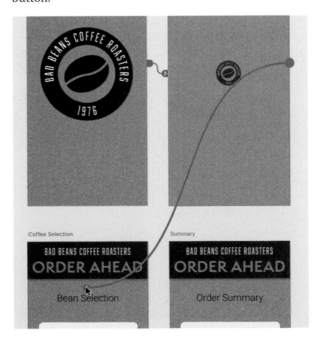

Once the splash screen animation completes, we take the user into the experience proper.

5   In the Property Inspector, ensure Trigger is set to **Time** and give it a delay of **0 s**. Set Type to **Transition** and Animation to **None**.

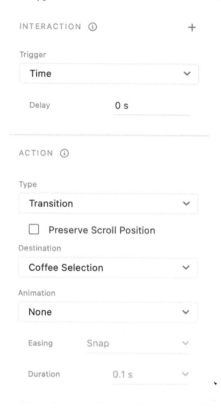

These settings ensure that once the animation completes, we jump straight into the Coffee Selection artboard.

6   Select the Splash Begin artboard by clicking its name and click Desktop Preview ▶ at the upper right of the interface.

The splash screen animation plays, leading to the coffee selection screen. Work your way through the experience to ensure everything works correctly, including scrolling, toggle selection, and navigation across screens.

Generating a share link

There are many ways to export content from XD for further use or to share your prototype for review, development, or user testing.

We'll create a basic share link URL using mostly default settings. Before generating a link to share our prototype, we must declare a flow.

Tip You can create many flows in a single XD document and name them all whatever you wish by double-clicking the flow name and typing a new one.

1 At the upper-left corner of each artboard in Prototype mode is a small gray tab with a house icon. Locate the Splash Begin artboard and activate this tab by clicking it.

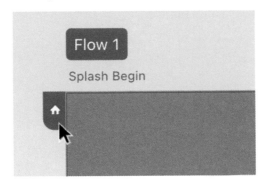

A new flow is created, and the tab becomes blue.

2 Click the Share tab along the upper left of the XD interface to enter Share mode.

Share mode is a bit simple compared to the other two interface modes, as its only purpose is the creation and management of share links.

3 Change the Link name to **Order Ahead**, leave View Setting at Design Review, and keep Link Access set to Anyone With The Link. Click the Create Link button.

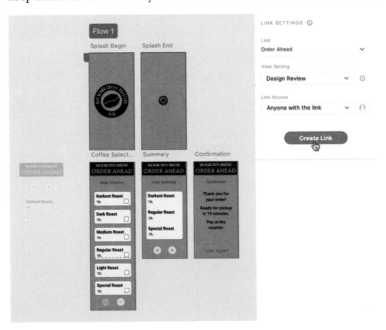

A link is generated according to the provided settings.

4   With the link created, either click it or copy and paste it into a web browser.

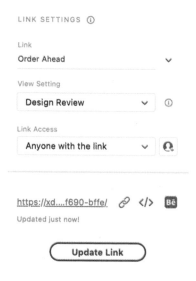

● **Note** Links can only be generated from declared flows. Objects on the pasteboard are never part of a flow—only artboards and their contents.

LINK SETTINGS ⓘ

Link
Order Ahead ⌄

View Setting
Design Review ⌄ ⓘ

Link Access
Anyone with the link ⌄ 🔒

https://xd....f690-bffe/ 🔗 </> Bē
Updated just now!

(**Update Link**)

Link settings can be changed from here after a link has been created.

5   In the web browser, the experience presents itself starting from the artboard marked as the beginning of the flow.

Interact with the experience, moving from screen to screen to preview the finished prototype. You can also use the bottom navigation to move between artboards.

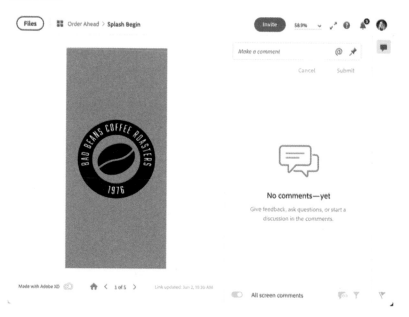

Next steps with Adobe XD

To further explore the creative options that XD has to offer, you can make use of Adobe's help resources available at www.adobe.com/products/xd/learn/get-started.html.

If you'd like to advance in your exploration of XD in greater depth, I encourage you to consider reading *Adobe XD Classroom in a Book (2021 Release)*, also available from Peachpit and Adobe Press.

Review questions

1 Why would you create a component out of a group of assets?

2 How can an artboard filled with design content be most easily selected?

3 How can you edit a Main component if one does not exist on any artboard or even the pasteboard?

4 What properties must be shared by an asset across artboards to perform a successful Auto-Animate?

Review answers

1 If you intend to use those assets across many artboards or if you want to manage multiple states.

2 Click the artboard name.

3 Choosing Edit Main Component from the Document Assets right-click menu will create a Main component and place it on the pasteboard if one does not exist in the document already.

4 The asset must be the same type of object and share the same name across artboards.

7 3D RENDERING WITH DIMENSION

Lesson overview

In this lesson, you'll learn how to do the following:

- Explore Adobe's various 3D software offerings.

- Create projects and scenes using Adobe Dimension.

- Understand how the camera and lighting impact a scene.

- Add models to a scene and adjust their position and rotation.

- Understand the design principle of proportion.

- Add realism to models with materials and graphics.

- Render a scene for use in Adobe Photoshop, allowing further customization.

 This lesson will take less than 1 hour to complete.

To get the files used in this lesson, download them from the web page for this book at www.adobepress.com/CreativeCloudCIB. For more information, see "Accessing the lesson files and Web Edition" in the Getting Started section at the beginning of this book.

Adobe Dimension is a compositing design software
application with an approachable, modern interface
for easy compositing of photorealistic graphics.

Getting started

● **Note** If you have not already downloaded the project files for this lesson to your computer from your Account page, make sure to do so now. See "Getting Started" at the beginning of the book.

Start by viewing the finished project to see what you'll be creating in this lesson.

1 Open the 07End.psd file in the Lesson07/07End folder to view the final project using Photoshop.

The file is a Photoshop document of a scene rendered in high-quality output from 3D models, materials, and graphics arranged as a scene in Dimension.

Dimension can render projects as a multilayered Photoshop file—such as 07End.psd—or as a flattened PNG. You can also use it to produce content for augmented reality experiences with Adobe Aero.

2 Close the file.

Understanding Adobe's 3D applications

Over the past few years, Adobe has greatly expanded the 3D toolset that is available through both Creative Cloud and the Substance 3D Collection. Let's begin with a brief overview of how everything is organized and which applications are meant for what purpose.

Adobe Dimension

Most Creative Cloud users are aware of Dimension, a rendering and design application intended to make 3D approachable for designers.

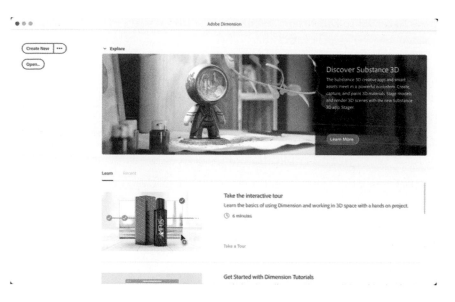

Dimension is available as part of a standard Creative Cloud subscription.

Adobe Substance 3D Collection

Adobe Substance 3D is a set of specialized software and assets for high-end 3D workflows. The collection is a separate offering from Creative Cloud that requires an additional subscription in most cases.

Substance 3D Stager

Like Dimension, Stager enables users to design and render 3D scenes. Using Stager's models, materials, lights, and cameras, you can create designs for virtual photography shoots.

● **Note** The Substance 3D Collection is included with enterprise-level Creative Cloud subscriptions for Higher Education as part of a single subscription.

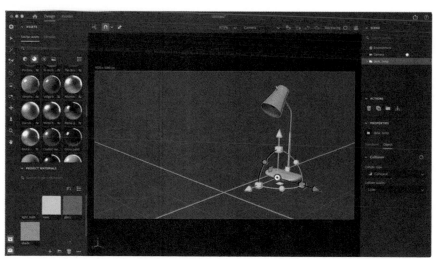

Stager is so similar to Dimension that nearly all of the exercises in this lesson can be completed interchangeably with either software application. Whereas Dimension is targeted toward traditional 2D designers, Stager is intended to be used by those engaged in a more focused 3D workflow.

We focus on Dimension in place of Stager in this lesson since Dimension is included with all Creative Cloud subscriptions and thus available to a greater number of designers.

Additional Substance 3D applications and services

● **Note** As of this writing, Substance 3D Modeler is in beta development.

While the focus of this lesson is on Dimension—and, to a lesser degree, Stager—it is good to know a little about the other Substance 3D applications and services and how you can use them.

- **Substance 3D Painter:** Painter enables workflows for texturing and painting 3D objects.

- **Substance 3D Designer:** Designer is focused on creating materials, patterns, filters, and environment lights for use in 3D workflows.

- **Substance 3D Sampler:** Sampler enables the creation and manipulation of materials sourced from real-world reference photography.

- **Substance 3D Modeler:** Modeler allows users to design 3D models with virtual reality interfaces and hardware.

- **Substance 3D Assets:** Accessible from https://substance3d.adobe.com/assets, you can source models, materials, and other assets from this resource for use in your 3D workflow.

Designing a 3D scene with Dimension

In this lesson, we are going to use Dimension to design a 3D scene that can be rendered in a realistic way. We'll populate it with a set of 3D objects branded and customized to our personal specifications.

Creating a new project

The first step, as with most design software, is to create a new project file to work in.

1 Open Dimension and view the Start screen.

2 Though you can simply click the Create New button to start off using Dimension's new project defaults, for this project click the ellipsis portion of the button to access additional options.

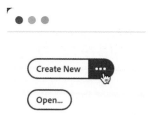

The New Document dialog box appears.

3 In the New Document dialog box, make the following adjustments to the size and resolution of your document canvas:

- Name the document **Scenic Render**.

- Set Canvas Size to **4000px** x **3000px**.

- Set Resolution to **300 Pixels/Inch**.

4 When finished, click Create.

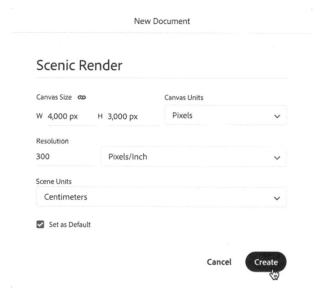

The increased canvas size and resolution will make your rendered output more adaptable to various media platforms like print or video.

5 Before beginning work on the new document, save the file by choosing File > Save from the application menu.

A simple save dialog box appears.

6 In the save dialog box, navigate to the Lesson07/07Start folder and click Save.

The Dimension project is saved with the file extension .dn in the chosen location.

Dimension and Stager differences

If you have a license for Substance 3D Stager, you can absolutely use it in place of Dimension for this section. The basics of working with models, materials, and the like are almost identical.

The main differences are that Stager includes more advanced features and boasts a more realistic and powerful rendering engine than Dimension.

Here are some other things to know if you choose to explore Stager:

1 Stager project files have the .ssg file extension.

2 Stager has a Ray Tracing toggle, which takes the place of Dimension's Render Preview.

3 Stager does not create a camera for your scene by default; you must create one manually.

4 Stager has many starter assets that are different from those found in Dimension.

5 Stager has many more options in the Render workspace.

Other than these considerations, anyone familiar with Dimension should feel right at home using Stager.

Exploring the Dimension interface

The newly established project is completely empty right now aside from Scene Environment settings and a camera. In Dimension, every new project makes both items available immediately upon creation.

Let's examine the Dimension interface.

Toolbar   Canvas   Scene panel

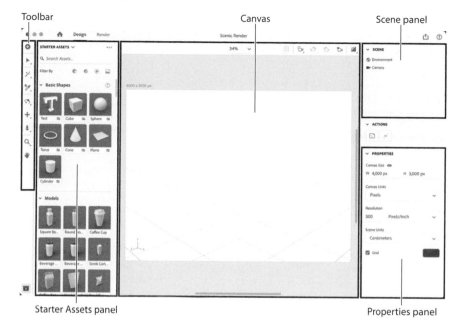

Starter Assets panel   Properties panel

- **Toolbar:** The Toolbar includes a set of tools for selecting and manipulating content, and zooming and panning the camera.

- **Canvas:** The Canvas is where all of your assets are rendered when using the Design workspace. Here you'll find an overview of your scene, and any cameras you use will change the view in this space.

- **Scene panel:** The Scene panel provides an outline of the various objects that make up a scene. As you add various models and other items to a scene, they will appear here as well since everything is part of the overall scene.

- **Properties panel:** As in many other Adobe applications, the Properties panel provides access for a designer to manipulate the various property values of selected objects. With nothing selected, Canvas properties are displayed.

- **Starter Assets panel:** This panel includes a wide variety of models, materials, lights, and images that you can use in a scene.

When nothing is selected in the Canvas or the Scene panel, the Properties panel will display properties pertaining to the document itself.

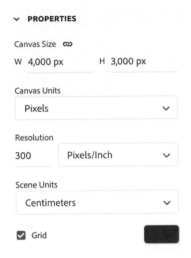

These properties reflect the settings you choose when you create your document. You can change them at any time, but it's good to settle on these parameters right away to avoid potential issues later.

In a new document, the Scene panel lists only Environment and Camera objects.

Choosing Environment will reveal properties addressing global lighting and how the ground plane appears on the Canvas.

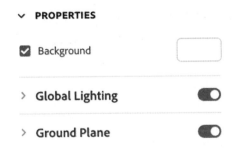

Choosing Camera will display the default camera properties.

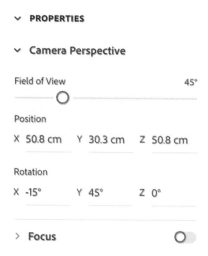

You can adjust all of these properties by tweaking values in this panel or by using the Orbit ↻, Pan +., and Dolly ↓. tools in the toolbar.

Manipulating the camera properties will visibly change the grid overlaying the Canvas, but if no models are present in the scene, little else will be visually noticeable.

The Dimension workspaces

Unlike other Creative Cloud applications like Photoshop, Illustrator, InDesign, and the like, Dimension has only two workspaces to choose from: Design and Render.

You can access both workspaces from the tabs at the top left of the Dimension interface.

You'll do most of your work in the Design workspace. The Render workspace comes into play once your design is complete and you want to render it to a file for use elsewhere.

Working with environmental elements

Elements of a scene such as a background image, camera perspective, and lights can always be set up and controlled manually, but Dimension can also make use of Adobe Sensei to determine lighting and perspective based on the selected background image.

Adding a background image

Let's select an appropriate background image for our scene.

1 If the Starter Assets panel is not visible, click the ⬚ button to open it.

The Starter Assets panel appears.

2 In the Filter By area at the top of the panel, click the Images icon 🖼 to show the starter background images.

The Starter Assets panel shows only images.

3 Drag the asset named Table onto the scene.

Dimension applies the image to the background of the scene. Note that the perspective grid does not quite match up with the tabletop.

4 To correct the perspective grid and adjust the lights per information gathered from your selected background image, click the Match Image button.

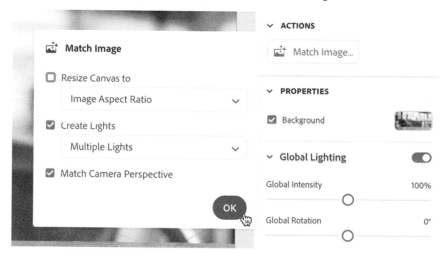

The Match Image dialog box appears.

5 Disable the Resize Canvas To option and ensure both Create Lights and Match Camera Perspective are enabled. Click OK.

Dimension inspects the image for light and perspective data and applies that data to the scene. The Canvas remains the same size because we chose not to resize it.

Understanding lights and the camera

You will likely have noticed some major changes within the Scene panel after enacting the Match Image process.

Not only have the ground plane and camera perspective changed in the canvas, but we also have a Directional lights asset present that did not exist before.

These lights were automatically generated and their properties set by the Match Image process. Clicking any of these Directional lights within the Scene panel will reveal adjustable properties within the Properties panel below.

You do not have to settle for the interpreted lights or their assigned properties. You can remove lights or make any adjustments you like to Height, Rotation, Intensity, and more.

You can access the Environment light from the Scene panel in a similar way. Like Directional lights, the Environment light is derived from the background image we established but has far fewer options.

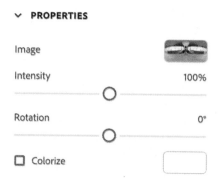

Adjusting any properties of these lights right now doesn't do anything to the scene itself that is apparent within the Canvas since no models are available for these lights to work against.

Selecting the camera from the Scenes panel will display the adjusted camera properties in the Properties panel.

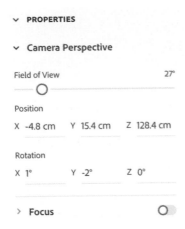

These properties have very different values from when we initially looked them over, as the camera has been adjusted to match the perspective information present in our background image.

The camera is set up perfectly for our scene, and everything is ready to start working with additional objects.

Adjusting the camera

While we have configured the camera settings for this project automatically based on data derived from the background image being used, you do have full control over the camera to set up perspectives for the scene.

You can change the camera perspective either by tweaking values in the Properties panel or by using the camera tools in the toolbar.

You can use these tools to adjust many aspects of the camera:

1 Orbit ⟳ moves the camera around freely.

2 Pan ⊕ shifts the Camera camera up, down, left, and right.

3 Dolly ↧ moves the camera toward the subject or backward, away from the subject.

Once you have set a particular view, you can save it for recall using the Camera Bookmarks button ⎘. Not only is this useful for recalling your perfect camera settings, but you can also save multiple settings for comparison later.

Working with 3D models

Now that we have created a new project in Dimension and established lighting and camera perspective based on background image data, we'll begin populating our scene with some 3D models.

Adding a coffee bag

Dimension includes several 3D models accessible through the Starter Assets panel. We'll add one of these models to the scene and reposition it with the Selection tool.

1 Within the Starter Assets panel, click the Models filter toggle ⬡ at the top of the panel to filter by models.

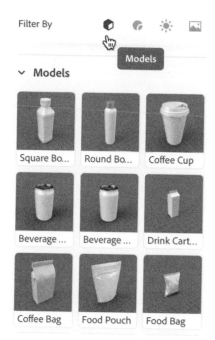

Now, only models are displayed for selection.

Tip You can also drag models from the Starter Assets panel onto the Canvas for custom placement, if desired.

2   Scroll down and locate Coffee Bag. Click it to add the model to the center of the scene.

Note You can also add models to a scene you've gotten from elsewhere through the Add And Import Content button ⊕ above the toolbar.

3   Using the Selection tool ▸., drag the Coffee Bag model toward the right side of the Canvas until the overlay displays an X offset of **19.5 cm**. Release the mouse button.

The bag is now positioned at the right side of the scene, but the Y and Z positions do not change.

Understanding the gizmo overlay

Whenever a 3D model is selected, a multidimensional gizmo overlay appears that allows you to adjust position, scale, and rotation across X, Y, and Z dimensions.

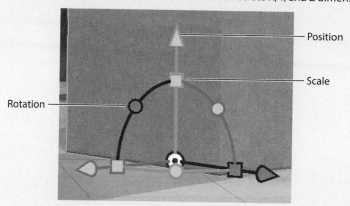

Position is identified by a cone, scale by a square, and rotation by a circle. This is the same icon used across all three dimensions, which are represented by different colors. X is pink, Y is green, and Z is blue.

Interacting with any dimension represented as part of the gizmo will also tell you which dimension and property you are currently adjusting.

Adjusting additional coffee bag properties

While using the Selection tool to move a model across the scene works well enough, making use of the gizmo overlay will enable a greater set of properties to be controlled in a more deliberate fashion.

Let's adjust the scale and rotation of the coffee bag.

1   If not already selected, use the Selection tool ▶. to select the Coffee Bag model.

    The bag is selected, and the gizmo overlay is visible on it.

2 Holding down the Shift key and dragging any of scale icons of the gizmo will adjust all dimensions equally. Do so now and adjust the scale to **120%** across all dimensions. Release the mouse button.

The informational overlay displays the difference as you make any adjustments.

3 Adjust the Y rotation property by dragging the green circle until the information overlay reads a change of **−30 degrees**. Release the mouse button.

The bag is now nicely positioned, scaled, and rotated for our virtual product shoot.

Adding a coffee cup and adjusting its properties

Alongside the Coffee Bag model, we'll add a paper Coffee Cup model as well, setting its position and scaling it so that the placement and proportions between both models are correct.

1 Within the Starter Assets panel, with the Models filter still active, locate the Coffee Cup model and click it.

The model is added to the center of the scene and is automatically selected, revealing the gizmo overlay.

2 Using the Selection tool ▶, drag the pink cone, which represents the X position, slightly toward the right side of the Canvas until the overlay displays an X offset of **3.5 cm**. Release the mouse button.

▶ **Tip** You can reposition models with greater accuracy using the gizmo overlay.

3 Let's bring the Coffee Cup model slightly closer to the camera as well. Drag the blue cone toward the bottom of the Canvas to adjust the Z position to **10.5 cm**. Release the mouse button.

The coffee cup is now closer to the camera than the coffee bag.

4 Lastly, hold down the Shift key and drag any of the square scale icons of the gizmo to adjust the scale property to 130% across all dimensions.

Now we have set the scene with a coffee bag and coffee cup, arranged nicely in the frame with appropriate proportion to each other and the background image being used in the scene.

Design principle: proportion

Proportion is one of the easier principles to grasp, as we can understand it by observing objects in the world around us. It refers to the comparative relationship between more than one object regarding size, primarily. But it can also be applied to something like quantity or even color to some degree.

When using any 3D software where more than one object is present in a scene, proportion is something that you will constantly be considering.

As we continue to work through this project, consider the importance of proportion when placing and sizing 3D models within the scene.

Working with materials and graphics

Most 3D models within Dimension have a very basic, default material applied to them that is not very realistic. It usually appears as a simple white material. You can see this by browsing the Starter Asset models as most include this default material.

The Coffee Bag model is different in that it includes a Paper material by default, which works well. But we will want to select a different material for our coffee cup.

Adjusting coffee cup materials

Now we'll select and apply a better material to use with the body of our Coffee Cup model.

1 The Coffee Cup model is actually a group of models as indicated by a folder ■ in place of a cube ⬡. Click the folder icon to the left of Coffee Cup in the Scene panel to expand it.

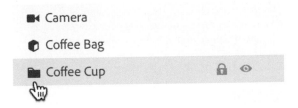

The Cup and Lid models now appear as nested beneath Coffee Cup.

2 Hover over Cup until a set of small icons appear to the right. Click the very last one, which is a right-facing chevron › .

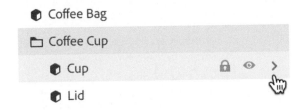

The Cup model properties open and the Scene panel changes to reflect this.

3 Any materials and graphics that are applied to the model appear in this view. Click Cup Material to select it.

4 In the Starter Assets panel, filter by materials by clicking the Materials filter selection.

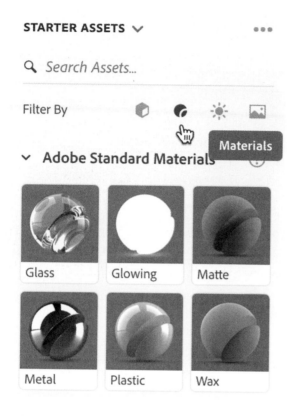

Only materials will now appear in the panel. They are divided into Adobe Standard Materials and Substance Materials.

5 Scroll down to locate the Cardboard material in the Substance Materials category.

6 Drag the Cardboard material from the Starter Assets panel onto the Cup material in the Scene panel. Release the mouse button.

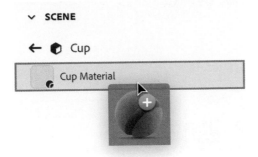

The existing material is replaced by the Cardboard material.

7 In the Properties panel, look over the various attributes that can be adjusted to refine the look of the material we've chosen. Click the Color preview square.

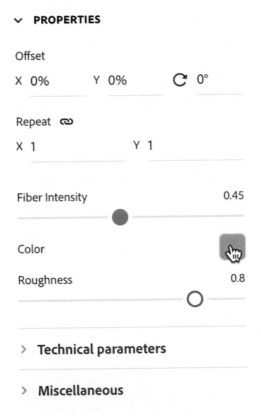

A small color picker overlay appears.

8 Select a different shade of brown for the cardboard color. You can click anywhere within the color space to choose, or you can enter the RGB values below it. Enter **122 92 50** for the RBG values and click outside the overlay to dismiss it.

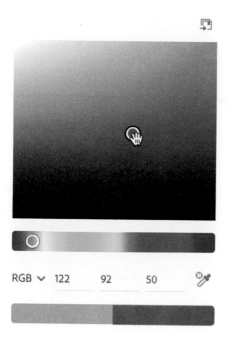

9 To exit the Cup model in the Scene panel, click the left-facing arrow ← at the upper left of the panel.

The Cup model in the Coffee Cup model group now exhibits a cardboard material with a modified base color. Note that we left the Lid model alone since it already has a plastic-like material applied to it.

Exploring the Illustrator file

The next step in this project is to apply branding assets to the Coffee Cup and Coffee Bag models we've so carefully assembled within the scene. For this purpose, we've created a set of branding assets in Adobe Illustrator.

If you'd like to view the assets, open the coffee_branding.ai file in the Lesson07/07Start folder.

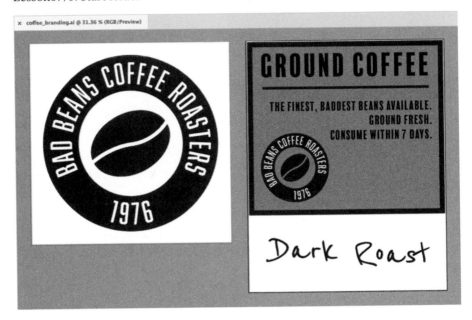

Note Dimension can make use of a wide variety of image formats as graphics within the software. Some of the more commonly used file formats are AI, PSD, JPG, PNG, TIF, EPS, BMP, and SVG.

You are likely already familiar with these assets from our previous exploration of Illustrator in Lesson 4. We have a logo and a label for Bad Beans Coffee Roasters, which are separated across two distinct artboards.

Dimension can leverage Illustrator files directly as placed graphics on models and even distinguish between artboards.

Adding a logo to the coffee cup

We'll begin branding the models with content from Illustrator by applying graphics as decals to our models.

Let's start by applying the logo image to the Coffee Cup model.

1 In the Scene panel, expand the Coffee Cup model group and select the Cup model.

The Actions panel changes to display quick actions specific to this model.

2 In the Actions panel, choose the quick action for Place Graphic On Model .

A file browser dialog box appears.

3 Locate and select the coffee_branding.ai file in the Lesson07/07Start folder and click Open.

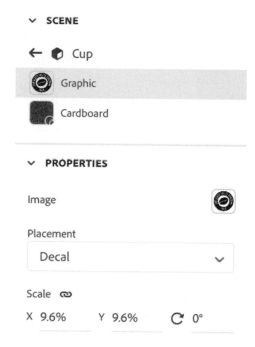

The graphic logo is placed above the Cardboard material.

4 Using the transform overlay that appears over the graphic logo, hold down the Shift key and drag any of the four square handles to preserve the image aspect ratio and scale the graphic down slightly so it fits better on the Cup model.

5 Select the full Coffee Cup model group and drag the green circle on the gizmo overlay to adjust the rotation property by **–13 degrees**.

The entire Coffee Cup model rotates to better match the rotation of the Coffee Bag model.

Adding a label to the coffee bag

Adding a label to the Coffee Bag model will include steps very similar to the ones we used when adding our logo to the Coffee Cup model. Of course, there will be small details that differ because of the difference in models and graphics.

1 Select the Coffee Bag model in the Scene panel and then choose the Place Graphic On Model  quick action from the Actions panel.

A file browser dialog box appears.

2 Locate and select the same coffee_branding.ai file that we used for the Coffee Cup model from the Lesson07/07Start folder and click Open.

The logo is placed on the coffee bag and the Properties panel changes to display materials and graphics for the selected model.

Dimension will use the first artboard from Illustrator by default, but we can adjust this.

3 Locate the Image thumbnail preview in the Properties panel and click it.

An artboard selection overlay appears.

4 Using the Artboard menu, select Artboard 2 and click outside of the overlay to dismiss it.

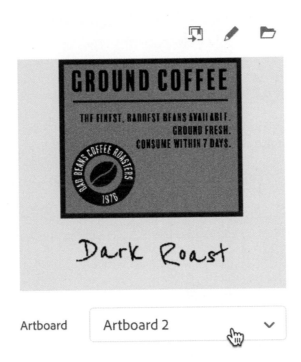

The correct artboard is now selected, and the label asset appears on the Coffee Bag model.

5 Using the Selection tool ▶, drag the label graphic and reposition it to better conform to the shape of the coffee bag. Release the mouse button once the graphic is placed.

Our 3D scene is now complete!

Replacing and removing graphics

If you ever decide to remove or replace a graphic from a model, the task is fairly straightforward.

The process of replacing a graphic is the same as selecting a different artboard, as we did for our coffee bag label. In the overlay, instead of selecting an artboard, you click the Select A File icon ▬ and browse to the new file.

To remove a graphic entirely, in the Scene panel in a model, select the existing graphic and then click Delete 🗑 in the Actions panel.

Using render preview

Dimension has a feature called Render Preview that you can toggle on and off using the Render Preview toggle ▣ located in the upper-right corner of the interface.

With Render Preview off, working in your project will be less intensive for your system, as objects are rendered more simply. Toggling off Render Preview also simplifies lighting and shadows quite a bit.

Turning Render Preview on will give you a better idea of what the final render will look like, and shadows will appear much more realistic.

Render Preview Off   Render Preview On

It is beneficial to enable Render Preview at certain times throughout the design process. But I recommend leaving it off when you are actively working on arranging and refining model attributes in your scene.

Rendering your 3D scene

There are a few options for getting your design out of Dimension and into a state that can be shared with others or worked on further. Let's close this lesson with a look at some of these options.

Exporting for augmented reality

Adobe Aero is an augmented reality (AR) design application that is available for mobile devices. Adobe even has a desktop version currently in development.

The software allows you to layer 3D models, multilayered Photoshop documents, animations, still images, and more into a live view using the mobile device camera.

To export your completed models from Dimension for use in Aero, choose File > Export > Selected For Aero from the application menu.

Export For Aero

Your file will be converted for use in Augmented Reality. This process can take several minutes if your file is more than 50 MB. Once completed, you can save your Aero-ready file to Creative Cloud Files to view it in the Aero Mobile app or to your file system to transfer it to your mobile device.

✓ Ready

Cancel   Export

The Export For Aero dialog box appears and translates your content for use in AR.

Clicking Export will allow you to save the selected models to your Creative Cloud sync folder or to any other location that can be accessed easily by Aero on your mobile device.

In an Aero project, the exported models can be loaded in and placed into the scene. Using Aero, these models can also be adjusted and programmed with behaviors.

● **Note** You can find Aero system requirements by visiting https://helpx .adobe.com/aero/ system-requirements.html.

Once you've created an AR experience using Aero, you can share it with others by providing a URL or by generating a scannable QR code.

● **Note** You can also quickly share your 3D scene as a web-based experience by clicking the Share 3D Scenes button ⬧ in the upper right of the interface. A link is generated that provides a simplified view of your scene.

Go ahead and try it out with your compatible mobile device. Enjoy the coffee!

Using the render workflow

The primary way of getting your scene outside of Dimension is to make use of the Render workspace.

Let's render our scene as a multilayered Photoshop document for further manipulation.

1   Switch to the Render workspace by clicking Render at the top left of the Dimension interface.

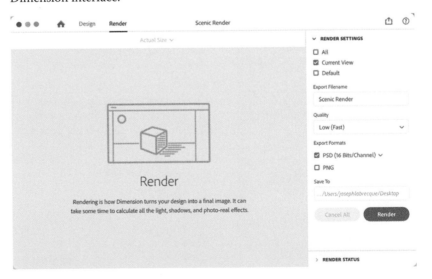

The Render workspace appears.

2 Review the Render Settings panel to the right and make any changes you would like:

- If you have created additional camera bookmarks, choose a camera bookmark or the Current View.

- Enter the desired Export Filename.

- Select a Save To location for your rendered file.

- Choose a Quality setting for your render.

- Choose PSD as the Export Format to create a layered Photoshop document.

When finished with your settings, click Render.

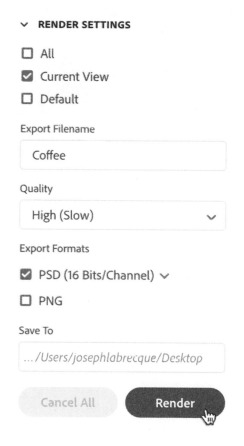

The 3D scene will begin to render and the majority of the screen will fill with a preview of the render process.

Tip The higher the quality you choose in Render Settings, the longer your scene will take to render. This is a very intensive process, and you may notice your system hardware struggling somewhat during the render.

3 Monitor the Render Status panel so that you know when the render is complete. Dimension will display a progress bar and time estimate to assist with this.

Once the render is complete, you can locate the PSD file in the location you chose and open it in Photoshop to add text or shape elements, modify the background image, or perform a variety of other manipulations that Photoshop is capable of.

Next steps with 3D

To further explore the creative options that Dimension has to offer, you can make use of Adobe's help resources available at https://helpx.adobe.com/support/dimension.html.

To discover more advanced 3D workflows, explore the Adobe Substance 3D Collection: www.adobe.com/products/substance3d/3d-augmented-reality.html.

To learn more about Adobe Aero, visit www.adobe.com/products/aero.html.

Review Questions

1 What is the difference between Substance 3D and Dimension?

2 What does Match Image do?

3 What is the difference between models and materials?

4 Which properties can you manipulate through interaction with the gizmo overlay?

Review Answers

1 Substance 3D is a professional, focused 3D designer's set of tools. Dimension is part of Creative Cloud and meant for use by designers more comfortable with applications like Photoshop and Illustrator.

2 Match Image makes use of Adobe Sensei to interpret aspects of a still photograph like perspective and lighting, and then apply those attributes to a scene in Dimension through the addition of lights and adjustments to camera perspective.

3 Models are the 3D forms of objects that can be placed within a scene. Materials are the textures and looks that can be applied to those models.

4 Properties that can be manipulated through the gizmo overlay include Position, Scale, and Rotation across the X, Y, and Z dimensions.

8 PRODUCING AUDIO CONTENT WITH AUDITION

Lesson overview

In this lesson, you'll learn how to do the following:

- Configure your hardware for recording and playback of audio.

- Meter and record clean audio at appropriate levels.

- Edit audio files and perform noise reduction.

- Layer and blend audio tracks in a multitrack session.

- Gain an understanding of the design principle of Emphasis.

- Create a multitrack mixdown and produce audio files for distribution.

This lesson will take less than 1 hour to complete.

To get the files used in this lesson, download them from the web page for this book at www.adobepress.com/CreativeCloudCIB. For more information, see "Accessing the lesson files and Web Edition" in the Getting Started section at the beginning of this book.

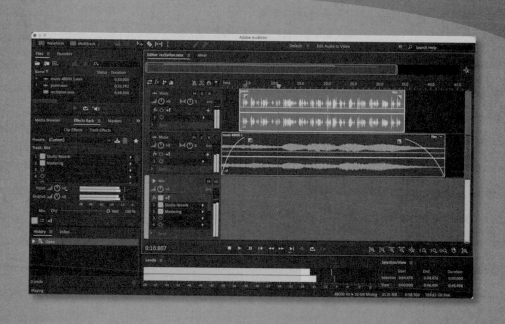

Audition can be used to created single waveform and
multitrack arrangements for the production of music,
podcasts, voiceover, film scores, audio restoration,
and more.

Getting started

● **Note** If you have not already downloaded the project files for this lesson to your computer from your Account page, make sure to do so now. See "Getting Started" at the beginning of the book.

Start by listening to the finished project to see what you'll be creating in this lesson.

1 Open the 08End.mp3 file in the Lesson08/08End folder to view the final project in a media playback application such as QuickTime, Preview, or VLC.

The project is an audio production that blends poetic recitation and musical accompaniment into a single, distributable file. Care has been taken that the levels of each part work well with the other, that any mistakes have been edited out, and that everything fades nicely to create a professional production.

2 Close the 08End.mp3 file.

Introducing Audition

Audition is part of the digital audio, video, and motion group of Creative Cloud software. It functions as a dedicated audio editor and arranger and is used stand-alone or in conjunction with other applications like Adobe Premiere Pro.

Audio editing applications like Audition generate visuals based on audio file amplitude across time. This creates a visible waveform that you can interact with through the different tools and workflows available—making the invisible, visible.

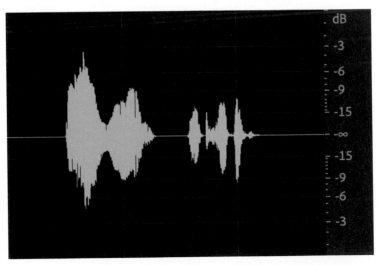

Being effective when working with sound, as you might imagine, is being a careful listener. Even with the visual aids on display in Audition, do not rely solely on them. Be sure to listen to the audio often as you work across your projects to monitor how changes you make affect the project.

Audition workflows

Audition provides three different ways of working with audio:

- Using the Waveform Editor to record and edit single audio files
- Using the Multitrack Editor to sequence single audio files as clips within tracks to be mixed together
- Editing a CD layout for the production of a compact disc using multiple, sequenced audio files

The Audition interface

Audition's user interface is fairly straightforward. We will remain in the Default workspace throughout this lesson, so I suggest you choose this as well.

If you're not already in the Default workspace, click Default at the top of the interface to switch to that workspace.

I'll highlight some of the important areas of the interface that we'll use in this lesson:

- Files panel: This panel displays any audio files, recordings, and session projects you are currently working with.
- Effects Rack: This is used to add effects to single waveforms or session tracks.
- History panel: This panel keeps a history of the steps you've taken when editing and arranging.
- Levels panel: This panel displays the volume (measured in decibels) of audio being recorded or being played back.
- Waveform Editor/Multitrack Mixer: This is where most of the visual waveform and clip data appears and where you can edit and sequence your audio. If you're using the Waveform Editor, you will be working with single recordings. If you're working in the Multitrack Mixer, you will be able to sequence and blend clips in a multitrack environment.

● **Note** While CD Layout does still exist in Audition, we will not be exploring it in this lesson since it is not applicable for most modern workflows and tasks.

Note We have closed the Essential Audio panel when working in Audition to make more room for other visual elements in the workspace.

Files panel Waveform Editor/Multitrack Mixer

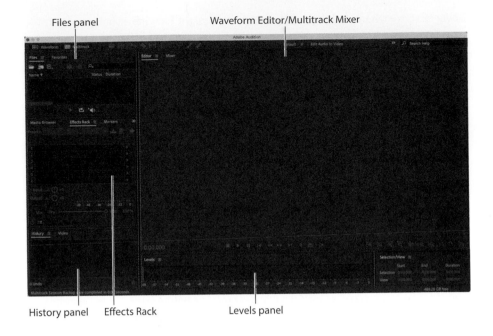

History panel   Effects Rack   Levels panel

Working in the Waveform Editor

Note If you do not have an audio file open when you click the View Waveform Editor button, Audition will prompt you to create one.

The Waveform Editor enables the recording and editing of single audio files. You may choose to record to a new audio file through this editor, and any audio file can be opened for editing and further manipulation using the same editor.

You can switch between the Waveform Editor and the Multitrack Editor by clicking either of the two buttons along the upper left of the interface.

Audio hardware configuration

Before any recording or playback takes place, it is important to gain an understanding of how Audition works with your hardware, such as microphones and speakers. If the audio hardware is not configured correctly, you will not be able to record or play audio in the software.

1 Choose Audition > Preferences > Audio Hardware on macOS or choose Edit > Preferences > Audio Hardware on Windows.

The Preferences dialog box appears with the Audio Hardware category selected.

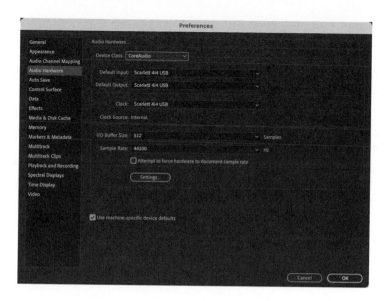

2 The most important settings here are Default Input (to control which microphone input is used for recording audio) and Default Output (to determine which set of speakers your audio will output to).

You can choose from built-in hardware or use an external audio interface if you have one on hand. Be sure to select the best hardware for your setup.

3 Choose the Audio Channel Mapping category just above the Audio Hardware category. This determines specifically how various input and output channels from your selected hardware are mapped in Audition.

4 Be sure to check your Default Stereo Input settings first. Most microphones are monaural in nature, meaning they capture only one channel of sound.

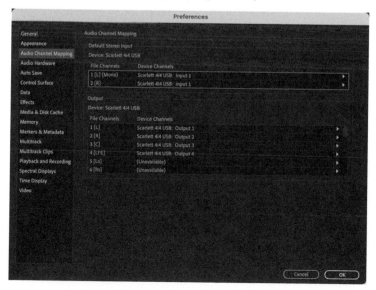

● **Note** If you want to capture stereo sound—where audio includes both a left and right channel—you can set both 1 [L] and 2 [R] values to map to the same microphone input. For your Output settings, this largely depends on your hardware capabilities, but you will generally select at least a set of stereo channels for both 1 [L] and 2 [R].

5 Click OK to close the dialog box.

Monitoring audio input

To test your audio input configuration before recording, right-click the Levels panel and choose Meter Input Signal from the menu that appears. Audition will then present the currently detected levels, in decibels, that are being interpreted by the microphone input.

Generally, your audio levels should be peaking somewhere between −12 and −3 dB for narrative recording. If everything registers lower, you should increase the gain on your hardware inputs. If you are registering above −3 dB, it would be a good idea to dial back the gain.

Recording audio

Now that you have configured your audio hardware and confirmed your inputs are working, we can proceed in this project by recording some audio.

In this example, we'll be reciting the poem "This Living Hand" by poet John Keats:

> This living hand, now warm and capable
>
> Of earnest grasping, would, if it were cold
>
> And in the icy silence of the tomb,
>
> So haunt thy days and chill thy dreaming nights
>
> That thou wouldst wish thine own heart dry of blood
>
> So in my veins red life might stream again,
>
> And thou be conscience-calmed, see here it is
>
> I hold it towards you.

You can choose another poem or anything else to recite when recording.

Let's begin by creating a new audio file:

1 To create a new audio file, click the New File icon ▣ in the Files panel, and choose New Audio File from the menu that appears.

2 In the New Audio File dialog box, enter **poem** in File Name, or choose another name that makes sense to you.

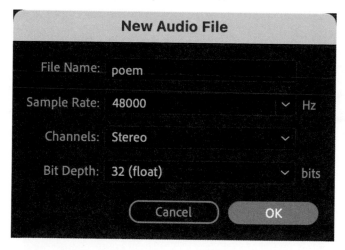

3 From the Sample Rate menu, select 48000; for Channels, choose Stereo; and for Bit Depth, choose 32 (Float).

This tells Audition to record audio as a 48000 Hz stereo file at 32 bits per sample.

4 Click OK to dismiss the New Audio File dialog box.

A new audio file is created in the Files panel and opens in the Waveform Editor.

5 Once you are prepared to record your voice, click the red Record button in the transport controls below the Editor and the recording will begin immediately.

6 Now that you are actively recording, recite the poetry. Leave a pause at the beginning, before you speak, and at the end, after you finish the recitation. Additionally, take your time and pause between lines.

As you record, you will notice a waveform being generated. We'll clean up any pauses during the editing phase, so don't worry about pausing too often.

7 Once you have competed the recitation, click the Stop button below the Waveform Editor to stop the recording.

8 Save your newly recorded file by choosing File > Save from the application menu.

Audition will prompt you for some information through the Save As dialog box that appears, including the filename and location.

9   To save this file as high-quality, uncompressed audio, select Wave PCM as the file type.

● **Note** You can change additional properties like Sample Type and File Name if you like, but we configured these when the file was created.

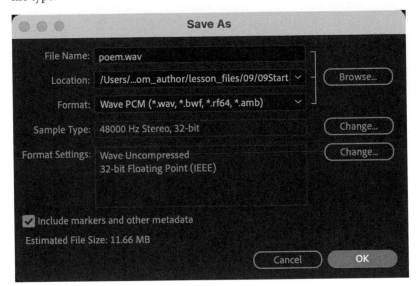

10 Change the location to the Lesson08/08Start folder.

11 Click OK to save the file.

Audio file properties

You may be wondering what all these properties refer to when creating a new audio file.

1   Sample Rate refers to the frequency that digital audio samples are recorded from an analog source.

2   Channels specifies whether you want to record in monaural sound, which is a single audio channel, or in Stereo sound, which includes both left and right channels.

3   Bit Depth indicates how dense each data sample is when captured. The greater the bit depth, the more audio data within each sample is acquired.

Editing audio

Now that your audio is recorded and saved to a local file, let's look at the visual waveform displayed in the Waveform Editor to get an idea of what you may need to edit.

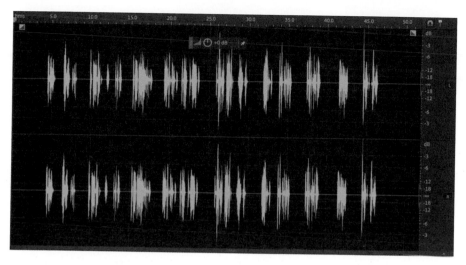

The waveform indicates audio amplitude across time and is measured in decibels from top to bottom. Time itself is represented from left to right and is measured in standard minutes and seconds.

Above the waveform is the navigator. This tool represents your current view of the waveform. You use it to examine particular segments across time to perform edits when necessary.

You can increase the waveform detail by adjusting the navigator from each side and by scrubbing along to target specific areas of the waveform.

Now you'll perform some edits on the audio file to clean things up a bit:

1   You should be able to play back the audio at any point by moving the blue playhead ▮ across the waveform and pressing Play or tapping the spacebar.

2   Listen to your recording to locate any long pauses in your audio that can be shortened, and using the Time Selection tool ▮, drag to select portions of time for removal.

3 A small amplitude dial will appear over the selection via an overlay. Use this dial to increase or decrease the amplitude of your current selection.

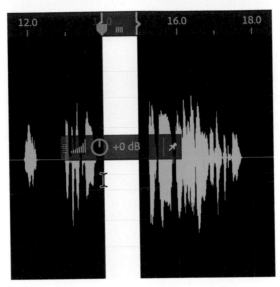

4 Now we want to remove the entire selection from the waveform to decrease the lengthy pause in speech. Press the Delete key on your keyboard to remove it entirely.

5 Proceed to remove any long pauses from your audio file, including those at the beginning and end of the recording. When you are finished, the narration should play back naturally with no obvious pauses or gaps.

Comparing the original state of the audio recording with what you have now, it should be obvious that this is a much tighter, edited production.

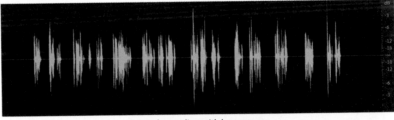

Original recording with large pauses

Recording with pauses edited out

Audio cleanup

Aside from excising long pauses and dead space from your recording, there are also mechanisms within Audition to help you clean up a recording that may be on the noisy side. In fact, one of the primary uses of Audition is to restore audio recordings through a variety of noise reduction techniques.

Let's remove some of the background noise from the recording we've been working on by using a process effect.

1 Using the Time Selection tool, select a segment of your audio waveform where it is quiet and without any recorded speech.

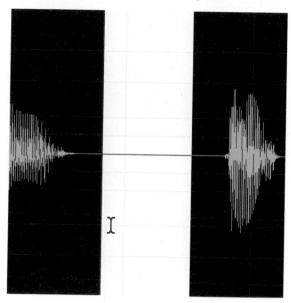

We can use this to generate a noise print for this process that contains only unwanted background noise.

2 Select Effects > Noise Reduction/Restoration > Capture Noise Print from the application menu.

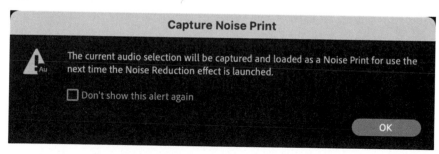

The noise print will be captured.

Note There is also an Output Noise Only option that allows you to listen only to the noise being removed.

Note Certain effects are very processor-intensive and cannot be stacked during real-time playback and must be applied first. Any such effects will contain the word "process" in the name, indicating they must be used immediately and cannot be used in the Effects Rack.

3 With the noise print captured, select Effects > Noise Reduction/Restoration from the application menu. Click Noise Reduction (process).

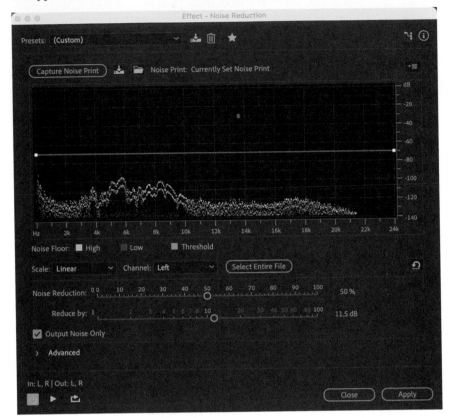

The Effect – Noise Reduction box dialog appears.

The captured noise print will be automatically loaded into this effect.

4 Playing back your audio will now make use of the effect. Listen to see how it may have been improved by using noise reduction.

5 Using the Noise Reduction slider, adjust the strength of the noise reduction applied to your audio. This specifies how many decibels the noise should be reduced by. Once you find the settings you desire, click Apply to commit the changes.

You can also view and edit your audio recording in the Waveform Editor through either Spectral Frequency Display or Spectral Pitch Display .

These alternate displays are useful when you need to perform precise editing across a specific frequency with tools like the Spot Healing Brush and related selection and cleanup tools 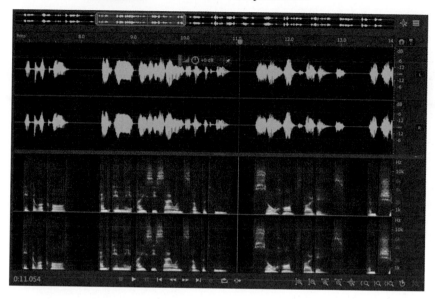 or to view detected pitch data.

Working in Multitrack View

While working on a single file is useful, you can also use Audition to layer and sequence multiple audio recordings in order to compose a multitrack mixdown involving voice, music, and more.

Creating a multitrack session

To begin working in the Multitrack Editor, you must first create a multitrack session file. This is essentially a data file that tells Audition where your audio files are located and how various effects and other settings are applied across the session.

1   Click the New File Icon in the Files panel and choose New Multitrack Session from the menu that appears.

● **Note** Just as when creating a single audio file, you can make choices for Sample Rate, Bit Depth, and channel Mix. Audition will automatically convert any audio files that do not fit the session criteria—so no pressure!

2 In the dialog box that appears, provide the session with a name and the folder location you want to save it to. You can choose an existing template to use, but I suggest selecting None for this exercise.

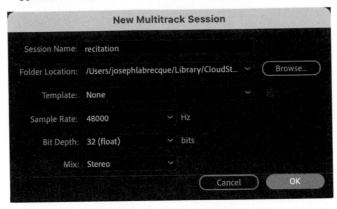

3 Click OK to save your Multitrack Session SESX file to the Lesson08/08Start folder and open it in the Multitrack Editor. You will see a stack of around six empty tracks ready for you to work with.

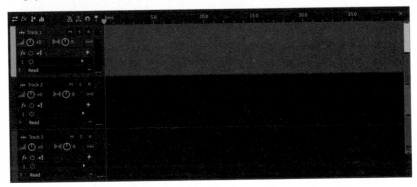

Working with multitrack audio

We will begin working on our multitrack session by adding audio files to our empty tracks and naming them appropriately.

1 Click the name of the top track, Track 1, to select it for renaming. Type **Voice** and click outside the name to commit your change.

2 From the Files panel, drag the poem.wav file into the Voice track and drop it in. The waveform will then appear as a clip within the track.

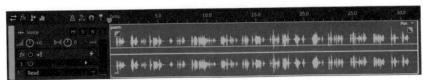

3 Click Track 2 and rename it Music.

I've supplied a short musical piece in the exercise files for this lesson named music.wav. You can, of course, select another piece of music from your own collection or from various stock media websites for use in a project like this.

4 Drag music.wav from the Lesson08/08Start folder into the Music track. Audition warns you that the sample rate of the music.wav file does not match the sample rate of the session. Click OK.

Audition resamples the clip and saves it as a copy of the original file named music 48000 1.wav. The waveform of this audio file then appears as a clip.

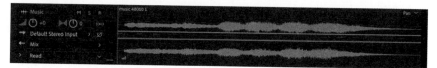

● **Note** Audition is great at conforming files with different properties such as sample rate to allow for their convenient inclusion within a multitrack arrangement.

Observe that we now have a set of two tracks each populated by a unique audio file clip—one for our voiceover and another for the background music.

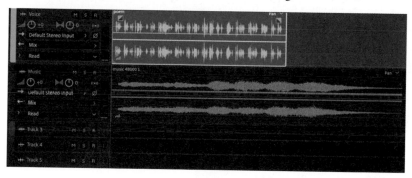

Removing empty tracks and trimming clips

We have now filled all the tracks needed for this project and are left with a few that are not needed. We also have to adjust the length of our clips so that they conform better to the intended overall length of the project.

Let's first remove the empty tracks from the session.

1 Choose Multitrack > Tracks > Delete Empty Tracks from the application menu.

Any tracks without clips are removed from the session.

Next, we'll trim the longer music clip to better conform with our narrative recitation.

2 Hover your mouse cursor over the left edge of the clip within the Music track. A small red bracket with a black arrow appears. Drag to the right to trim the beginning of the clip by a few seconds.

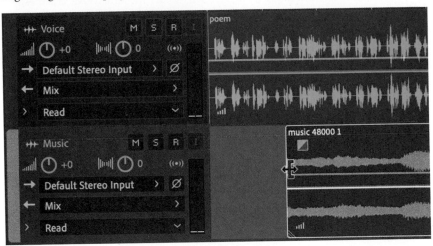

3 The end of the clip within the Music track needs to be trimmed back as well. Hover your mouse cursor over the right edge of the clip within the Music track.

● **Note** Trimming a clip in this way does not actually trim the original audio file; it only adjusts the amount of the audio file and its placement within the clip container.

4 When the red bracket with the arrow appears, click it and drag to the left to trim the ending of the clip by a few seconds, just as you did with the beginning.

5 Drag the clip in the Music track to reposition it to begin at 0 seconds.

Fading clips in and out

If you play the session back from the beginning, you'll notice the music begins abruptly. Better to fade it in for a nice transition.

Now you'll create a nice fade-in for the music clip.

1   Locate the small, two-tone gray rectangle ■ in the upper-left corner of the clip and drag it to the right to create a smooth fade in place of the abrupt start we have now.

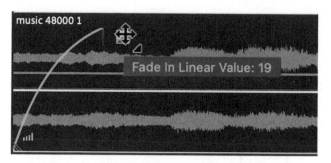

● **Note** Dragging up or down will also adjust the fade curve to fade in slower or more quickly, and pulling farther right will extend the length of the fade.

2   Apply a fade to the end of the clip in the Music track as well so that it doesn't end so abruptly. Use the fade icon ◣ like before to adjust the fade.

3   The last thing we need to do is adjust the position of the clip in the Voice track so that it appears just after the fade-in of the Music track is complete. Drag the clip in the Voice track to shift it over to an appropriate place within the timeline.

Your project should appear similar to the following figure.

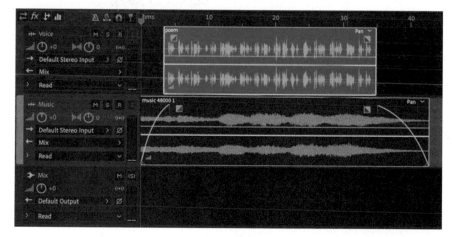

Design principles: Emphasis

In either a purely visual or purely sound-based work, emphasis is achieved by creating a point that stands out from the rest. This might entail a splash of color, the use of contrast placement or isolation of objects or sound, or the use of size or scale. In audio work, you can achieve this effect through a drastic change in amplitude or the introduction of a new sound.

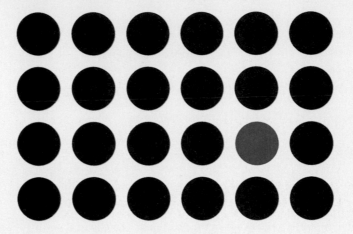

With creative audio work in particular, emphasis can be achieved through the use of recorded audio that punctuates an otherwise placid score. For instance, in the example we've been working through, we might add a single thunderclap or a door slamming somewhere within the recording to emphasize a certain point. In a musical arrangement, we could make use of a sequence of notes that stand out from the rest. These are simple ways to incorporate the design principle of emphasis.

Creating a multitrack mixdown

Once you have sequenced your clips across tracks and adjusted your fades, it's time to add some effects to the overall mix and output a multitrack mixdown for distribution.

You may have noticed that in addition to the numbered or named tracks in your multitrack session, there exists a special track at the very bottom of the stack named Mix.

By default, this is the track into which all other tracks feed their outputs. This means that any effects or adjustments you attribute to the Mix track are essentially applied to all other tracks since they all converge through this one track for final output.

We'll now add some mastering effects to the overall mix and then render it to a new file for distribution:

1 Look to the top left of the multitrack session to locate Inputs/Outputs ▣ and the Effects switcher. Click fx 𝑓𝑥 to reveal the Effects Rack on each track in the session.

With Effects chosen in the switcher, we now have access to an Effects Rack for each track, including our overall Mix track.

Effects can be added to any of the visible effect slots within the rack, and adding them to the Mix track will apply them to all tracks, since they all pass through Mix.

2 Click the arrow to the right of the first slot and choose Reverb > Studio Reverb.

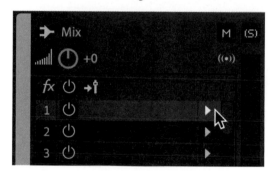

● **Note** You also have the ability to switch to Sends ▣ or EQ ▪ from the same switcher. Sends will allow you to channel multiple tracks to a single bus track in order to effectively share effects among those tracks or control volume, pan, and so forth across tracks using the send bus. EQ will bring up a small EQ control directly within the track without having to add in an EQ effect.

The Studio Reverb effect is added to the Effects Rack for the Mix track, and the Rack Effect – Studio Reverb dialog box appears.

Here, you can choose from a number of presets or make adjustments to various effect properties using the array of sliders available.

Note You can also
make adjustments to
the effect properties
and even play back your
audio to hear the results
with the effects dialog
box still open. This
makes it easy to tweak
the effects and know
what is happening in
your session.

▶ **Tip** Adding a small
bit of reverb to the
overall mix will help
bind your various tracks
together in a pleasing
way. Adding too much
reverb will muddy the
mix, though, so be
careful!

3 From the Presets menu, select Vocal Reverb (Small) to add a bit of reverb to the overall mix.

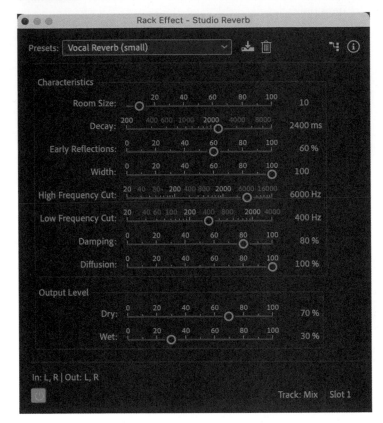

4 Close the dialog box when finished.

Let's add one more effect to the Effects Rack for our Mix track. You'll generally want to apply some mastering effects to your overall mix in order to tweak various parameters like overall EQ, adjustments to loudness, and so on.

5 Click the arrow to the right of the second slot and choose Special > Mastering.

The Rack Effect – Mastering dialog box appears and presents a number of controls.

6 From the Presets menu, select Make Room For Vocals to adjust the overall mix. Play with other parameters to see how they affect the final output. You can always choose the preset again if you mess up!

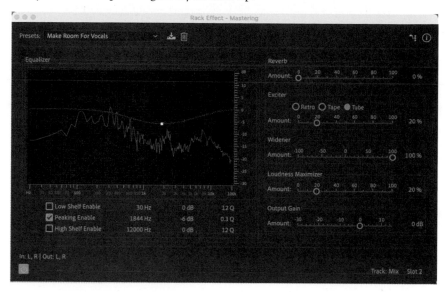

7 When finished, close the dialog box.

You now have both a Studio Reverb and a Mastering effect slotted into the Effects Rack for your Mix track. Since all other tracks pass through the Mix track on their way to final output, you can affect the entire mix through any controls or effects present in this track.

> ▶ **Tip** The green power icon next to each effect allows you to toggle the effect on or off as desired.

Processing the mix

The final step to creating our multitrack mixdown is to process our mix to a single waveform and export it as a file for distribution.

Creating a mixdown is simple. Let's go ahead and create one from our multitrack session:

1 Within the Multitrack Editor, choose Multitrack > Mixdown Session To New File > Entire Session from the application menu.

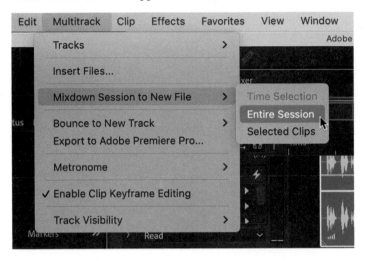

A temporary waveform is produced from your multitrack session and opens in the Waveform Editor.

2 Choose File > Save As from the application menu to save your file as a WAV, an MP3, or whatever other audio file format you desire.

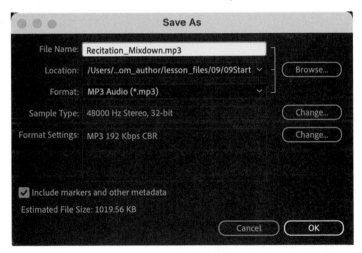

Next steps with Audition

For a deeper look at everything Audition has to offer, including workflows and techniques not presented in this lesson, take a look at *Adobe Audition CC Classroom in a Book, 2nd Edition* from Peachpit and Adobe Press.

Review questions

1 Why is configuring your input and output hardware so important?

2 What is a waveform in Audition?

3 What is a good decibel range for your audio designs?

4 If you want to isolate specific frequencies in your recording for cleanup, what feature should you enable?

5 What is the Mix track used for within a multitrack mixdown?

Review answers

1 If not correctly configured, your audio input or output can be too loud or too soft. It is best to get it properly set up before you begin a project.

2 A waveform is a visual representation of amplitude across time.

3 A good range is somewhere between –12 dB and –3 dB. This will ensure that the listener will not have to manually adjust their speaker volume very much to listen comfortably.

4 Enable Spectral Frequency Display.

5 All other track output will pass through the Mix track so you can affect all track attributes through this single track.

9 SEQUENCING VIDEO CONTENT WITH PREMIERE PRO

Lesson overview

In this lesson, you'll learn how to do the following:

- Create a new Premiere Pro project and import media for sequencing.

- Edit clips and manage tracks within a sequence.

- Perform audio leveling between tracks.

- Create motion using still images through keyframes.

- Apply transition effects between clips.

- Gain an understanding of the design principle of rhythm.

- Create titles and credit sequences with text and motion graphics templates.

- Export your video for distribution.

 This lesson will take less than 2 hours to complete.

To get the files used in this lesson, download them from the web page for this book at www.adobepress.com/CreativeCloudCIB. For more information, see "Accessing the lesson files and Web Edition" in the Getting Started section at the beginning of this book.

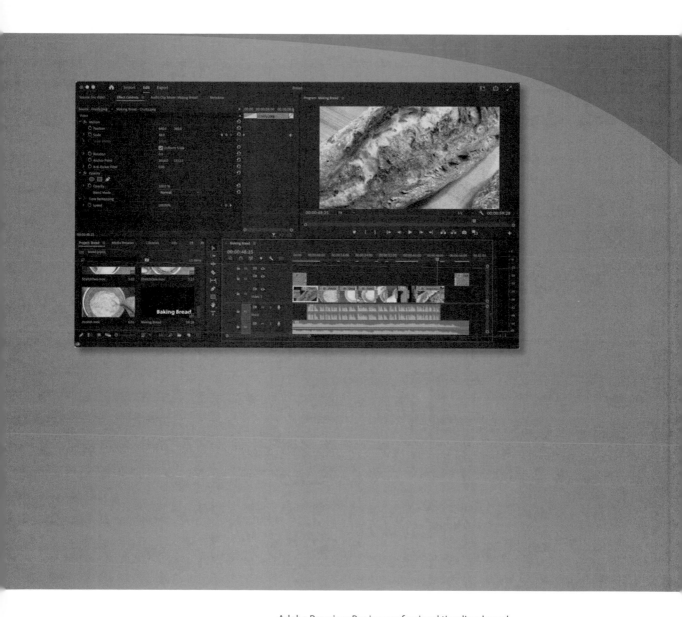

Adobe Premiere Pro is a professional timeline-based media sequencer that enables video production for personal projects, social media, television, documentary, and film. This software is an all-in-one solution for organizing, sequencing, refining, and exporting your video productions.

Getting started

● **Note** If you have not already downloaded the project files for this lesson to your computer from your Account page, make sure to do so now. See "Getting Started" at the beginning of the book.

Start by viewing the finished project to see what you'll be creating in this lesson.

1 Open the 09End.mp4 file in the Lesson09/09End folder to view the final project.

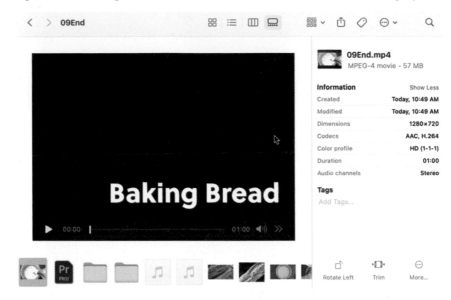

The project is a rendered video sequence created in Premiere Pro demonstrating a few tips for baking bread at home. It consists of imported audio voiceover and music files, imported video files, and some still photographs that have been given slight motion. The video exhibits both beginning title and end credit text overlays.

2 Close the video file.

Understanding Premiere Pro

When considering video editing software as part of Creative Cloud, you generally have two choices: Premiere Pro and Premiere Rush. While this lesson focuses on Premiere Pro exclusively, it's good to have an understanding of where each piece of software fits into the overall picture—especially in relation to each other.

About Premiere Pro

Adobe Premiere Pro is a professional video editing and production application used across industries such as television and film. It can also be used on smaller, more focused projects for social media, short documentary films, or personal activities.

When you open Premiere Pro, the start screen will look very familiar to you if you've worked with other Adobe desktop applications like Adobe Photoshop or Adobe Illustrator.

Premiere Pro is desktop-based software, and projects being edited and arranged within the software are meant to remain there through the duration of the production.

About Premiere Rush

Adobe Premiere Rush functions very much like Adobe Lightroom in that it is available on both desktop and mobile and has the ability to sync your content to the cloud for use across all devices.

The focus of Premiere Rush is on putting together shorter sequences quickly for distribution over social media channels. This is different, of course, from Premiere Pro, which is more suited to full-scale, professional projects and workflows.

A common way of working within the Premiere Rush ecosystem is to first capture content and perform a rough edit on your Apple iOS or Google Android device.

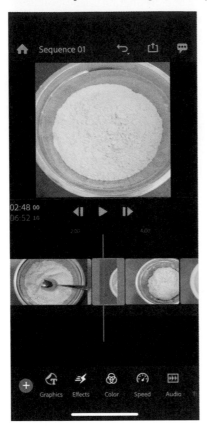

Premiere Rush will sync the project to the cloud. Later, with your laptop or desktop computer, you can open the rough project, refine it, and publish it to social channels directly.

 **Tip** If you start a project with Premiere Rush, you can import that project sequence into Premiere Pro to take advantage of advanced tools and workflows.

Creating a new project

In this lesson, we'll create a new Premiere Pro project based on preexisting footage. Basing a new project on existing footage will enable us to create a video sequence with proper settings as we move forward.

Starting a Premiere Pro project

Let's create a new Premiere Pro project and import our media into a sequence.

1   In the upper left of the Premiere Pro start screen, click New Project.

Premiere Pro launches Import workflow mode and prompts you to name the project and choose a location to save the project.

2   In the Project Location field, browse to the Lesson09/09Start folder.

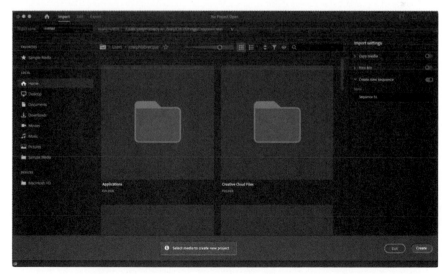

3 In the Project Name field, enter **Bread**.

The project has not been created yet, since we still need to import our media and create a sequence.

4 Along the right-hand side of the Import workflow mode interface, you will find a set of Import settings choices. Toggle on Create New Sequence if it is not already activated.

5 Enter **Making Bread** in the Name field to reflect the sequence topic.

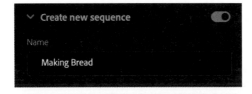

6 Using the file explorer to the right of the Import workflow mode interface, browse to the Lesson09/09Start folder.

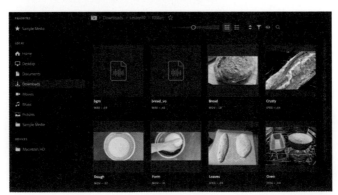

This folder contains all the video, still images, and audio files that we will use in our project.

7   From here, you can select the files to import into the sequence. Click to select the checkbox in the upper-left corner of each file preview.

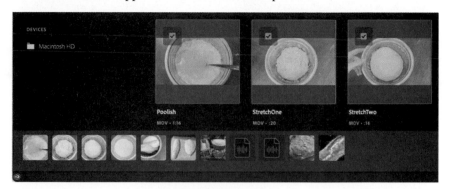

▶ Tip If you want or need to adjust your sequence settings later, you can access them at any time by selecting a sequence and choosing Sequence > Sequence Settings from the application menu.

Be sure to select a piece of video footage first, because your sequence will be created based on the properties of the first video file you select.

8   In the lower-right corner of the Import screen, click the Create button.

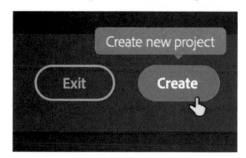

▶ Tip If you want to create a project without any media or sequences ready to work on, simply click Create and Premiere Pro will create an empty project.

Premiere Pro creates a new project file named Bread.prproj in the Lesson09/09Start folder and switches to Edit workflow mode. We will spend most of our time in this lesson in this workflow mode.

The Premiere Pro interface

Now that we have created a new Premiere Pro project and sequence and imported associated media, let's take a look at the overall Premiere Pro UI where you'll do your editing.

We'll begin by working in the Assembly workspace. If you are not currently in the Assembly workspace, you can switch to it by clicking the workspace switcher █ in the upper-right corner of the main UI and then choosing Assembly from the menu that appears.

Program Monitor

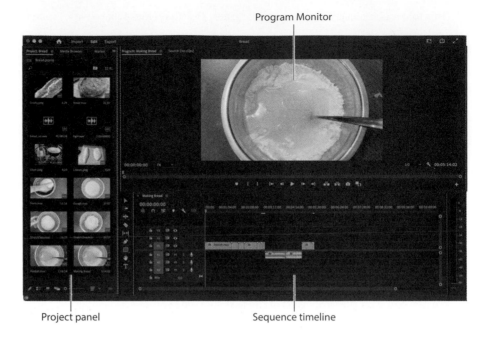

Project panel   Sequence timeline

In most workspaces, we can identify the three main panels when working in Premiere Pro:

- **Project panel:** This is the panel that contains any media we've imported into the project, as well as content like sequences and other native Premiere Pro assets.

- **Sequence timeline:** This is the timeline of the currently selected sequence. Here you'll arrange media, in the form of clips, across video and audio tracks in order to arrange your video project.

- **Program Monitor:** Here you'll see a preview of what is visible at the playhead's current position in the timeline and control overall sequence playback.

Premiere Pro has many workspaces that align to certain tasks. Let's switch to the Editing workspace and see how it differs from the Assembly workspace; you'll be spending a lot of time with this particular configuration.

- Switch to the Editing workspace by clicking the workspace switcher ▣ in the upper-right corner and then choosing Editing from the menu that appears.

Source Monitor   Program Monitor

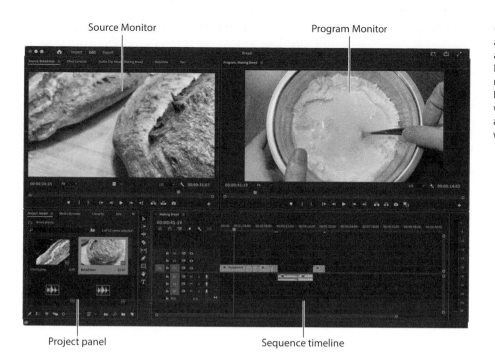

Project panel   Sequence timeline

● **Note** Workspaces and workflow modes are different things in Premiere Pro. Workflow modes consist of Import, Edit, and Export whereas workspaces all exist within the Edit workflow mode.

In addition to the Program Monitor, we get immediate access to the Source Monitor in the Editing workspace. The Source Monitor is where you load individual pieces of media to define specific clips to use in your sequence.

Exploring the sequence timeline

The concept of tracks is likely somewhat familiar from what we were working on in Lesson 8, "Producing Audio Content with Audition." The concept is basically the same: clips are sequenced within a track. But unlike Audition, Premiere Pro keeps audio and video tracks separate from each other.

By default, Premiere Pro creates a sequence with three video tracks (labeled V1, V2, and V3) and three audio tracks (labeled A1, A2, and A3). Video files and still images are imported to V1 as clips, and any audio files are imported to A1 as clips. Any video files that include audio will be placed across both track types.

Time representation in Premiere Pro

As we work through the timeline in this lesson, you will notice that Premiere Pro represents time in a way that you may never have encountered before.

Premiere Pro always displays time units as 0:00:00:00. This is HOURS:MINUTES:SECONDS:FRAMES. So, 3 minutes and 30 seconds would be represented as 0:03:30:00.

The number of frames in the last unit of the sequence is dependent on the frames per second (fps) setting of your sequence. So, a half-second for a 30fps sequence would be represented as 0:00:00:15.

Managing imported media

● **Note** When working in Premiere Pro, your project file references all your media through external reference links. Your source media files don't become embedded within your project file. Because of this, it's a good idea to approach project creation and media management in an organized and deliberate way.

When you selected clips in Import workflow mode, the media was imported into the sequence as clips within either audio or video tracks in the order in which you selected them. All of the video clips are considerably longer than what we'll use in our project.

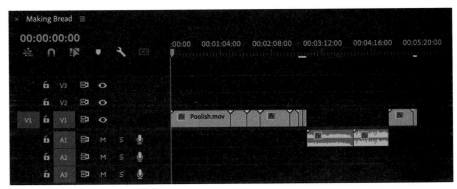

We are going to select segments of clips to match the length of our audio narration and use its content as a guide.

We currently have the following media files in our project bin and representative clips placed along the timeline:

Audio files:

▶ **Tip** If any of your media files become unlinked at any time, you can resolve this by right-clicking the unlinked media in the project bin and choosing Link Media from the menu.

- **bgm.wav:** The background music for our project

- **bread_vo.wav:** A narrative audio recording describing the breadmaking process

Video files:

- **Poolish.mov:** Video of the poolish preferment being prepared
- **Dough.mov:** Video of the poolish being mixed with the remainder of ingredients to form the dough
- **StretchOne.mov:** Video of the initial strength-building exercises
- **StretchTwo.mov:** Video of the second set of strength-building exercises
- **Form.mov:** Video of the slap-and-fold technique before the main bulk fermentation period
- **Bread.mov:** Video of the baked loaves of bread after emerging from the oven and cooling for some time

Still images:

- **Crusty.jpeg:** A photograph of the baked loaves
- **Loaves.jpeg:** A photograph of divided and formed loaves of bread dough
- **Oven.jpeg:** A photograph of the prepared oven

Note There is also a sequence named Making Bread in the Project panel alongside all the media that you imported. This is the sequence that is currently open and displayed in the timeline.

Creating additional bins

All of our media files exist within the root of the Project panel. If you want, you can create additional bins to contain specific types of media or to organize various media groups.

To create a new bin within the main project bin, click the New Bin button ■ at the bottom right of the Project panel. This will create a new bin that you can then drag media into in order to more finely organize your overall project.

Although this is useful for larger projects, this lesson's project is small enough that there is no need for additional bins.

Let's remove the video and still image clips from the timeline so that we can re-sequence them later in a more organized manner.

1   Hover over the line between tracks and you'll see the cursor transform to display a set of arrows pointing both up and down. Drag up on the track borders to make the various tracks taller.

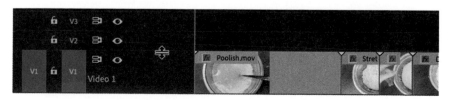

When the tracks are tall enough, you'll be able to see a small preview thumbnail, which is helpful in visual tracks.

2   We'll now move the audio tracks into position, since they will remain as full clips exactly as they presently are. Drag the bgm.wav clip in track A1 to 00:00:00:00 in track A2 and release the mouse button.

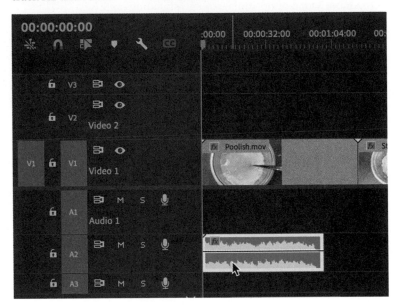

This is the background music track for our project. You can always drag clips from one track to another in this way.

3   Drag the bread_vo.wav clip over to 00:00:05:00 within the A1 layer.

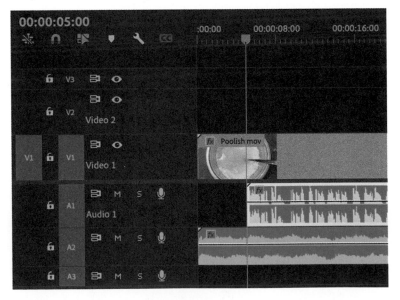

This will ensure that the background music plays a bit before the voiceover narration begins.

4   Using the Selection tool 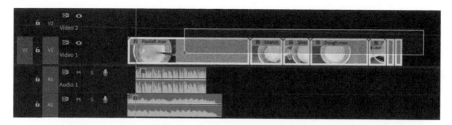, drag a rectangular selection across all clips in V1 to select them.

5   Remove the selected clips from the track by pressing the Delete key.

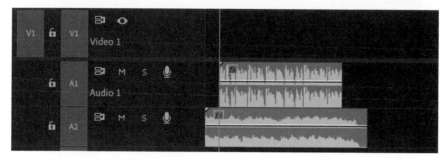

The video clips are removed from V1 and we retain audio voiceover and music within the A1 and A2 tracks. We will create new clips from the imported video and stills in a more deliberate way.

Working within a sequence

Now that we have created a new Premiere Pro project, adjusted audio clip tracking and position, and removed clips we do not intend to keep, we can begin sequencing our project in earnest.

Adjusting audio levels

We are going to build the visuals for this project by defining clips that illustrate what is expressed through the voice narration. We do not want the background music to overpower the narration because it will be more difficult for the viewer to understand what the narrator is saying, and it will be unpleasant to listen to as well.

Since we will be using audio as the framework for everything we do in this sequence, let's make sure our levels are correct.

1   Switch to the Editing workspace with the workspace switcher if you are not viewing that workspace already.

2   Click the Audio Clip Mixer tab at the top of the Source Monitor to view the audio mixer controls.

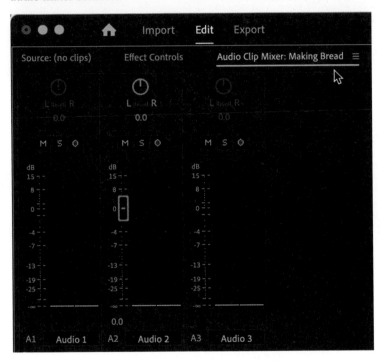

Premiere Pro assigns an audio channel in the mixer to each audio track in the sequence.

3   Rename Audio 1 to **Voice** and Audio 2 to **Music**.

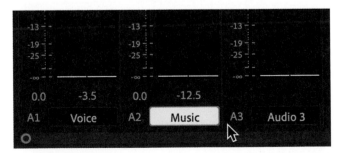

Audio 3 doesn't have any audio clips associated with it, which means you can safely ignore it.

4　Pressing the spacebar on your keyboard initiates playback within the sequence and allows you to monitor audio levels within the mixer. Press the spacebar and listen to the audio playback.

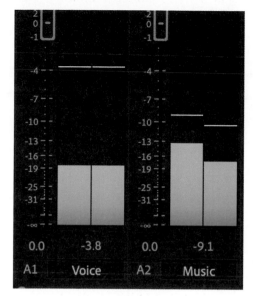

It isn't terrible, but the music could definitely be lowered a bit, and perhaps the voice slightly as well.

5　Using either the levels slider or the blue numeric indicator below it, set Voice to −2.0 decibels (dB) and Music to −13 dB.

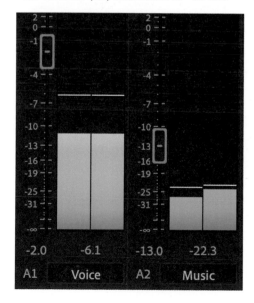

Note If your audio tracks are tall enough, you will also see an amplitude envelope across your audio clip. Dragging this up or down will increase or decrease the volume as well.

Tip If you'd rather remove empty tracks from a sequence that you have no intention of using, you can do so by right-clicking anywhere to the right of the track name and choosing Delete Track.

Now, the voice and music no longer in conflict, and you should find testing the audio playback a much more pleasant experience.

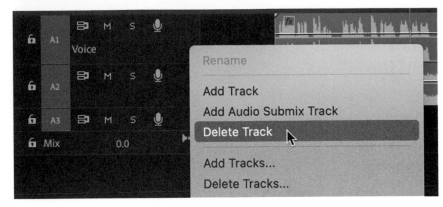

Working with still images

With the audio playing back at appropriate levels, it's time to start populating the video tracks with clips from our imported media.

We'll begin by adding an image of crusty bread for the intro.

1   Listen to the first 9 seconds of audio in the timeline by pressing the spacebar or by using the Play-Stop Toggle button ▶ below the Program Monitor.

    The music plays and the narration explains that baking a nice loaf of bread isn't difficult. We will use the still image of crusty bread to cover these 9 seconds.

2   Locate Crusty.jpeg within the Project panel and drag it into the V1 track of the sequence timeline.

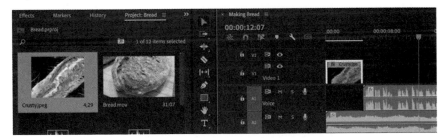

Premiere Pro adds the still image to the sequence as an image clip that persists for 5 seconds. We want this image to remain on screen for 9 seconds to cover the intro narration.

3 Hover your cursor over the right side of the clip until it transforms into a red bracket with an arrow. Select the clip in the timeline, drag it to around the 9-second mark, and release the mouse button.

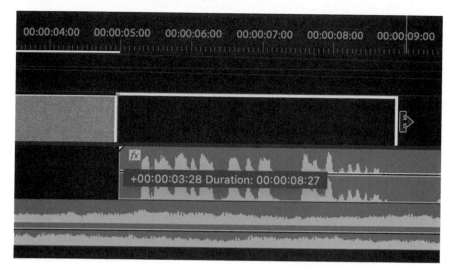

▶ **Tip** The default length for still images placed on the timeline is 5 seconds. To change this setting, choose Premiere Pro > Preferences on macOS or Edit > Preferences on Windows to open the Preferences dialog box and choose the Timeline category. You can adjust Still Image Default Duration from this location.

The still image now remains visible for about 9 seconds as the intro is spoken.

Using the Source Monitor

A still image works fine for the intro, but we'll need to work in some video clips for the next steps explained in the narration.

For this, we'll make use of the Source Monitor.

1 Starting at 9 seconds, listen to the narration up to the 15-second mark.

The narration explains that we'll be making a poolish. Let's add a trimmed clip of poolish being made.

2 Click the Source tab to open the Source Monitor in the Editing workspace.

In the Source Monitor, you can set in and out points in your source media files so that only specific portions are included in the clips you add to your sequence.

3 Locate the video named Poolish.mov in the Project panel and drag it up into Source Monitor.

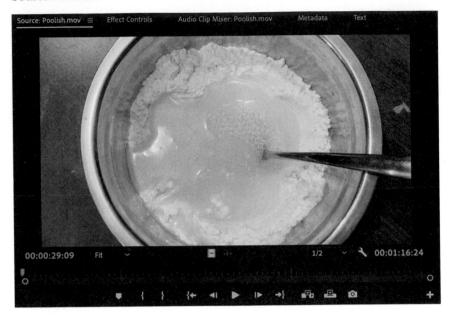

The Source Monitor now displays the Poolish.mov video file. We can scrub the playhead within the Source Monitor to preview the video. It is far too long! We only need 6 seconds of footage.

4 Move the playhead within the Source Monitor to the 1 minute and 18 seconds mark (00:01:18:00). Click the Mark In button  to mark where the clip should begin.

5 Move the playhead in the Source Monitor forward to 00:01:24:00. Click the Mark Out button  to mark where the clip should end.

We have now defined a span of time between these marks that encompasses 6 seconds of media from the much longer source video.

6 Drag the video preview down into the timeline, placing the generated clip directly following the existing still image clip in the sequence by releasing the mouse button.

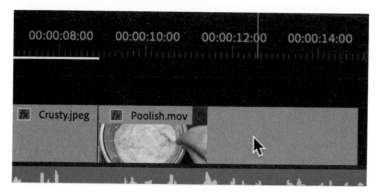

The 6-second clip is added to the sequence. Looking at the timeline, you may notice our clip is a bit shy of the audio that it needs to cover.

7 Just as we did with the still image, hover your cursor over the right side of the clip until it transforms into a red bracket with an arrow. Drag the clip to the right to extend it ever so slightly and release the mouse button while using the audio waveform shown here as a guide.

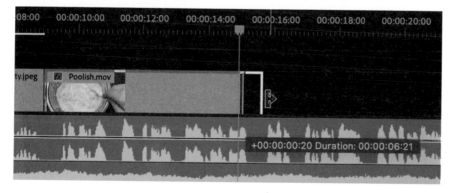

We are now certain that the poolish video continues for the duration of the narration regarding poolish.

Additional Source Monitor clip options

If a source video has audio associated with it, dragging from the preview in the Source Monitor down to the timeline will add both video and audio to the appropriate tracks.

If you want only video clips created from media with both video and audio content, you can drag from the Drag Video Only button ⬛ instead. Similarly, if you want only clip audio, you can use the Drag Audio Only button ⬛ to add the audio to the sequence.

The clip we're working with has no audio associated with it, so only video clips would be created either way.

Add the remaining clips

We will now fill in the remainder of the sequence by using the methods we've already worked with to add video clips and still images using the narration as a guide. Pay attention to the start time and duration in the source monitor as you define your clips.

Clip Start Time

Clip Duration

As you proceed with the following steps, you can use the suggested time markers and lengths to create each clip, and everything will be close to perfect.

1 Drag Dough.mov from the Project panel to the Source Monitor. Then create a clip starting at a bit shy of 21 and a half seconds (00:00:21:15) that is 6 seconds in length, and add it as the next clip in your sequence.

2 Drag StretchOne.mov from the Project panel to the Source Monitor, create a clip starting at 2 seconds and 10 frames (00:00:02:10) that is just over 6 seconds in length, and add it to the end of your sequence.

3 Drag StretchTwo.mov from the Project panel to the Source Monitor, create a clip starting at 8 seconds that is a bit over 3 seconds in length, and add it to the end of your sequence.

4 Drag Form.mov from the Project panel to the Source Monitor, create a clip starting at 1 minute and 13 seconds that is 3.5 seconds in length, and add it to the end of your sequence.

5 Drag Loaves.jpeg directly into the timeline at the end of the sequence and change the duration to 3 seconds.

6 Drag Oven.jpeg directly into the timeline at the end of the sequence and change the duration to about 2 and a half seconds.

7 Finally, drag Bread.mov from the project bin to the Source Monitor, create a clip starting at 5 seconds that is 9 and a half seconds in length, and add it to the end of your sequence.

8 Listen to the entire sequence to be sure that the various clips switch from one to another at appropriate times in the narrative and make adjustments with the Selection tool as needed.

Your full sequence in the timeline should look similar to the following figure. It's okay if things are a little different, but it's likely close if you've followed the suggested clip parameters.

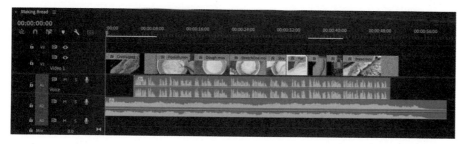

Adjusting still images

You may have noticed when adding still images to the timeline sequence that they are much larger than the frame in the Program Monitor. That's because our sequence resolution is smaller than the image resolution.

We'll now adjust the still images to fill the frame in a more meaningful way.

1 With the Selection tool, click the Crusty.jpeg clip in the sequence to select it.

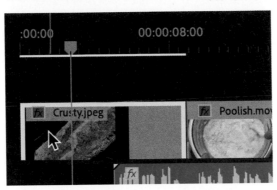

▶ **Tip** If the effect controls are empty, be sure to select the desired clip within the sequence and they will appear.

2 Click the Effect Controls tab to view the effect controls for the selected clip.

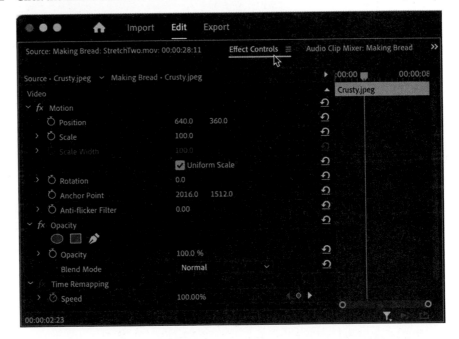

Because we have a clip selected, effect controls appear for properties of Motion, Opacity, and Time Remapping.

3 Adjust the Scale property of Motion to a value of **38**.

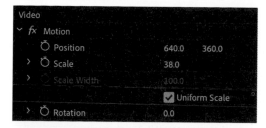

4 Move the playhead in the sequence to around 2 and a half seconds to view the change in scale in the Program Monitor.

We now see much more of the image in frame.

5 Click the Loaves.jpeg clip in the sequence to select it and adjust the scale property to a value of **70**.

▶ Tip If you'd like to focus on a particular portion of an image, you can always adjust the Position property along with Scale.

▶ Tip In addition to adjusting the scale numerically, if you prefer to manually scale your content with transformation handles, you can do so by double-clicking the media in the Program Monitor.

6 Click the Oven.jpeg clip in the sequence to select it and adjust the Scale property to a value of **34**.

All three still images are now more appropriately sized for the frame. The image of prepared bread loaves will appear too large for now, but we'll adjust additional properties to fix this later.

Adding motion to clips

When you play back the sequence as it currently exists, you'll see a rather distinct difference between video clips and still image clips in that the stills remain still and unmoving.

A trick used by documentary filmmakers to make images feel more integrated and cinematic within a video sequence is to add just a touch of zoom or pan to the images. This is often referred to as the "Ken Burns effect," as it was made popular by the documentarian Ken Burns through extensive use of pan and zoom in his work.

Let's add some movement to our stills.

1 Using the Selection tool, select the first image clip, Crusty.jpeg. Then click the Effect Controls tab in the Source Monitor to open that panel if it's not already open.

2 Ensure that the playhead is positioned at the beginning of the clip in the Effect Controls panel and click the Toggle Animation stopwatch button ⏱ aligned with the Scale property to activate it.

The stopwatch turns blue, and a small diamond called a *keyframe* is added at the playhead position. A keyframe holds data values for the property it is aligned with at a specific point in time.

3 We are going to insert another keyframe at the end of the clip, so move the playhead in the Effect Controls panel to the very end.

4 Adjust the Scale value to 48.

A new keyframe is automatically created at the playhead position.

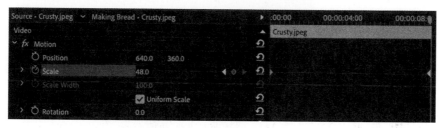

We now have two keyframes aligned to the Scale property with different values. Premiere Pro will change the scale from one value to another upon playback, creating a smooth zoom motion on the still image.

5 Now select the second image clip, Loaves.jpeg. Recall that this image was scaled up higher than the others. We will create a panning animation for this clip.

6 Position the playhead at the very beginning of the clip and click the Toggle Animation stopwatch button ⏱ aligned with the position property to create an initial keyframe and set the first value—the x position—to **30**.

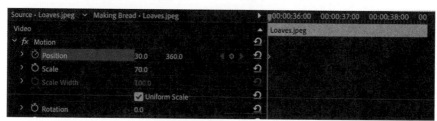

The clip is now focused on one of the loaves in the image.

7 We will once again insert another keyframe at the end of this clip, so move the playhead in the Effect Controls panel to the very end.

8 Change the x position value to **185**. A new keyframe appears at the playhead.

A smooth pan across the still image is created as the x position value changes from the beginning of the clip to its end.

▶ **Tip** When trying to precisely align your playhead to existing keyframes, you can use the keyframe navigation arrows ◄○► for any property to jump from one keyframe to the next, ensuring the playhead is positioned correctly.

9 Select the third image clip, Oven.jpeg, and create a subtle zoom motion similar to what you applied in steps 1–4 when manipulating the Crusty.jpeg clip. But in this instance, set the final Scale value to **38**.

Play back your sequence to view the zoom and pan action that the three still images now exhibit.

Adding transitions to clips

The video clips and still image clips are now fully sequenced against the audio playback. Whenever one clip ends and another begins, however, we get a very abrupt cut.

We can improve the flow of our sequence by making use of transitions between clips.

● **Note** The various workspaces available in Premiere Pro contribute greatly to the overall project workflow. Make use of them to quickly switch between your focused tasks!

1 Using the workspace switcher ▣, choose the Effects workspace.

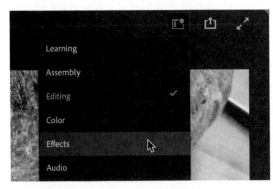

Premiere Pro switches from the Editing workspace to the Effects workspace.

2 The Effects panel is now accessible in the upper-right corner of the interface and displays a number of effect folders. Open the Video Transitions folder and then the Dissolve folder within it to access the collection of dissolve transition effects.

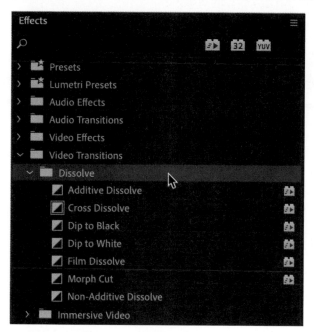

3 Locate the first clip in the sequence move the playhead back to the beginning of the sequence, and drag the Dip To Black effect from the Effects panel so that the mouse is positioned at the beginning of the clip. The cursor will change to a transition icon and the first bit of the clip will highlight. Release the mouse button to apply the effect.

4 Since this effect is opening the entire video sequence, we want to lengthen its duration a bit. Hover your mouse over the right side of the effect indicator, which now overlays the beginning of the clip, until it turns into a red bracket. Drag to the right to increase the duration of the transition slightly.

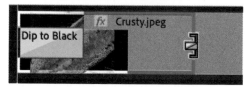

Note You can also change the duration of an effect from this panel, preview the effect in isolation upon the clip, and see the exact duration of the effect with finer control overall.

5 Click the effect indicator that overlays the beginning of the clip and open the Effect Controls panel. Make any necessary adjustments to the effect so its duration is 2 seconds and 20 frames.

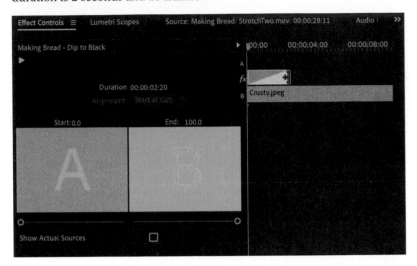

▶ **Tip** If one clip or the other does not receive a highlight when applying a transition effect, that usually indicates there are not enough extra frames in the clip to perform the transition effect successfully. Adjusting the clip start and end with the Selection tool or through the Source Monitor can fix this.

6 For the remainder of the clips in the sequence, we will use a Cross Dissolve effect so that one clip dissolves through to the next in a pleasant way. Drag the Cross Dissolve effect from the Effects panel so that the mouse is positioned at the junction between each remaining set of clips. The cursor changes to a transition icon and a highlight appears on the last bit of the previous clip and the first bit of the clip that follows. Release the mouse button to apply the transition.

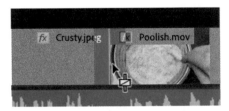

▶ **Tip** You can also apply a default transition between all the clips arranged on the timeline by selecting all clips and choosing Sequence > Apply Default Transitions To Selection from the application menu. Cross Dissolve is the default video transition in Premiere Pro.

7 Add Cross Dissolve transition effects between each remaining clip in the sequence.

8 Finally, apply another Dip To Black effect at the very last clip.

The beginning and end clips of the sequence now open and close with a Dip To Black effect, and each and every clip transition within the sequence displays a Cross Dissolve.

Although Premiere Pro offers many other transition types, you generally want to apply only a few to establish a steady and consistent rhythm between clips.

Design Principle: Rhythm

When you're considering illustrative or graphic design, the principle of rhythm can only suggest a sort of repetition, transition, or flow from one state to another.

You can accomplish this by repeating certain visual elements along the canvas, through gradual change as with a gradient fill, or through a flowing transition of properties from one state to another, as expressed in the following figure.

When working with video—or even audio—as a medium, rhythm can be expressed much more directly through repeating patterns and transitions across the timeline. The use of short clips that dissolve from one to the next in a consistent and repeatable way establishes a consistent rhythm in our Premiere Pro project.

Adding a title with the Text tool

There are a few ways to add text and titles to your project in Premiere Pro. We'll be exploring two of these methods in this lesson, beginning with use of the Type tool.

1   Move the playhead to the beginning of the sequence.

    This will ensure that any text we create using the Type tool begins at 0 seconds along the timeline.

2   Select the Type tool **T** from the toolbar and click anywhere within the Program Monitor to create a new text clip. Type **Baking Bread** for your text content.

▶ **Tip** You can also create a text clip by dragging across the Program Monitor to create a clip with a defined width. For longer text, this technique is useful since you can easily redefine the text box width.

3 Switch to the Selection tool and click the new text clip in the V2 track to select it.

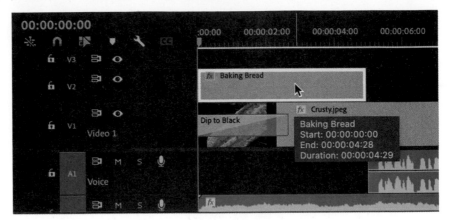

The clip was added to track V2 because track V1 was occupied by the Crusty.jpeg still image clip.

4 Open the Effect Controls panel and choose the Text (Baking Bread) option.

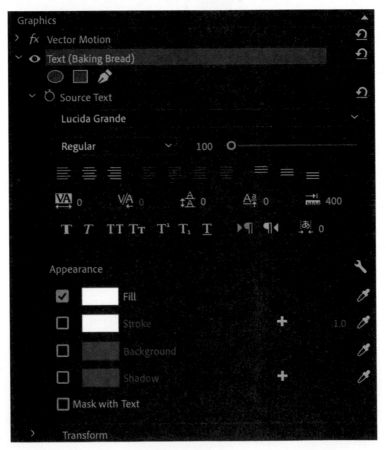

Properties are exposed such as the typeface, size value, alignment, color, and more. We'll change some of these values to better integrate the text into the sequence as a title.

5 Let's make changes to our text properties. Choose a new typeface such as Soleil, an Adobe Font. Adjust the size value to something close to 130. Change the fill color to pure white (#**FFFFFF**) and add a simple drop shadow.

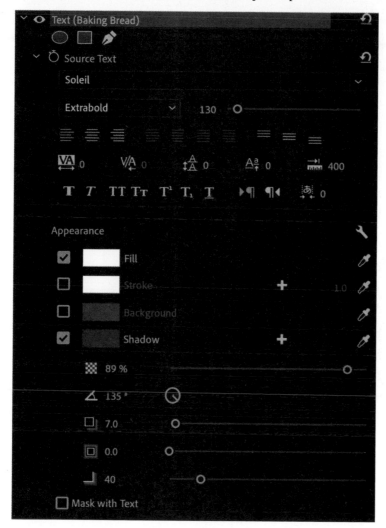

Of course, you can always tweak these settings to your own designs, and if you select a different font, you will probably have to because of the differences across typefaces.

6 Using the Selection tool, drag the formatted text in the Program Monitor to reposition it into the lower-right corner of the frame.

▶ **Tip** You can always jump over to Adobe Fonts to explore and sync different typefaces for use in your Premiere Pro project.

7 To complete your titles, add a Cross Dissolve transition effect to the end of your text clip.

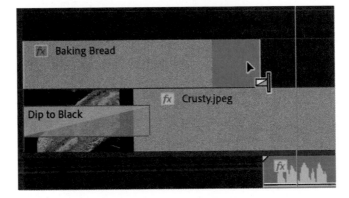

Adding end credits with Motion Graphics templates

In addition to the title text at the beginning of our video sequence, we want to design end credits for placement at the end of the sequence.

For the end credits, we'll make use of a Motion Graphics template through the Essential Graphics panel.

1   Open the Essential Graphics panel by choosing Window > Essential Graphics from the application menu or by switching to the Captions And Graphics workspace.

2   In the Essential Graphics panel, type **credits** in the search field and press Enter to perform the search.

A set of templates appears below that contain the word "credits" in the title.

3   Scroll down and locate the template named Modern Credits and drag it to the end of the sequence in the V2 track. Release the mouse button to place it.

A clip appears within the V2 track.

4 Using the Selection tool, select the clip and, in the Essential Graphics panel, select the Edit tab to make sure that you are in Edit mode and that you have a number of properties available to tweak.

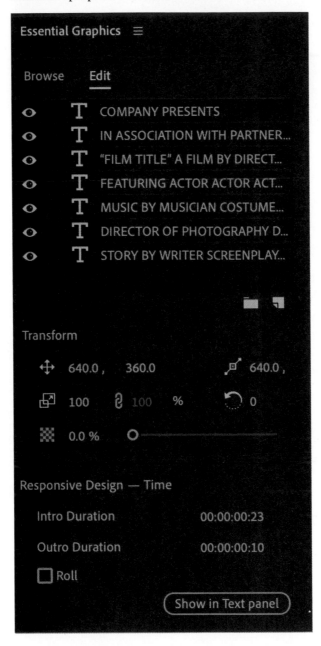

You have access to each line of text, transform properties for the clip, and the ability to adjust the timing of the intro and outro animations that are part of the template.

5 Select and delete the bottom four text objects from within the Essential Graphics panel by pressing the Delete key.

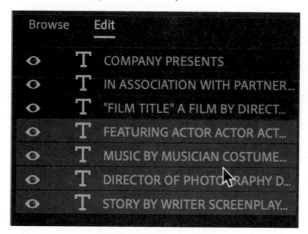

After you delete the bottom four lines of text, only the top three will remain.

6 With the Selection tool still chosen, double-click the first line of text in the program monitor and change it to read **FRACTURED VISION MEDIA PRESENTS**.

7 Triple-click the second line of text in the Program Monitor and change it to read **IN ASSOCIATION WITH ADOBE PRESS AND PEACHPIT**.

8 Triple-click the third line of text in the program monitor and change it to read **"BAKING BREAD" A FILM BY JOSEPH LABRECQUE**.

● **Note** Feel free to use your own name and production company info here as well. We don't mind!

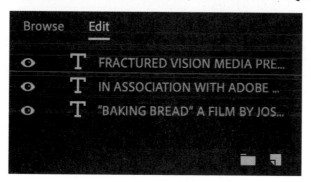

The text value changes are reflected in the Essential Graphics panel as well as in the Program Monitor.

9 Using the Selection tool, select all three text objects in the Program Monitor, and in the Essential Graphics panel, change the fill color to white.

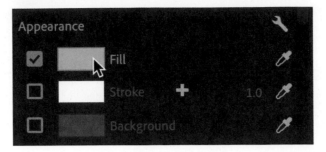

10 Deselect all objects in the Program Monitor and select the graphics clip in the timeline. Adjust the following properties in the Essential Graphics panel:

- Position: **640, 422**
- Anchor Point: **437**
- Scale: **159**

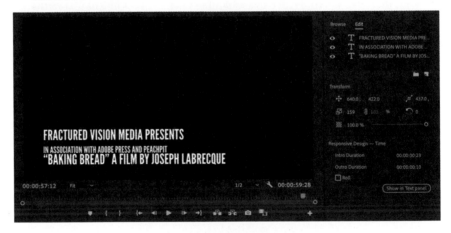

These settings scale up the clip so that the text appears larger and is positioned at the bottom-left edge of the frame, refining our end credits.

Our entire sequence is now complete.

Exporting your completed video

With our video sequence completed, now we have to export it so that we can share it as a distributable video file. There are a few methods of doing this in Premiere Pro, and we'll be examining two of them.

First, though, play the sequence back in Premiere Pro to be sure that there is nothing left unfinished.

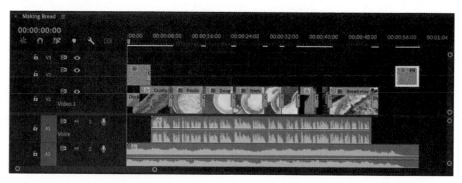

All clips should transition smoothly from one to another, matching the narrative audio content. Titles set the stage and ending credits give attribution. It should all flow as a unified work.

Using quick export

Likely the most straightforward way of exporting a video file from a Premiere Pro sequence is to use Quick Export.

1   Click the Quick Export icon ⬆ at the upper right of the interface to initiate an export.

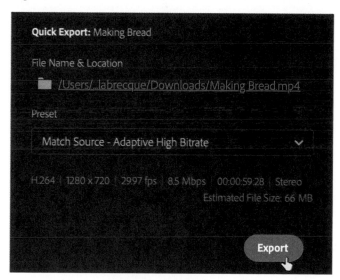

The Quick Export dialog box appears. You can adjust the export location and select an encoding preset, but the defaults will work in this example.

2 Click the Export button to initiate an export.

A dialog box appears letting you know the export progress.

3 Once the export completes, a blue popover box appears at the lower right of the interface. Click in the file path to open the system-level file explorer and access your distributable MP4 file.

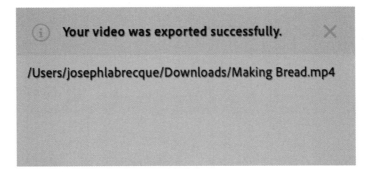

This video file can be distributed across social media, video sharing sites, or wherever else you'd like to share it. The MP4 file format is one of the most ubiquitous video formats around.

MP4 and H.264

The terms MP4 and H.264 are often used interchangeably, but it is important to understand the role of each and how these terms differ.

- H.264 is a video compression codec that is supported by many software applications and even much of the hardware we use in everyday life.
- MP4 is a file container format whose video contents most often make use of the H.264 codec.

Using the Export workflow mode

If you would prefer more control over the export process, you can make use of the Export workflow mode.

1 With your sequence completed, switch to the Export workflow mode by clicking the Export tab at the top of the interface.

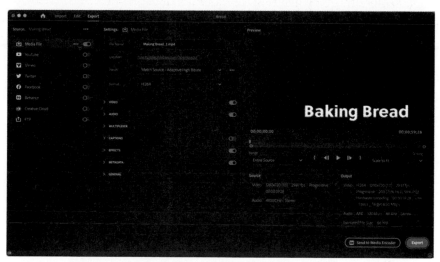

Premiere Pro switches from the Edit workflow mode to the Export workflow mode.

2 In the left column, you can choose from a variety of export and publish options. We will produce a simple video file that can be used anywhere, so ensure that the Media File option is toggled on.

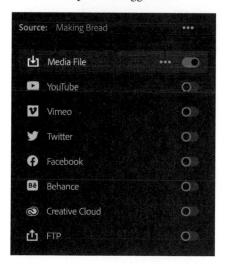

Optionally, you can enable additional publish targets from this area. But for any social network or service, you will be prompted to authenticate and give permission.

3 The center column exposes a number of categories containing properties you can tweak to modify specific aspects of your output file. Ensure that you choose H.264 for the Format option.

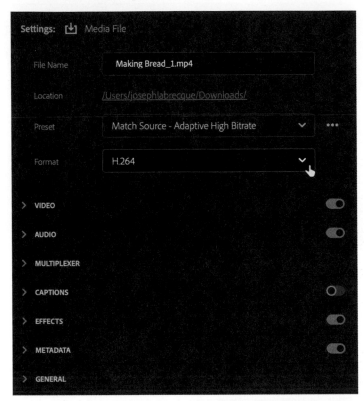

Adjust any other properties as necessary, including file name and location, so that you will be able to locate the video file that is produced through this process.

4 The right column presents an opportunity to preview and trim the video output. It also provides a set of data values related to how the video will be processed in accordance with the choices made in the other two columns.

Scrub the playhead across the timeline to ensure everything looks okay in accordance with your chosen settings.

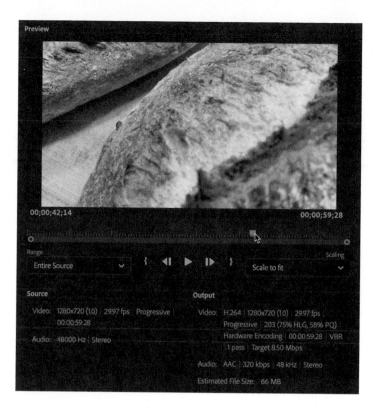

5　After you've confirmed that the sequence and appropriate settings are in place, click the Export button in the lower right to render your sequence to a distributable video file.

Congratulations—you've edited, arranged, and produced a short video!

Next steps with Premiere Pro

To further explore the creative options that Premiere Pro has to offer, you can make use of Adobe's help resources available at https://helpx.adobe.com/support /premiere-pro.html.

If you'd like to advance in your exploration of Premiere Pro in greater depth, I encourage you to consider reading *Adobe Premiere Pro Classroom in a Book (2023 Release)*, also available from Peachpit and Adobe Press.

Review questions

1   How are imported files handled within a Premiere Pro project?

2   What are the three workflow modes you can switch between in Premiere Pro?

3   What are the differences between the Source Monitor and the Program Monitor?

4   What is the Project panel used for?

5   What does the stopwatch toggle next to properties in the Effect Controls panel enable?

Review answers

1 Imported files are linked from within the project and are not embedded, so you must be careful when moving, renaming, or deleting them.

2 Import, Edit, and Export.

3 The Source Monitor is used to generate clips from media files, whereas the Program Monitor is used to preview the sequence timeline playback.

4 Organizing both imported media along with content like sequences or graphics generated within the project.

5 The stopwatch toggle enables the use of keyframes across the clip timeline in order to animate a change in properties from one keyframe to the next.

10 COMPOSITING MOTION GRAPHICS WITH AFTER EFFECTS

Lesson overview

In this lesson, you'll learn how to do the following:

- Create empty compositions and form compositions from imported assets.

- Create text elements and modify their attributes.

- Animate properties across time using keyframes.

- Apply easing to animated properties.

- Adjust and animate 3D layer properties.

- Add effects and animate effect properties.

- Learn about the design principle of variety.

- Render your composition as a video file.

 This lesson will take less than 2 hours to complete.

To get the files used in this lesson, download them from the web page for this book at www.adobepress.com/CreativeCloudCIB. For more information, see "Accessing the lesson files and Web Edition" in the Getting Started section at the beginning of this book.

Adobe After Effects is the industry-standard motion graphics and video compositing software that lets you design engaging title sequences, produce rich visual effects, and create compelling scenic compositions.

Getting started

● **Note** If you have not already downloaded the project files for this lesson to your computer from your Account page, make sure to do so now. See "Getting Started" at the beginning of the book.

Start by viewing the finished project to see what you'll be creating in this lesson.

1 Open the 10End.mp4 file in the Lesson10/10End folder to view the final project.

The project is a 10-second motion graphic to promote a fictional book being released soon. It employs several common features of After Effects, including keyframing, effects, and even 3D motion.

2 Close the file.

Understanding After Effects

Since both Adobe Premiere Pro and After Effects can work with video content, you may be confused about when you would choose one over the other. It is important to know the most appropriate application for your project.

For instance, if you are sequencing several video clips across a project, Premiere Pro is better suited for this task. After Effects excels at motion composition, asset manipulation, effects generation, and more advanced treatments.

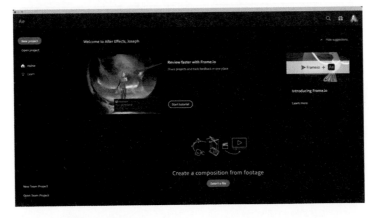

When you first open After Effects, you'll see a start screen that should look very familiar by this point in the book. Everything you'd expect is here: the ability to create a new project, open an existing project, and engage with a variety of learning content.

Managing projects and compositions

The basics of working in After Effects are very simple. You work in a single project that can include multiple compositions. In these compositions you manage your media content.

Creating an After Effects project file

We'll now create and save a new After Effects project file to work with across the duration of this lesson.

1   Launch After Effects and click New Project on the Start screen.

The Start screen disappears, and an untitled project opens.

2   Choose File > Save As > Save As from the application menu and save your project file to the Lesson10/10Start folder.

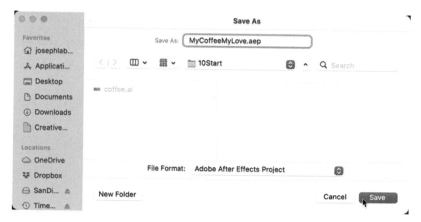

I've named my file **MyCoffeeMyLove.aep**, with the .aep file extension identifying it as an After Effects project file.

The After Effects interface

Despite After Effects being one of the most complicated and robust applications in Adobe Creative Cloud, the interface and management of workspaces are very approachable.

We will use the Default workspace for all the exercises in this lesson, and that workspace will appear in all the figures. I suggest you switch to it from the available workspaces selection along the top of the interface.

With the Default workspace selected, take a look at the variety of panels and how they are arranged across the interface.

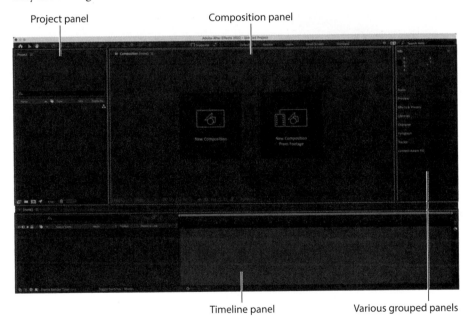

You will be using most of these panels often in this lesson, so let's examine briefly what each is used for:

- **Project panel:** This panel contains all imported media, compositions, and other project assets. When dealing with applied effects, the Effects panel will also reside here as a grouped panel.

- **Composition panel:** This panel functions primarily as the composition viewer, but you can directly interact with assets in a composition through this panel as well.

- **Timeline panel:** This panel is arranged by a layer stack, similar to other applications like Adobe Photoshop, but it also includes a time-based dimension. You can expand all properties of a particular layer and manage keyframes in the Timeline panel as well.

- **Various grouped panels:** This is a column of various grouped panels that include the Effects and Presets panel, Character panel, and Paragraph panel. Generally, any additional panels you might be working with (beyond the three just described) will be grouped in this column.

Creating a new composition

With an After Effects project file created and saved, we can move on to establishing a new composition in it.

1 In the Composition panel at the center of the interface, since there is no composition open, After Effects prompts you to create a new composition. Click New Composition.

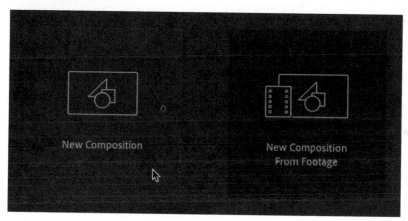

The Composition Settings dialog box appears.

Note See the "Time Representation in Premiere Pro" sidebar in Lesson 9 for an explanation of how to read and enter timecodes in After Effects.

2 In the Composition Settings dialog box, After Effects prompts you to make decisions about particular properties of the composition to be created. In the Composition Field, type **Main**. Set the width to 1280px and the height to 720px. Ensure that Pixel Aspect Ratio is set to Square Pixels and set the Frame Rate to 30. The Duration setting should be 10 seconds: 0:00:10:00. Click OK to create the composition.

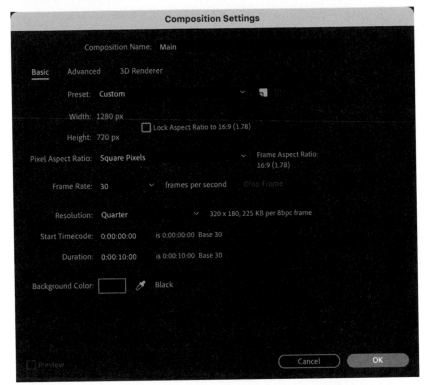

A new composition is created using the property values we chose. The Composition panel and the timeline are now aligned with this new composition, and the composition is added to the Project panel.

3 Click the Main composition, which has appeared in the Project panel, to view its properties.

● **Note** In After Effects, compositions always have a predetermined duration, unlike a Premiere Pro sequence, where the duration is determined by the timeline contents.

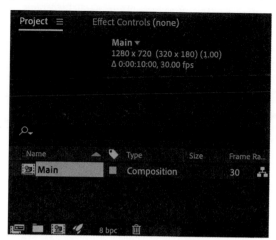

We can verify that the composition measures 1280x720 and has a duration of 10 seconds.

Creating a composition from an Illustrator file

We have a single composition created and ready to go in our project, but you have likely noticed that it is completely devoid of any content.

You can import media assets like video, images, and audio and create a composition out of those assets in a very convenient way.

For this purpose, you will find an Adobe Illustrator file named coffee.ai in the Lesson10/10Start folder. If you open this file in Illustrator, you will see it includes an artboard measuring 1280x720 with various pieces of artwork laid out across the canvas.

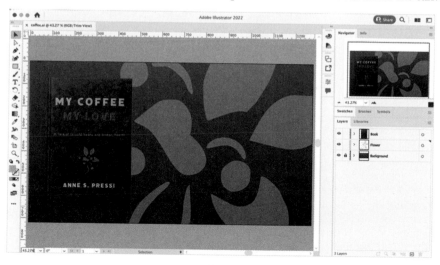

Aside from the visual media elements present in this file, pay particular attention to the Layers panel. There are three layers that have been explicitly organized to contain each individual visual element we'll be working with in After Effects: Book, Flower, and Background.

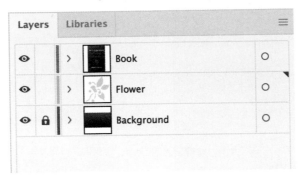

We want to keep these assets on separate layers so that they can be animated separately. If they were all on a single layer, the assets would transfer to After Effects as a single asset.

Okay! Now that we've gotten familiar with the Illustrator file, let's make an After Effects composition out of it.

1   In After Effects, choose File > Import > File from the application menu.

A file browser appears.

<blockquote>▶ **Tip** Because we chose to retain layer sizes on import, each layer will be the width and height of the content it contains. If you choose not to retain layer sizes, each layer will include invisible pixels that make each one the size of the artboard instead.</blockquote>

2   Locate the coffee.ai file in the Lesson10/10Start folder and select it. In the Import As menu, choose Composition – Retain Layer Sizes ensure that Create Composition is selected, and click Open.

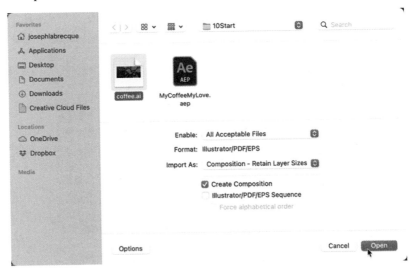

The Illustrator file is imported and translated according to our choices.

3 In the Project panel, note that there is a new composition named "coffee" that has been created. Select this new composition.

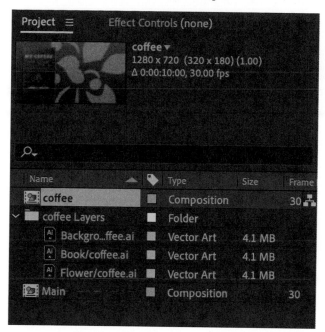

The coffee composition includes the layers and related assets from each of those layers in it. The same layers are included in the folder that After Effects has created, named "coffee Layers."

4 Double-click the coffee composition.

The Timeline and Composition panels are now aligned with the coffee composition.

The empty Main composition still exists, and you can switch between compositions using the tabs along the top of the timeline.

Adjusting composition settings

You can always adjust any of the settings of your composition at any time while working on your project.

To do so, choose Composition > Composition Settings from the application menu with the desired composition open in the timeline.

The same Composition Settings dialog box that appears when you create a composition appears again, enabling you to change any aspects of it you like.

You can use this dialog box to adjust the composition size, frame rate, or duration, among other settings.

Nesting compositions

After Effects is very versatile in that compositions can exist as content within other compositions. This allows you to create fine-grained edits in one composition that is then added to a container composition, where you can make additional edits.

We are going to nest the coffee composition in our Main composition.

1   Open the Main composition by double-clicking it in the Project panel or by switching to the Main composition tab in the timeline.

The Main composition is currently empty.

2 Drag the coffee composition from the Project panel into the Main composition timeline.

The coffee composition appears as a layer in the Main timeline.

3 Scrub the playhead across the Main composition timeline to see how the coffee composition fits perfectly within it.

Even with no internal motion, the coffee composition can be manipulated externally from the Main composition timeline.

Working with composition elements

With our compositions created and nested in the overall project, we'll turn our attention to working with the various elements in the compositions.

Adding text elements

The coffee composition includes several visual assets. Let's add some text as well.

1 If you are still viewing the Main composition, switch back to the coffee composition by clicking its tab above the timeline.

2 Choose the Horizontal Type Tool **T** from the tools arranged at the top of the After Effects interface and drag a large text element across the empty space next to the book in the Composition panel. Release the mouse button.

The text element is activated. The size doesn't matter too much. We can adjust it later.

3 Enter MY COFFEE MY LOVE and press Enter/Return to add a line; then type A Tale of Ground Beans and Broken Hearts.

This is the title and subtitle of the book we are promoting. They are contained in the same text element.

4 Click outside the layer to deactivate the selected text element. With the Horizontal Type Tool **T** still chosen, drag another text element across the bottom area beneath the existing text. Release the mouse button.

Again, the exact size and position of the text element doesn't much matter right now.

5 Enter Available November 1 for the text element value.

6 Click outside the layer to exit the text element editor.

Modifying text properties

With our two text elements created and the correct values entered, we'll next adjust the character and paragraph properties of each line.

1 Click in the top text element and drag across the entire first line to highlight it.

The second line should remain deselected.

● **Note** The Europa font family is part of the Adobe Fonts collection that can be accessed at https://fonts.adobe.com as part of your Creative Cloud subscription.

2 In the cluster of panels along the right-hand side of the interface, locate the Character panel. Change the font to **Europa-Bold** with a Size value of **71px** and click the color chip to enter a value of **#EBEBEB**, a light gray.

The title is now big and bold.

3 With the top text still active, drag across the entire second line to highlight it.

The first line will be deselected.

4 In the Character panel, set the font to **Europa-Light** with a Size value of **35px**. Set the color of the text to **#EBEBEB**.

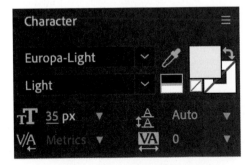

5   With the second line of text still selected, open the Paragraph panel, toggle the Center text option on, and set the Space Before Paragraph value to **38px**.

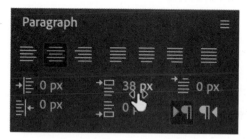

6   Click anywhere in the first line of text and center-align it as well using the Paragraph panel.

7   Click outside the text box to exit the text element editor.

8   Select all text in the second text element. In the Character panel, set the font to **Europa-Regular** and the size to **54px**. Set the color of the text to **#EBEBEB**.

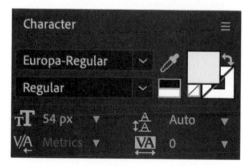

9   In the Paragraph panel, center-align the text as before. Press the Esc key to exit the text element editor.

Text width and positioning

Once you have configured your character and paragraph properties, you may need to adjust your text elements in the composition window in order to better match the figures shown here.

Here are some ways to go about this:

1 **Selection tool:** Using the Selection tool ▶, you can drag any element in the composition window to adjust its position. If you need to make any text elements wider, the Selection tool will only scale your elements, so you probably won't want to do that!

2 **Horizontal Type tool:** To adjust the width of any text element, use the Horizontal Type tool to activate the text element and resize handles will appear along the sides. Drag these handles to adjust the width so that the text fits better.

3 **Align panel:** By selecting multiple elements in the composition and choosing Window > Align from the application menu to access the Align panel, you can align your elements to one another—or alternatively to the composition itself.

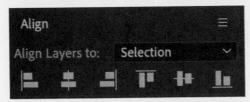

4 **Grids, Guides, and Overlays:** You can access a wide array of options at the bottom of the Composition panel that enable different sets of guides and grids that you can activate to assist in positioning elements exactly how you need them.

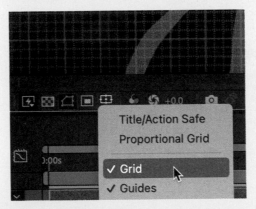

No matter what combination of tools you use to achieve proper sizing and positioning of your text elements, After Effects has options for all preferences.

Keyframing the primary text

We need the text to appear at a certain point in our motion graphic and can make it appear in a very elegant way through keyframes and easing.

1 Position the playhead at exactly 3 seconds as a marker and drag the primary text layer across the timeline to the right.

This ensures that the text will not be visible until 3 seconds have passed.

2 Expand the Layer properties by clicking the small chevron to the left of the layer name. Expand the Transform properties as well.

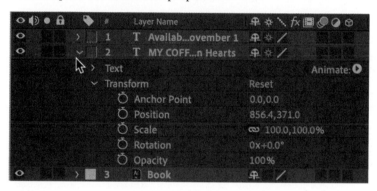

Nearly any visual element will have Transform properties that include Position, Scale, Rotation, and Opacity, among others.

3 In order to produce motion, you must enable the stopwatch toggle for any properties that you wish to change across time. Enable the stopwatch for both Position and Opacity.

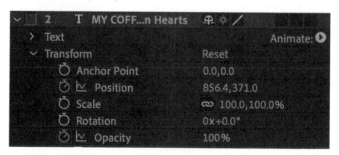

A diamond-shaped keyframe is automatically inserted into the timeline, aligned with the selected property.

4 Move the playhead to 4 seconds on the timeline and click the Add Or Remove Keyframe At Current Time button  at the left of each stopwatch to insert keyframes in Position and Opacity.

New keyframes are established at the 4-second mark. These keyframes contain the final property values of this keyframe set.

● **Note** If there is a green line present at the top of the timeline, this indicates that animation is in memory and that playback will be in real time. If the line is not green, then those frames need a bit more time to render before they will play back smoothly.

5 To adjust the initial keyframe values, click the Go To Previous Keyframe button ◄ at the left of either stopwatch to go back to the keyframe at the 3-second mark. Adjust the Y Position value (the second of the two values) to 300.0 and the Opacity value to **0%**.

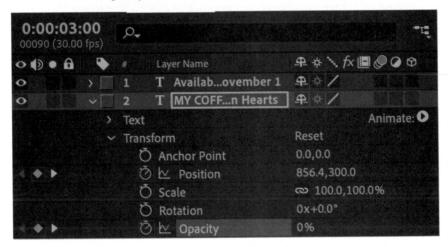

These changes will make the text transparent, initially, and place it slightly above its final Y position.

Adding eases to the text motion

If you play back the timeline, you will notice that nothing happens until the 3-second mark, when our text drops into place and appears. The motion is fine, but it could be even smoother with easing applied.

We'll finish up this motion with some easing.

1 Choose the Selection tool ▸ and drag a rectangular selection around all four keyframes to select them.

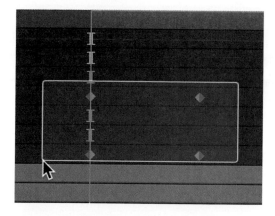

Selected keyframes appear blue.

2 Choose Animation > Keyframe Assistant > Easy Ease from the application menu.

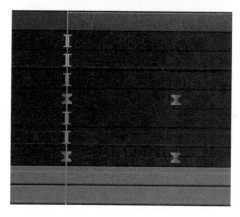

● **Note** An Easy Ease changes the motion to start slow, speed up toward the middle of the animation, and slow down again at the end.

● **Note** There are a variety of ease types in After Effects. You can perform fine-grained, custom easing by activating the Motion Graph toggle ▣, accessible above the timeline.

The appearance of all four keyframes changes to indicate that an Easy Ease has been applied.

3 Collapse the layer properties and press the spacebar to play the timeline. As you can see, the motion appears smoother now that easing has been applied.

Keyframing the secondary text

Our primary text element motion is complete, and it looks pretty good! We will do something similar—and simpler—with the secondary text element that states the book release date.

1 Move the playhead across the timeline to 4 seconds and 15 frames. Drag the layer that represents the secondary text element over to the right so that it begins at this point.

2 Expand the Layer properties by clicking the small chevron to the left of the layer name. Expand the Transform properties as well.

3 Activate the stopwatch ⏱ for Opacity and set the value to 0%.

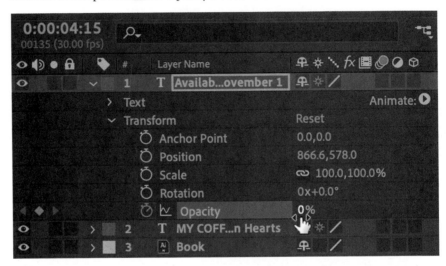

This will ensure the text begins as fully transparent.

4 Move the playhead to 5 seconds and 15 frames and change the Opacity value to **70%**.

A keyframe is automatically inserted when the associated property value changes.

5 Select both keyframes and choose Animation > Keyframe Assistant > Easy Ease from the application menu.

6 Collapse the layer properties and press the spacebar to play the timeline and preview the text motion.

The secondary text appears following the primary text, and both sets of text fade in nicely.

Keyframing the floral design

With the text elements now in motion, we'll turn our attention to those assets imported from Illustrator. The background itself will not have any motion applied to it, but the floral design and the book definitely will.

Let's begin by animating the floral design.

1 Move the playhead to the beginning of the timeline at 0 seconds and expand the Flower layer Transform properties as we've done before.

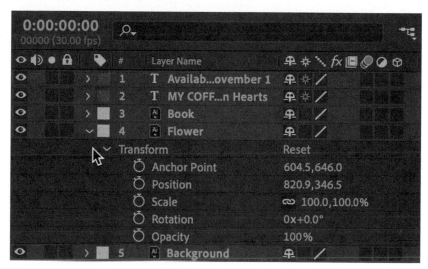

2 Activate the stopwatch toggle for both Scale and Opacity. The Scale property has values for both vertical and horizontal scale. Since we want to adjust them in unison, be sure the link toggle is activated. Set the Scale value to **120%** and bring the Opacity value down to **0%**.

3 Move the playhead to the very end of the timeline at 9 seconds and 29 frames. Adjust the Scale setting back to **100%** and set Opacity to **45%**.

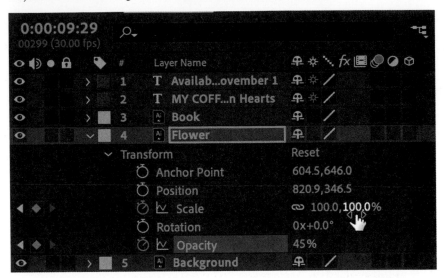

The floral design animation lasts for the entire duration of the composition timeline.

4 Collapse the Layer properties and press the spacebar to play the timeline and preview the floral design motion.

The flower appears slowly and gradually increases in opacity while decreasing in scale.

Keyframing the book position

After the primary text fades into place, we will have the book itself slide in from the right—out of frame—to settle at its present location in the composition.

1 Move the playhead across the timeline to 2 seconds. Drag the layer that represents the book over to the right so that it is visible at this point.

2 Expand the Transform properties and activate the stopwatch toggle ⏱ for the Position property.

▶ **Tip** It is possible to treat the X and Y Position properties as completely separate from each other. To do so, right-click the Position property and choose Separate Dimensions from the menu.

A keyframe is created that holds values for both X and Y Position properties.

3 Move the playhead across the timeline to 4 seconds and click the Add Or Remove Keyframe At Current Time button ◆ at the left of the stopwatch in the Position property to insert a keyframe.

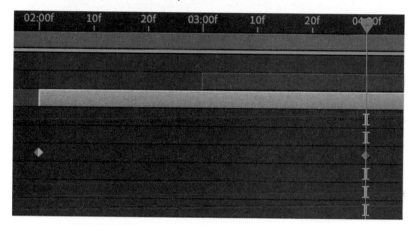

This duplicates the previous keyframe and is where we want the book to end.

4 To adjust the initial keyframe values, click the Go To Previous Keyframe button ◀ at the left of the stopwatch to go back to the keyframe at the 2-second mark. Adjust the X Position value to **1530**.

The book will begin completely out of frame. But since we added that secondary keyframe at 4 seconds, it will settle into position once the animation has completed.

5 Select both keyframes and choose Animation > Keyframe Assistant > Easy Ease from the application menu to apply some smooth easing.

Note Frames are represented in the timeline as the last pair of numerals displayed within the 0:00:00:00 time display.

Because we are changing position over time, a motion guide appears in the composition window, displaying the path of motion. Since we are using an Easy Ease, the small dots—which represent frames—are closer to one another at the beginning and end and farther apart toward the middle.

Keep the properties for the Book layer open for now. We are not done with this asset yet.

Working with 3D layers

After Effects includes some powerful 3D tooling and workflows. We are going to touch on the basics of 3D manipulation in this project by keyframing the Orientation property of our Book layer.

1 The first step to working with any 3D properties is to declare an existing layer as a 3D layer. To do so, click the 3D Layer toggle 🔲 to the right of the layer name in the Book layer.

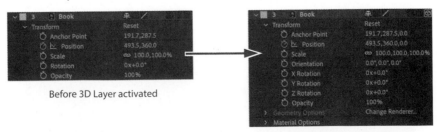

Before 3D Layer activated

After 3D Layer activated

With the 3D Layer toggle activated, the Book layer becomes a 3D layer and the number of Transform properties increases substantially to allow for manipulation of the 3D properties it now exhibits.

2 We are going to focus on the Orientation property. Move the playhead to 3 seconds and 14 frames and enable the stopwatch for Orientation.

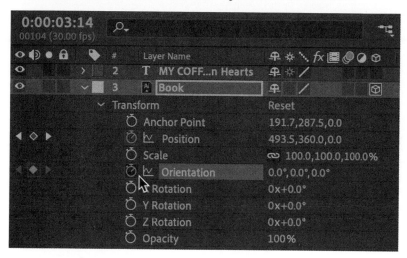

A keyframe is inserted with Orientation values in the X, Y, and Z dimensions all set to the default of 0 degrees.

3 Move the playhead to 2 seconds in the Book layer, where the motion begins. Keep the X value at **0** degrees and change the Y value to **30** degrees and the Z value to **350** degrees.

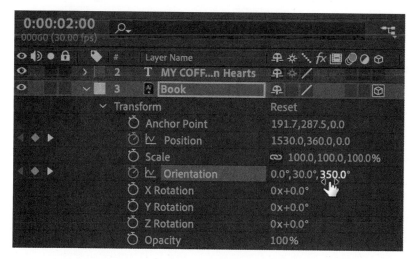

These changes will make the book look slightly lifted and rotated as it appears in the composition from off frame, as if being slid over by an unseen hand.

4 Collapse the Layer properties and press the spacebar to play the timeline and preview the improved book motion.

The book still appears from off-screen and moves to the correct position, but now its movement has a bit more realism and dimension.

Working in 3D space

Since activating the 3D Layer toggle for the Book layer, you may have noticed a multicolored gizmo appear. You interact with this gizmo to modify all three dimensions of the 3D orientation of the book visually.

The results are the same regardless of whether you use the gizmo with the Selection tool or you adjust these properties numerically, as we've done in this lesson.

You may note too, that when the book is out of frame at the starting position it is not entirely visible. So it can be difficult to manipulate precisely using either method.

Enabling the Draft 3D toggle 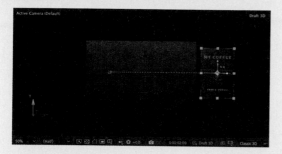 at the bottom of the composition window will make 3D Layer content visible via an Extended Viewport—even when out of frame. It also attempts to render any 3D Layer content more quickly and accurately than if not enabled.

There are many other workflows to explore with 3D in After Effects through the use of cameras, lighting, and more. If interested in pursuing these workflows in more depth, take a look at the references at the end of this lesson.

Adjusting layer timing

When playing back the composition timeline, you may have noticed that the primary text appears a bit too soon and distracts from the motion of the book sliding into view.

Let's fix the timing of our composition elements.

1 If you scrub the playhead, you can find the exact time when the book clears the incoming text. Set the playhead to 3 seconds and 20 frames.

2 If you adjust the timing of the primary text layer, you need to do the same for the secondary one. Shift-click both text layers in order to select them and then drag the primary text layer to the right until it begins at the playhead position you've set.

Since both layers are selected, they both shift over into their new positions.

3 Play the composition timeline once again and see how everything is sequenced nicely now. Note that not only did the visible layers themselves shift over, but also the keyframes you so painstakingly set earlier.

This is something that everyone working in After Effects should know how to do, as adjusting the timing of elements is a crucial part of the overall workflow.

Adding effects to composition elements

Up to this point in the lesson, we've dealt with a good number of things that After Effects can do. But we haven't really applied any actual effects. Let's change that by completing our motion composition with some effects.

Adding drop shadow effects

Adding a bit of drop shadow can help visual elements by providing additional contrast or by creating a greater sense of physical realism.

We'll make use of the drop shadow in our composition to achieve both ends.

1 Open the Effects & Presets panel in the right-hand column of various panels by clicking its name.

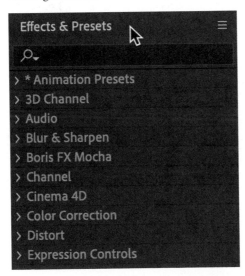

An intimidating list of effects and presets appears within categories. If you are unfamiliar with what is available and simply begin browsing effects through this panel, you may become overwhelmed with the choices.

2 Thankfully, there is a search mechanism at the top of the panel to make things a bit simpler. Click in the search field and type **drop shadow**.

The Drop Shadow effect is the only one that matches both terms, and so it appears.

3 Move the playhead to the end portion of the composition when all assets are visible and drag the Drop Shadow effect from the Effects & Presets panel onto the book asset in the Composition panel. Release the mouse button once the cursor displays a green plus (+) icon and a highlight appears across the asset.

You can apply effects by dragging them onto elements in the Composition panel or onto the individual layers in the timeline, which can be a more accurate method.

4 Drag an additional Drop Shadow effect onto the layer in the timeline that represents the primary text element.

This will help in giving the light-colored text a greater degree of contrast with the background.

Each layer that has an effect placed on it gets a small Effect toggle 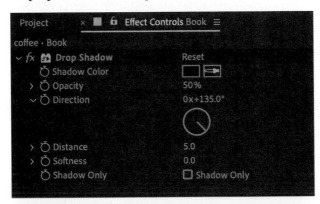 in the Effect column of the timeline.

Adjusting effect properties

When you add an effect to layer content, it is applied using the effect's default properties. You'll want to adjust these properties to meet your project's specific needs.

1   To adjust the properties of applied effects, do one of the following:

- If the Effect Controls panel isn't opened automatically when you apply an effect, choose Window > Effect Controls from the application menu.

- Select the Book layer to view the effect properties for the Drop Shadow effect we applied earlier.

- In the Book layer, expand the Effects property group, and then open the properties for the Drop Shadow effect.

> **Note** Each effect has its own custom set of properties, and they vary widely from effect to effect.

> **Tip** Keeping the different effect properties exposed in the timeline will assist with keyframe placement if you choose to animate any effect.

If multiple effects are added, they will all appear in the Effects group.

2 We will not be animating this effect, so it may be simpler to adjust the Drop Shadow effect properties from the Effect Controls panel. Change the Distance value to **15** and the Softness value to **70**.

Distance offsets the Drop Shadow effect based on the Direction property. Softness will blur the Drop Shadow effect.

3 Select the primary text element and adjust its Drop Shadow Opacity value to **70%**. Leave all other values at their defaults.

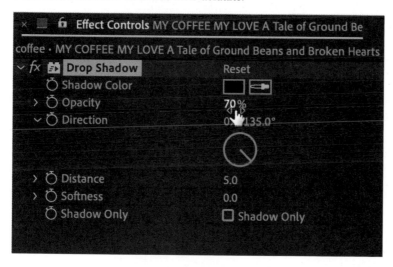

An increase in the Opacity value will make the shadow effectively more prominent.

● **Note** We didn't
add motion to any of
these effects, but any
effect property can be
animated if a stopwatch
exists to enable
keyframing.

4 Survey the results of your effect adjustments to see how the book appears to have a slight shadow against the background now. Additionally, the primary text element received a distinct, close shadow, giving it a bit more contrast against the background.

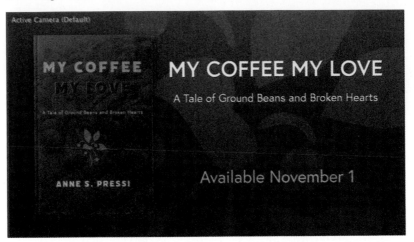

Generating animated noise effects

The background and floral design are both very sharp and simple. Let's use an animated noise effect to blend them together and create a bit of texture.

We could apply a noise effect to both layers separately, but that would double our work. We will make use of an adjustment layer to make things easier and more organized.

1 To create an adjustment layer, right-click in the empty space below your existing layers in the Timeline panel and choose New > Adjustment Layer from the menu.

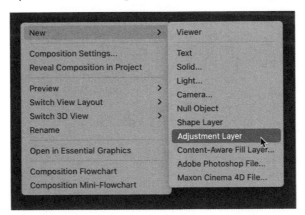

The adjustment layer is added to your Project panel and to the top of your composition layer stack.

2 Drag the layer just above the Flower layer and release the mouse button to reposition it.

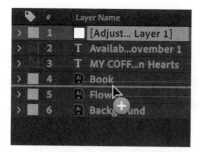

Since an adjustment layer affects only layers below it, we need to position it just above the Background and Flower layers and below all other layers.

3 In the Effects & Presets panel, perform a search for the term noise to locate the Noise effect.

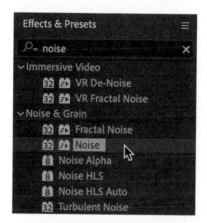

4 Drag the Noise effect from the Effects & Presets panel and onto the adjustment layer in the Timeline panel.

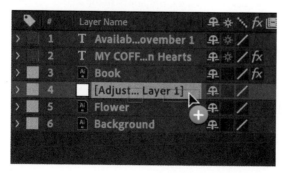

5 Be sure the adjustment layer is selected. In the Effect Controls panel, adjust the Amount Of Noise value to **20.0%** to create some subtle grain.

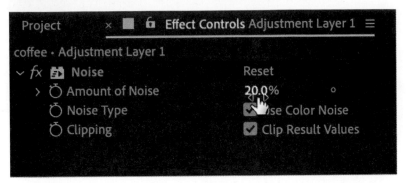

Note If you want an adjustment layer to affect only certain layers in a composition, create a nested composition that includes the adjustment layers and also the layers to which you want to apply the adjustments.

6 Reposition the playhead and press the spacebar to view the results.

Even though we did not add any keyframes to this effect, the noise is still animated across the entire composition on both layers below the adjustment layer.

Some effects do require keyframes for motion to occur, but you can still adjust the intensity of the effect with keyframes if desired.

Design principle: variety

We've made use of a lot of different effects and techniques in our After Effects composition. Even in applying the same Drop Shadow effect to two visual elements, we adjusted the values of certain properties so that they exhibit the same properties differently.

This is an example of the design principle commonly known as variety.

Variety can be expressed in a single composition or canvas using different colors, values, textures, shapes, effects, and so on. It is sometimes seen as in opposition to the principle of unity, but in truth, the two can be used together to retain the viewer's interest.

The important thing to know about variety is that it should be used with intent. Otherwise, chaos ensues—and that is not a design principle in any way. Chaos is the opposite of design!

Adding effects to an entire composition

Adjustment layers are great for adding effects to a set of layers and can certainly be used to affect an entire composition. But there are other methods that are a bit more organized.

Recall that one of the first things we did in this project was create an empty composition named Main. Later, we nested the coffee composition within Main, but we haven't addressed it since that time.

The coffee composition resides in the Main composition as a layer, and just like all the other layers we've been dealing with, we can add effects to it in the same manner.

Let's add some intro and outro effects to the entire composition using this workflow.

1 Click the Main tab in the Timeline panel to edit the Main composition.

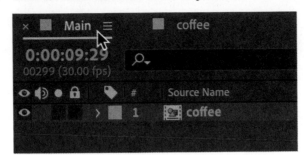

The coffee composition is nested in this composition as a layer.

● **Note** A vignette in photography or videography is a darker area around the edges and corners of the frame, usually due to lensing in hardware. It is often employed as a stylistic choice when it comes to purely digital work.

2 In the Effects & Presets panel, perform a search for the term vignette to locate the CC Vignette effect.

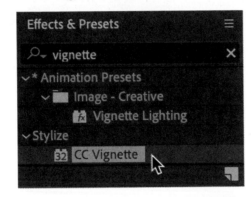

CC Vignette is a stylistic effect that darkens the corners and edges of a frame by applying a vignette—just like with photography in Adobe Lightroom or Photoshop.

3 Drag the CC Vignette effect from the Effects & Presets panel and onto the coffee layer in the Timeline panel.

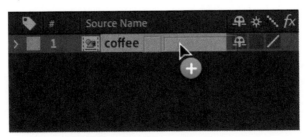

4 Move the playhead to the very start of the timeline at 0 seconds and expand the layer property groups until you are in the CC Vignette properties. Activate the stopwatch for the Amount property.

A keyframe is added at 0 seconds specifying the Amount property as 100. This indicates that a large amount of vignetting will be visible.

5 Move the playhead over to 2 seconds and set the Amount value to **100**.

This decreases the amount of vignetting from 100 to 40 over the first 2 seconds of playback, providing an introductory effect before the book or text elements begin their motion.

6 In the Effects & Presets panel, perform a search for the term burn to locate the CC Burn Film effect.

The CC Film Burn effect will give the appearance of burn marks across the frame, as though film has been left in a projector for too long and the heat from the projection bulb is causing the film to melt and burn.

7 Move the playhead to 8 seconds, drag the CC Burn Film effect from the Effects & Presets panel, and release it onto the coffee layer in the Timeline panel.

We will create an outro animation after all internal motion has ceased that performs a stylistic burn effect.

8 Locate and expand the properties for CC Burn Film in the coffee layer and activate the stopwatch for the Burn property.

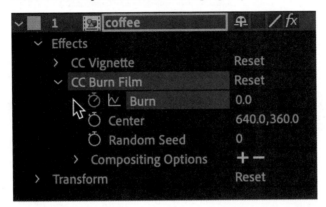

A keyframe is inserted at 8 seconds that holds a value of 0 for the Burn property. This will ensure that we see no burn effect whatsoever at this point on the timeline.

9 Move the playhead to 9 seconds and set the Burn value to 100%.

From 8 seconds to 9 seconds, the CC Film Burn effect will flare up and quickly burn out the image to complete black for the last second of our 10-second composition, creating a dramatic outro.

10 Play the entire Main composition from the beginning to see how these effects apply to the nested composition.

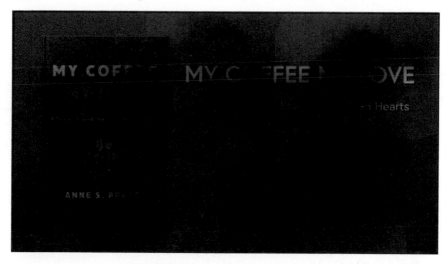

Everything flows smoothly, from the subtle vignetting serving as the intro, to the animation in the coffee composition, and closing with a stylized burn effect. The project is complete.

Publishing your composition

To distribute your completed work, you'll need to render it as a video file for playback.

We will render our Main composition for playback over YouTube.

1 With the Main composition active, choose Composition > Add To Adobe Media Encoder Queue from the application menu.

Composition	Layer	Effect	Animation	View	W
New Composition...				⌘ N	
Composition Settings...				⌘ K	
Set Poster Time					
Trim Comp to Work Area				⇧ ⌘ X	
Crop Comp to Region of Interest					
Add to Adobe Media Encoder Queue...				⌥ ⌘ M	
Add to Render Queue				⌃ ⌘ M	
Add Output Module					

Adobe Media Encoder opens.

▶ **Tip** If Adobe Media Encoder does not open immediately, try opening it manually and then issue the Export command again. Also, be sure that your software is completely up to date.

● **Note** There are
many other formats
and presets you can
choose from. We are
using H.264 for the
near-universal support
it receives, and YouTube
for its popularity.

2 In Media Encoder, the composition appears in the Queue panel in the upper-right quadrant of the interface. Apply the following settings:

- **Format:** H.264.

- **Preset:** YouTube 720p HD.

- **Output File:** Set this to a location and filename of your choosing.

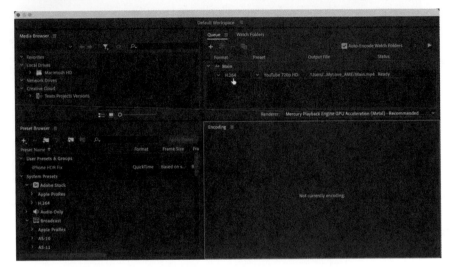

3 Click the Start Queue button 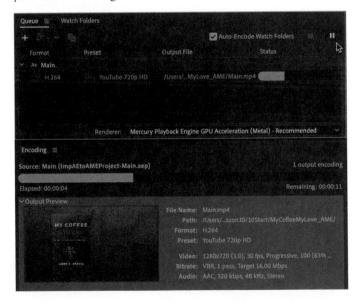 to begin processing your video according to your chosen settings.

The Encoding panel will show your progress and even give you a preview of the video as it is rendered from your composition.

4   Locate the file in the location you previously specified and play it back to ensure everything looks good.

● **Note** You can also get a native rendering of your composition by choosing Composition > Add To Render Queue, but the files produced are not suitable for distribution. Rather, they can be used in other creative workflows.

Next steps with After Effects

To further explore the creative options that After Effects has to offer, you can make use of Adobe's help resources available at https://helpx.adobe.com/support/after-effects.html.

If you'd like to advance in your exploration of After Effects in greater depth, I encourage you to consider reading *Adobe After Effects Classroom in a Book (2023 Release)*, also available from Peachpit and Adobe Press.

Review questions

1 What must you do when organizing an Illustrator file if you want to animate different Illustrator layers individually in After Effects?

2 How do you enable animation for a layer property?

3 What does Easy Ease do to your motion?

4 How do you gain access to a layer's 3D properties?

5 How do you apply effects to layers in a composition?

Review answers

1 Ensure that your Illustrator file has distinct and organized layers established, since layers from Illustrator will translate into timeline layers in an After Effects composition.

2 Activate the stopwatch toggle for that specific property.

3 Changes the motion to begin more slowly, get faster toward the middle, and slow down toward the end.

4 Activate the 3D Layer toggle for that layer.

5 Drag the desired effects onto a layer in the timeline or a visible object in the Composition panel.

11 ANIMATING INTERACTIVE CONTENT WITH ANIMATE

Lesson overview

In this lesson, you'll learn how to do the following:

- Target multiple platforms with Adobe Animate.

- Import bitmap images onto the stage.

- Draw and manipulate vector content.

- Create shape tweens and apply easing effects.

- Gain an understanding of the design principle of movement.

- Work with frames, keyframes, and blank keyframes.

- Create symbols from existing content.

- Make content interactive through the Actions Wizard.

- Understand publish and export workflows.

 This lesson will take 2 hours to complete.

To get the files used in this lesson, download them from the web page for this book at http://adobepress.com/CreativeCloudCIB. For more information, see "Accessing the lesson files and Web Edition" in the Getting Started section at the beginning of this book.

Animate is a platform-agnostic animation, motion design, and interactivity software used to create animation for television, apps, and games for the web and mobile platforms, and a wide variety of additional engaging experiences through native web technologies and even virtual reality.

Getting started

● **Note** If you have not already downloaded the project files for this lesson to your computer from your Account page, make sure to do so now. See "Getting Started" at the beginning of the book.

Start by viewing the finished project to see what you'll be creating in this lesson.

1 Open the 11End.fla file in the Lesson11/11End folder to view the final project.

2 Choose Control > Test Movie from the application menu to run the interactive animation in a web browser.

3 Click the animation's initial screen to begin playback.

The project is an animation of a lively ball that rolls across an elevated cliff and down to the ground below. In this lesson, you'll learn to assemble and design all the assets involved, give them life through the various tools and workflows available in Animate, and enable interactive elements for the user.

4 Close the project file.

Introducing Animate

Adobe Animate is a platform-agnostic animation, motion design, and interactivity application. Animate is used across industries but is most known for its use in a variety of television and web content. You can also design and develop interactive experiences, including games and applications using the software.

Animate differs from Character Animator in that it allows for a much more diverse platform set and a more varied assortment of animation styles. Animate, unlike Character Animator, does not use live performance capture.

Animate differs from After Effects in that, again, it supports a greater variety of target platforms. Animate also allows for interactivity, whether in the form of interactive displays, applications, or games.

There will always be similarities between applications like this. The power comes in knowing the strengths of one over the other and taking advantage of that.

Animate document types

Animate supports a multitude of document types, both natively and through the use of extensions. Which platform you choose will depend on what sort of project you wish to create. Here are some of the most important native platforms to be aware of:

1 HTML5 Canvas: Targets native web browser technologies with the <canvas> HTML element and JavaScript for interactivity.

2 ActionScript 3.0: A format native to Animate most often used for noninteractive animation. It can be effectively rendered as HD video or brought directly into After Effects for compositing.

3 AIR: Maintained by HARMAN through an Adobe partnership. AIR (https://airsdk .harman.com) is used to create apps and games across desktop and mobile platforms, including Windows, macOS, iOS, Android, and more.

4 WebGL glTF (beta): Targets the native web through standard or extended implementations of glTF via WebGL GPU-accelerated technologies.

5 VR (beta): Targets the native web through use of WebGL specifically with panoramic and 360-degree virtual reality environments.

● **Note** Animate was formerly known as Flash Professional and was rebranded to reflect the multiplatform nature of the software as the industry began moving away from the single-runtime Flash platform.

▶ **Tip** You can also install third-party extensions that add additional document types to Animate, such as exporting your animations as LottieFiles.

Launching Animate

When you launch Animate for the first time, if you haven't used it before you will be asked whether you are new to Animate. How you answer has a number of consequences in terms of how the interface appears and how various panels are arranged.

If you have already made this choice previously, don't worry. Either way, you'll see how to configure everything to align with what you see a bit further on in this lesson, once we create a new file and start working.

When you launch Animate without any project files open, you will be presented with a Home screen just as in other Creative Cloud applications like Photoshop and Illustrator.

From this screen you can create new projects based on presets or custom properties, click the Learn tab to view tutorials, and see what is new with the software.

Creating a new project and working with content

In the next few exercises, you will create a new document in Animate and begin to populate it with both imported bitmap content and vector content that will be designed within the software.

Creating a new Animate document

The first step in any Animate project is to decide which platform to target and then create a new document based on that decision.

To begin, we'll create a new document in Animate targeting HTML5 Canvas as a platform.

1 With Animate open and the Home screen visible, click the Create New button or choose the More Presets option to open the New Document dialog box.

2   Click the Advanced tab and choose HTML5 Canvas from the Platforms category. Leave the properties in the Details area at their defaults and click Create.

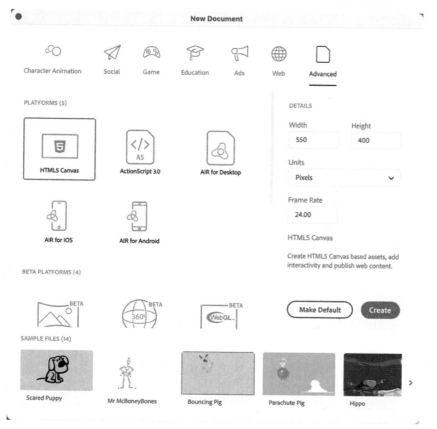

Animate creates the document.

Note You can always convert from one platform to another by clicking File > Convert To and choosing the target platform you want to use. Animate will create a copy of your existing document that targets the alternative platform.

3 Choose File > Save to open the Save prompt and navigate to the Lesson11 > 11Start folder. Enter a meaningful filename and click Save.

▶ **Tip** The FPS (frames-per-second) setting applies to the entire document and determines how many frames of content it takes to establish one second of time across the document timeline.

Your project is saved as an Animate document (with the filename extension *.fla) on your local computer and the Save dialog box closes.

The Animate interface

Now that we have created a new file within Animate, you'll find a set of common panels and other interface elements that will always be present when you're working in the software.

We'll refer to these throughout this lesson, so it's good to identify them now.

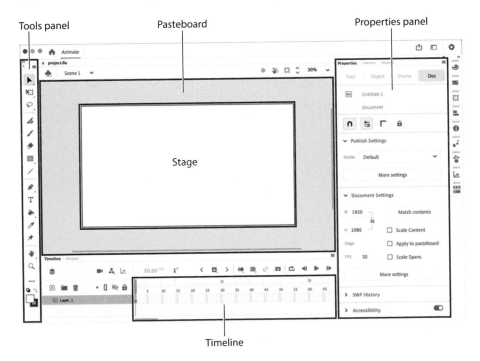

Earlier, you learned that the interface may appear differently depending on the answer given to a prompt the first time Animate is launched. No matter which choice you have made, you will want to check the following settings so that your workspace appears similar to what you'll find referenced in this lesson.

1   Choose Animate > Preferences > Expert Preferences on macOS or Edit > Preferences > Expert Preferences on Windows.

    This will configure a lot of elements like the Tools panel configuration and set your workspace to Essentials.

2   In the upper right of the Timeline panel, open the Options menu ☰ and choose Standard from the top three options.

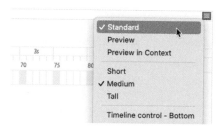

    This determines how frames appear within the timeline.

3   Navigate to Edit > Preferences > Edit Preferences on Windows > General (Windows) or Animate > Preferences > Edit Preferences (macOS) and change UI Theme to Light.

    Changing the UI theme isn't critical like steps 1 and 2, but you may find it helpful since we are using the setting for all the figures in this lesson.

With all that taken care of, we are ready to resume!

Importing bitmap images

For this project, we'll start by importing a photographic bitmap image of a cloudy sky as our background to appear behind all other layers.

1   To begin, let's rename the existing layer named Layer_1 to something that is more descriptive. Double-click the layer name to highlight it and type **Sky**.

2   Click outside the layer name or press Enter (Windows) or Return (macOS) to commit the change.

3 To import the bitmap image of a cloudy sky into this layer, go to the application menu and choose File > Import > Import To Stage.

4 From the file browser that appears, navigate to the Lesson11/11Start folder, choose the file named CloudySky.png, and click Open.

● **Note** Recall that our document was created at the HTML5 Canvas default width and height of 550x400 pixels. The photograph is 1280x720 pixels.

The photograph of a cloudy sky appears across the stage. You'll notice it is actually far too large and extends onto the pasteboard.

5 To resize the document stage to match the image you've imported as a background, ensure that the Doc tab is selected in the Properties panel and click Match Contents in the Document Settings section.

Animate resizes the document stage to match the size of the content you've imported.

6 To better see the entire stage and its contents and have it automatically scale based on the available space, choose Zoom > Fit In Window.

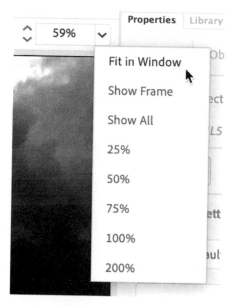

Drawing the cliff

Now we'll draw a cliff face in a new layer using a series of vector rectangles.

1 Create a new layer by clicking the New Layer icon ⊞ at the top of the timeline.

2 Double-click the layer name to highlight it and rename the layer **Cliff**.

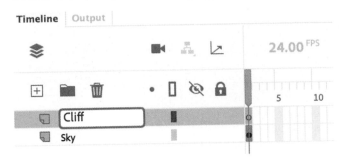

The newly created layer remains selected.

3 Select the Rectangle tool ▪ from the Tools panel.

4 On the Tools tab of the Properties panel, choose a color that you like for your cliff fill and stroke.

⬤ Note When Object Drawing is activated, you will not be able to merge shapes together as they are drawn. They will, instead, be placed into Drawing Object containers.

∨ **Color and Style**

| ▬ | Fill | ▨ | 100 % |
| / | Stroke | ▨ | 100 % |

I've chosen a brown color for my fill and to disable the stroke.

5 Ensuring that Object Drawing ◉ is not selected, drag across the lower part of the stage, from one side to the other, to create a rectangle representing the ground. The height doesn't matter.

6 Drag to form another rectangle to the side about halfway across the screen. It should overlap the previous rectangle so that they merge together.

7 Choose the Selection tool from the Tools panel and hover over the vertical edge of the cliff until the cursor changes to display a small arc. Drag to pull the cliff wall inward, creating a nice curve.

8 Adjust other portions of the cliff face in a similar manner to give some natural slope and incline to the environment.

Drawing the ball

With the cliff face created, we can now draw the ball element, which will eventually become our primary motion asset for this piece.

1 Create a new layer by clicking the New Layer icon ⊞ at the top the timeline.

2 Double-click the layer name to highlight it and rename the layer **Ball**.

The newly created layer remains selected.

3 Select the Oval tool ● from the Tools panel.

4 In the Tools tab of the Properties panel, choose a color that you like for your ball fill and stroke.

I've chosen a red radial gradient ■ fill and no stroke.

5 Holding down the Shift key, drag across the rightmost area of the stage on top of the cliff to draw a circle of about 140px in diameter.

The gradient is okay right now, but we can improve its application upon the circle we've just drawn.

6 Select the Gradient Transform tool ▦ from the Tools panel (noting that it might be grouped with the Free Transform tool) and click the ball to select it.

7 Using the Gradient Transform tool, adjust the scale of the gradient by dragging the scale icon in the overlay ⊘ outward in order to increase the amount of red in the gradient and decrease the darker coloring, making it less severe.

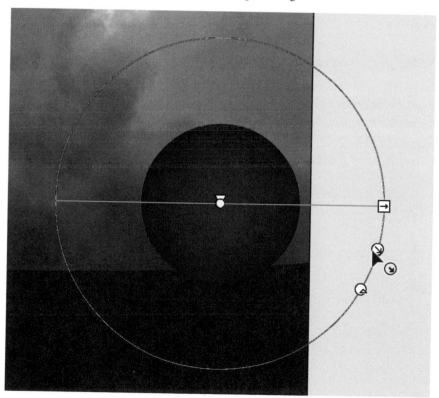

► **Tip** The Shift key will create a perfect circle instead of an oval when used alongside the Oval tool. Similarly, holding down Shift when drawing with the Rectangle tool produces squares.

● **Note** If need be, you can select this shape and change its width, height, and position using the Object tab of the Properties panel.

● **Note** You can continue adding assets to your scene such as grasses, clouds, and stones. Just be sure to create each set of assets in its own layer.

► **Tip** All content that you add to the stage should be in its own layer if you intend to animate it later. Including more than one object on the same layer can be problematic for the tweening engine in Animate.

Making your content move

Now that we have a set of layers and assets to make up the visual aspects of our animation, it is time to add motion to the ball in order to make it move across the clifftop in a natural way.

Extending the timeline

You will notice that we currently have only a single frame as part of our project timeline. If we try to scrub the blue playhead or click the Play button ▶ above the timeline, nothing happens, since an animation must effectively include at least two frames.

Let's extend the frame span across the timeline to establish one second of time.

1   Drag across all three layers at frame 24 starting with the Ball layer until the selected frame across all layers is highlighted. Then release the mouse button.

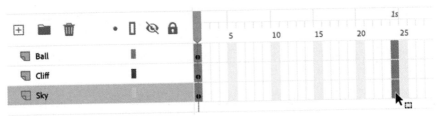

The blue highlight indicates that these layers are now selected.

2   Next, you'll insert frames in all layers up to and including the selected frames. Click the Insert Frames Group button ◘ above the timeline and choose Frame from the options that appear.

Gray frames appear from frame 1 to frame 24 across all three layers.

3 Scrub the playhead by dragging it across the timeline.

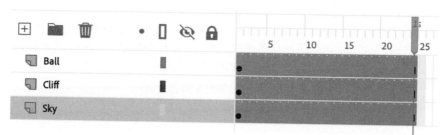

● **Note** The time markers above the timeline are calculated using the FPS value of the document. In this case, the document is set to 24 FPS, so the 1s marker is visible at frame 24.

While you can now scrub and play across the timeline, nothing changes yet on the stage. This is because the state of all objects remains identical across all frames. We need to make changes across time in order to produce motion.

Inserting keyframes

To create any sort of animation in Animate, you must make use of keyframes. A *keyframe* is a special frame that exhibits a change in some property for the content on that layer.

Now we'll add a keyframe to the Ball layer and adjust the properties of the associated object.

1 Select frame 15 in the Ball layer, click the Keyframes icon ◼ above the timeline, and select Keyframe to insert a new keyframe.

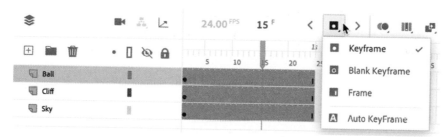

A new keyframe is inserted at frame 15, indicated by a filled circle.

2 At frame 15, use the Selection tool ▸ to move the ball from the side of the stage to the edge of the cliff.

3 Drag the blue playhead between the keyframes to see how the ball on the stage jumps from one position to the next due to the change in properties held within the second keyframe.

Types of frames and keyframes

There are three types of frames within an Animate project timeline. Let's examine the differences between the three:

1 Frames: Simple frames ▮ extend the frame span across the timeline, determining where and when certain assets appear and disappear. Frames are designated by a plain, gray background.

2 Keyframes: These are special frames that contain information designating a change in property values such as position, scale, or rotation. Keyframes ▮ are easily identifiable by the filled black circle within the frame and a discreet border to the left.

3 Blank Keyframes: A blank keyframe ○ is simply a keyframe where either the object has been removed from the stage or none existed. Using blank keyframes, you can stop assets from appearing on the stage. Blank keyframes are easily identifiable by the unfilled black circle within the frame and a discreet border to the left.

Creating shape tweens

Animate will take any property changes from one keyframe to the next and fill in the frames in-between when instructed to do so.

Let's create a shape tween between the two keyframes on our project timeline.

1 First, select at least one frame between the two keyframes on the ball layer.

2 Click the Insert Tweens option above the timeline and select Create Shape Tween.

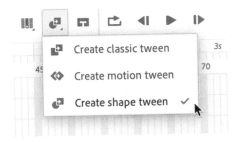

The appearance of the frames between the two keyframes changes in color, indicating that a shape tween has been created.

3 Drag the playhead across the shape tween to see how Animate adjusts the change in position of the ball shape across the in-between frames.

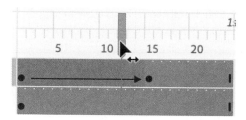

● **Note** Any object that is to make use of a tween in Animate—such as the ball shape—should exist on its own layer for the tween to work correctly. This is why we are so careful with creating new layers for each asset.

4 Click Test Movie ● to preview the animation in a web browser.

Animate tween types

We are using only shape tweens in this lesson, but there are two additional tween types you should know about when working in Animate projects. Let's briefly examine all three.

1 Shape Tweens: As you've seen, this tween type works by creating at least two keyframes across the timeline and changing the properties of an object on the stage at one of the keyframes. You can change position, rotation, scale, color, and opacity, and even morph from one shape to another. Shape tweens work only with shapes.

2 Classic Tweens: These are created in exactly the same way as shape tweens in that you have at least two keyframes with a change in properties of an object on the stage at one of the two keyframes. You can change position, rotation, scale, opacity, and additional properties like color effects, blend, and filters. Works only with symbol instances.

3 Motion Tweens: Similar to classic tweens in capability, motion tweens differ primarily in the way they are created and how they are expressed within a project. A motion tween only needs a single existing keyframe to function as the entire layer is converted to a motion layer. This allows for small, diamond-shaped keyframes to automatically be created as you change properties across the timeline. You also get access to the Motion Editor for more precise easing when using this tween type. These tweens work only with symbol instances.

Design principles: Movement

When working with static visual design, the principle of movement can only be implied through line and form. In the example below, there is no actual movement, but the form that the circles take makes it seem as though there is movement from the lower left to the upper right.

When working in design software like Animate, however, you can express movement through changes in visual properties across time by adjusting things like position and scale.

Add realism to motion with easing

When performing a test movie, you will have observed the ball in motion. You may also have noticed that the motion looks mechanical and rough right now. This is because our motion lacks any variance and exists as a linear execution across each frame.

We can improve the motion by adding variance and weight through easing.

1   Select any of the frames that make up the shape tween.

2   In the Frame tab of the Properties panel, click the Classic Ease button in the Tweening section.

An easing effect panel appears. You can choose an ease type from the categories to the left and a specific ease from the column in the middle. An ease graph displays how each ease is weighted from beginning to end to help you visualize each ease.

● **Note** A classic ease is the default, linear ease type without any variance whatsoever. You can see this by observing the straight line in the easing graph.

3 Choose Ease In from the ease category column and Sine as the ease type. Double-click Sine to apply the ease to a shape tween.

● **Note** An ease-in starts slow and then gets faster toward the end.

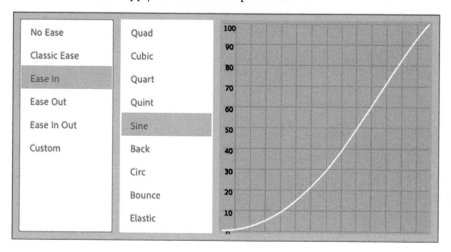

The ease effect button label changes to reflect the change we've made.

4 Preview the animation in a web browser by clicking Test Movie ●.

The movement of the ball is much smoother due to the ease that we've applied.

Applying personality with transformations

Even though the ball moves across the stage with some degree of variance through the easing effects we've applied, we can provide a more detailed animation that gives the ball a bit of personality and character through some simple transforms.

Now we'll use the Free Transform tool to apply basic animation principles to our ball as it interacts with the environment.

1 Select frame 16 in the Ball layer.

2 Create a new keyframe by clicking Insert Frames Group above the timeline and select Keyframe from the pull-down that appears.

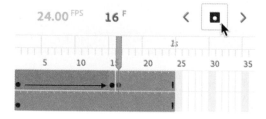

A new keyframe appears at frame 16.

3 Insert another keyframe at frame 19.

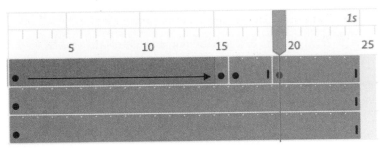

Both of these new keyframes are currently identical to the keyframe at frame 15.

4 Select the Free Transform tool ⊞ from the Tools panel.

5 Using the Free Transform tool, select the ball at frame 16 on the stage.

A transform rectangle appears.

6 Hover the Free Transform tool over the top or bottom edge of the transform rectangle until the cursor changes to indicate skew by arrows pointing in opposite directions. Drag to skew the transform slightly to the right.

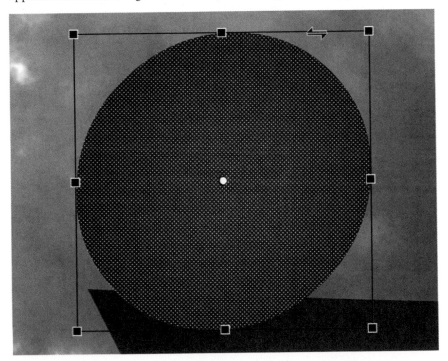

This will give the ball a bit of transformation as it pulls back from the edge, increasing the perception of weight.

7 With the Free Transform tool still active, select the ball at frame 15 on the stage.

A transform rectangle appears.

8 Hover the Free Transform tool over the top or bottom edge of the transform rectangle until the cursor changes to indicate skew by arrows pointing in opposite directions. Drag to skew the transform slightly to the left.

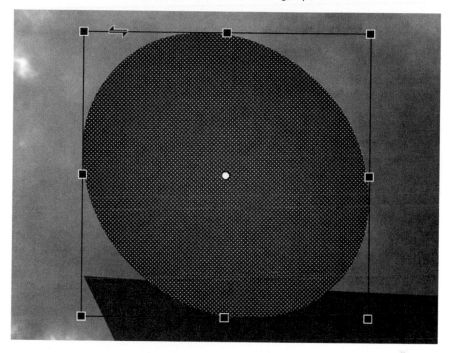

This will give the ball a bit of transformation as it initially rolls to a stop, indicating forward momentum.

9 Select any frame between the keyframes at frame 16 and frame 19.

10 Click the Insert Tweens option above the timeline and choose Create Shape Tween. If Create Shape Tween has been previously selected, there is no need to open the menu.

Animate creates a new shape tween.

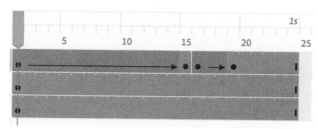

11 Preview the animation in a web browser by clicking Test Movie ⊙ .

Completing the animation

While we could go through completing the remainder of the animation step by step, this is a good opportunity to put into practice all the techniques we've gone over thus far.

Complete your animation with the following considerations:

- The ball is now at the edge of the cliff. Does it roll off? Jump down? Retreat off stage? Get creative in your intention.
- Establish keyframes across the timeline and adjust the position, scale, and transform properties to create a physical, weighted animation.
- Extend the timeline to 2 or even 3 seconds to include more action.
- Remember to add ease effects and transforms to refine the appearance of your animation and the feel of your tweens.

If you'd like to view a completed version of the animation, open the Lesson11/11Start folder and locate the file named project_animation.fla, which includes a two-second animation of the ball jumping off the cliff, smashing into the ground below, and bouncing off screen to the left. Use this action as a template for your own animation.

Making use of onion skinning

When completing your animation, it may be useful to employ a visualization feature in Animate called *onion skinning*.

This allows you to see where the ball has been, is, and will be across the timeline so that you can make better choices with your keyframes and their associated objects.

- Click the Onion Skin button ⬤ above the timeline to enable onion skinning.

Onion skinning for the ball is shaded differently depending on whether those frames come before or after the current position of the playhead.

- You can use the playback controls above the timeline to test your animation. Here is my completed timeline with a full set of keyframes and tweens as expressed in project_animation.fla:

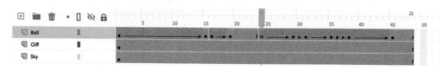

- Once you are happy with your animation, preview it in a web browser by clicking Test Movie ⊙.

Tip It is possible to make many changes to how onion skinning functions by opening the Onion Skin menu and choosing Advanced Settings.

Making your content interactive

Now that we have designed a complete animation, let's take things a step further and make the project interactive. In the next exercise, you will pause the playhead and provide a message to the user, letting them know to click to continue.

Draw an overlay prompt background

When you pause the timeline, you need to let the user know which action to take to proceed with playback.

Now you'll design a large overlay to cover the stage and obscure the animated content below.

1 Create a new layer and rename it prompt.

This layer will contain any assets that make up the user prompt overlay we will design.

2 Select the Rectangle tool  from the Tools panel.

Now you will create an overlay shape across the entire stage.

3 On the Tools tab of the Properties panel, set the fill color to black #000000 at 60% opacity and disable the stroke.

This will allow the user to see the underlying content through the overlay.

4 Using the Rectangle tool, draw a shape the same width and height as the stage.

You could even draw this object larger than the stage since its only purpose is to act as an overlay.

Create an overlay prompt message

With our overlay in place, we need to communicate to the user, letting them know they must click the screen to proceed with the animation.

We'll accomplish this with a simple text message.

1 Select the Text tool ▦ from the Tools panel.

2 Drag to draw out a text object. After releasing the mouse, type **Click to Play!** within the text object.

This is a direct message to the user, letting them know what needs to occur for playback to begin.

3 The text is likely pretty ugly at this point, so we must adjust its properties using the Object tab of the Properties panel. Change the font to Europa-Bold with a size of 96pts and a color value of #FFCC99. Center-align the text.

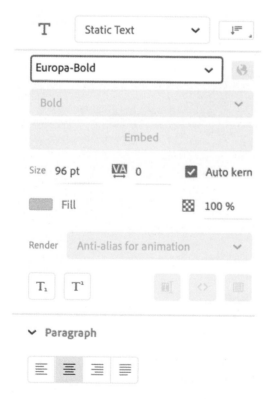

4 To position the text object at the center of the stage, open the Align panel by choosing Window > Align from the application menu.

5 Ensure that the Align To Stage option is enabled and click both Align Vertical Center and Align Horizontal Center.

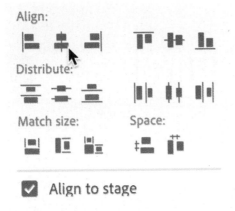

The text message is now aligned perfectly to the center of the stage.

We have created both elements necessary to build an interactive overlay. We cannot, however, add interactivity to the text or shape objects as they currently exist. For that, we must convert them into a symbol.

Creating a symbol

Symbols in Animate are special objects that feature their own internal timelines and exhibit a number of additional properties that simpler objects do not exhibit.

Let's convert our text and shape objects into a symbol.

1 Select both the text object and the shape overlay.

2 With both elements selected, click Convert To Symbol ✛ on the Object tab of the Properties panel.

The Convert To Symbol dialog box appears.

3 Name the symbol overlay and choose Movie Clip for the type. Click OK to create the symbol.

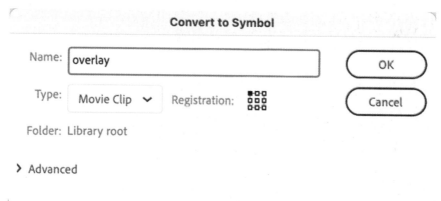

We've chosen Movie Clip because this symbol type can be made interactive.

Note An instance of a symbol exists on the stage after converting content to a symbol. Symbols themselves never exist on the stage—only instances of symbols are reflected across all of their instances.

Note Symbols exist within the Library panel and can be edited from there as well.

4 Choose Window > Library from the application menu to open the Library panel. Select the overlay symbol you just created to preview it.

5 We want the symbol instance on the stage to appear only on the first frame. Select frame 2 in the Prompt layer, click Insert Frames Group above the timeline, and choose Blank Keyframe from the pull-down that appears.

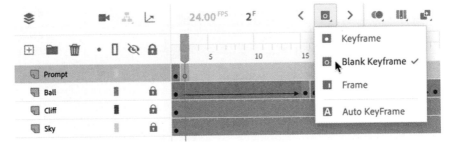

A blank keyframe is inserted, confining the overlay prompt symbol instance to frame 1 only.

6 Preview the animation in a web browser by clicking Test Movie ⊙.

The animation plays back as usual, but you'll see the single frame with the prompt overlay pass by through each loop.

We need to add some instructions to our animation through code to pause it at the overlay and wait for a user action.

Stopping the playhead

One of the best aspects of working in Animate is that the software enables a unique combination of visual design, motion design, and interactive design workflows.

As the project stands now, it plays back automatically. You will now add a bit of code to stop the playhead at frame 1.

1   Create a new layer at the top of the timeline and rename it Actions.

● **Note** Actions is a name that is generally accepted as the standard for adding code to an Animate project, but you can name it whatever you like. The idea is that you have a layer that is specifically set aside for holding code apart from any visual elements.

2   You create code in Animate in a special panel called Actions. Open the Actions panel by choosing Window > Actions from the application menu.

The Actions panel appears.

3   Ensure that frame 1 of the Actions layer is selected and type `this.stop();` into the script editor in the Actions panel.

This code instructs the playhead to stop immediately at the current frame, frame 1.

The script editor is the numbered space in the right pane of the panel that you can type in.

4   Preview the result of your code in a web browser by clicking Test Movie ●.

The animation will hold at frame 1 as we've instructed, effectively pausing the movie at the overlay prompt.

Adding interactivity

When testing the project in a web browser, you'll note that the playhead stops immediately at frame 1, displaying our prompt overlay. We need the user to be able to click the overlay to watch the animation.

Let's make the movieclip symbol instance we created at frame 1 into an interactive element.

1   Select the overlay movieclip instance on frame 1.

● **Note** Instance names can be applied to symbol instances only.

2   On the Object tab of the Properties panel, type **playprompt** in the Instance Name field.

An instance name allows you to target any element through code specifically by name.

3   Select frame 1 in the Actions layer and open the Actions panel if it isn't already open.

● **Note** The Actions Wizard can be used on web-based document types such as HTML5 Canvas, WebGL, and VR.

4   Instead of typing the code by hand, we will make use of the Actions Wizard. Click the Add Using Wizard button at the top of the Actions panel.

The interface switches from the script editor to reveal a step-by-step set of prompts.

Step 1 prompts you to select an action from a list of possible actions. We want the movie to play when the prompt overlay is clicked.

▶ **Tip** The list of actions is lengthy. You can type a term in the search box to filter the actions by keyword.

5   Locate the Play action and select it.

6 With the action selected, you're prompted to choose which object to apply the action to. Since we want the main timeline to play, select This Timeline and click Next.

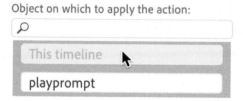

Object on which to apply the action:

At this point, the wizard moves on to Step 2.

7 Step 2 of the process prompts us to select a triggering event. Since we want the timeline to play once the user clicks the overlay prompt, select On Mouse Click.

Step 2:

Select a triggering event:

With this frame

On Double Click

On Mouse Click

On Mouse Out

On Mouse Over

8 The final step of the process is to select the object to apply the mouse click triggering event to. Since we provided an instance name of playprompt to our overlay instance, Animate presents that to us here. Select playprompt and click Finish And Add.

Select an object for the triggering event:

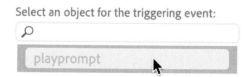

The wizard exits and automatically returns you to the script editor.

9   Take a look at the code that was constructed for us based on choices made through the step-by-step process of the Actions Wizard. Comments are included to describe what happens in each bit of code to help us understand what is happening. Close the Actions panel.

```
Actions:1                              Add using wizard  -◉  ⊕  <>  ≣  Q  ❷
1        this.stop();
2
3        var _this = this;
4      /*
5      Clicking on the specified symbol instance executes a function.
6      */
7      _this.playprompt.on('click', function(){
8      /*
9      Play a Movie Clip/Video or the current timeline.
10     Plays the specified movie clip or video.
11     */
12     _this.play();
13     });
14
15
```

10 Preview the completed interactive animation in a web browser by clicking Test Movie ◉.

The playback stops immediately at frame 1 and waits for a click interaction before playback begins. You've designed your first interactive animation. Congratulations!

Publish and export workflows

When your animation is finished, you'll want to share it with the world. Animate has a great number of options for doing so. We'll highlight a few here.

Publishing projects

When we publish content from Animate, we target the platform chosen when first creating the Animate document.

We have been using HTML5 Canvas in this lesson, so choosing File > Publish from the application menu will produce a bundle of web-native files such as HTML and JavaScript along with images and sounds, if included in the project.

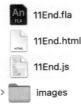

11End.fla

11End.html

11End.js

> images

Publish settings can be adjusted through File > Publish Settings and will vary based on the target platform. We discussed the various target platforms in the early portion of this lesson.

▶ **Tip** It is also possible to convert from one document type to another using File > Convert To, but any code will likely differ between platforms, so it will be commented out upon conversion. All assets and animation should convert nicely, though!

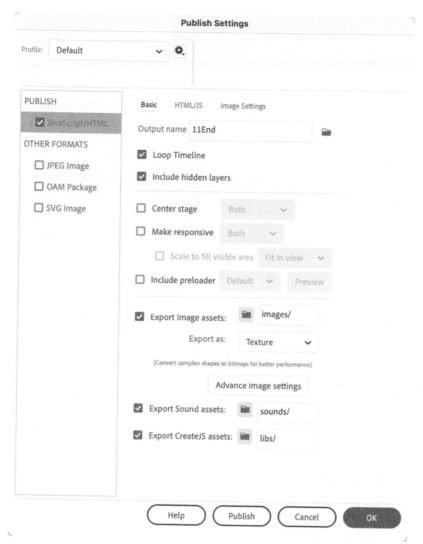

Exporting media

Exporting content is less tied to the document type and remains independent from the publish target. Generally, if you are using Animate for pure animation workflows, you will export rather than publish.

A number of locations allow export workflows in Animate, but the most direct way is to choose File > Export from the application menu.

You'll be presented with a small menu of export options:

- **Export Image:** Exports a still image derived from the current playhead position as PNG, JPG, or GIF files. It allows for lots of options in image quality and properties.

- **Export Image (Legacy):** A simpler and older version of the image export options that also allows for SVG export.

- **Export Movie:** Generates a sequence of image files in the format of JPG, GIF, PNG, or SVG, one image per frame. Alternatively, you can export as a SWF to bring into another application like After Effects for further compositing.

- **Export Video/Media:** This option offers a direct integration with Adobe Media Encoder. You use parameters to specify how you'd like to export the video, choose a format and preset from Media Encoder, and hand it off for processing.

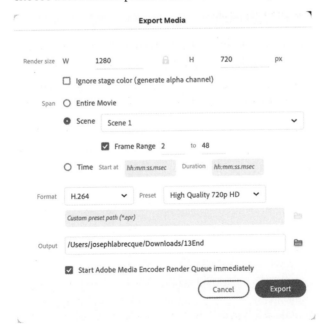

- **Export Animated GIF:** This is the same workflow as Export Image, but it will set all properties for an animated GIF file output instead of a still image.

- **Export Scene As Asset:** This option will package the entire scene as a special ANA asset file to be shared with other Animate users.

As you can see, the export options allow for many export workflows.

● **Note** Exporting content from Animate will generally not include any options for interactivity and coding because images, videos, and similar media types do not support interaction.

Quick share and publish

Before we conclude this lesson, we should also note that there is a Quick Share And Publish ⬆ option available in the upper right of the Animate interface.

This option provides a quick way for you to share content as animated GIF or video files to social channels like Twitter or YouTube, or as exported files to your local hard drive for distribution or use elsewhere.

It's a great feature for those who just want to get their content rendered quickly!

Next steps with Animate

To further explore the creative options that Animate has to offer, you can make use of Adobe's help resources available at https://helpx.adobe.com/support/animate.html.

If you'd like to advance in your exploration of Animate in greater depth, I encourage you to consider reading *Adobe Animate Classroom in a Book (2023 Release)*, also available from Peachpit and Adobe Press.

12 principles of animation

If you'd like to make your animations more engaging and fluid, I suggest studying the 12 principles of animation. We've used a handful of these principles in this lesson when animating the ball by using easing and transformations.

The 12 principles of animation include squash and stretch, anticipation, staging, straight-ahead action and pose-to-pose, follow through and overlapping action, slow-in and slow-out, arc, secondary action, timing, exaggeration, solid drawing, and appeal.

We won't define the principles in this book, but I encourage you to research one of the many online resources that cover them in detail.

As an exercise, try and discover which of these principles have been applied to the movement of our little ball. You may be surprised at how many are present!

Review questions

1 What target platforms are supported in Animate?

2 What does the document FPS value indicate?

3 What is the difference between a frame and a keyframe?

4 What mechanism is used to create motion between two keyframes?

5 What must be done to a movieclip symbol instance to make it addressable through code?

Review answers

1 Animate supports the native web through HTML5 Canvas, WebGL, and VR document types. ActionScript 3.0 and AIR are also supported, as are third-party extensions.

2 FPS is the frames-per-second value, which determines the number of frames that make up 1 second of playback in your animation.

3 A keyframe can signify that content has changed on the stage at a particular frame, whereas a frame extends that change over time.

4 Applying a shape tween to the tween span between keyframes.

5 It must be given an instance name.

INDEX

D

decibels, 296, 299

declared flows, 247–249

decorative shapes, 96–98

defaults
  Audition interface, 293, 295
  Dimension camera, 261
  Dimension new project, 257, 273
  Illustrator workspace, 112
  InDesign text styles, 177
  InDesign workspace, 162
  latest versions as, 11
  Photoshop workspace, 60
  Premiere Pro, 324
  Premiere Pro stills duration, 331
  XD Toggle vs. Default states, 226–229, 235, 236

deletions, album vs. photo, 43

Design mode, Dimension, 261

Design mode, XD, 203, 241

design principles
  balance, 237
  emphasis, 308
  hierarchy, 181
  movement, 420
  negative space, 93–94
  proportion, 273
  repetition, 145
  rhythm, 343
  rule of thirds, 31
  variety, 393

Desktop application. *See* Creative Cloud Desktop

desktop applications
  Creative Cloud, 2–21
  Photoshop, 54–55
  Premiere Pro as, 317

destructive editing, 61

Detail view, 30, 33, 34

Dimension, 252–289
  branding assets, 278
  environmental elements, 261–267
  importing Illustrator files, 278
  introduction to, 254–255
  lesson on, 252, 254, 289

  materials and graphics, 273–278
  new project file, 256–258
  render preview, 284
  replacing/removing graphics, 283
  scene rendering, 284–288
  Stager vs., 258
  3D models, 267–273
  user interface, 258–261

dissolves, 342

divider, horizontal, 188–189

DNG format, 28

Document window, 60

documents, new. *See* new documents/projects

drawing vector shapes, 115–117

Dreamweaver, 12

drop shadows, 386–388

duplicates
  Illustrator assets, 135
  shape duplication, 123–125

dust removal, 61–63

E

easing motion, 375, 376–377, 420–421

editing
  audio, 294, 299–300
  cropping, 38–39
  lighting, 36–38
  Lightroom Desktop, 25
  Lightroom tools and presets, 34–41
  masking, 40–41
  nondestructive, 24, 40, 65
  Photoshop, 58–77
  rule of thirds for, 31
  video, 316–318, 327–350

effect controls, 336, 342

effects, adding motion, 386–399

Ellipse Tool, 115

emphasis, 308

end credits, 346–350

environmental elements, 261–267

Eraser tool, 73

Essential Audio panel, 294

Essentials workspace, 60, 112

Europa font, 91, 372

The fastest, easiest, most comprehensive way to learn
Adobe Creative Cloud

Classroom in a Book®, the best-selling series of hands-on software training books, helps you learn the features of Adobe software quickly and easily.

The **Classroom in a Book** series offers what no other book or training program does—an official training series from Adobe Systems, developed with the support of Adobe product experts.

To see a complete list of our Classroom in a Book titles covering the 2022 release of Adobe Creative Cloud go to:
adobepress.com/CC2022

Adobe Photoshop Classroom in a Book (2022 release)
ISBN: 9780137621101

Adobe Illustrator Classroom in a Book (2022 release)
ISBN: 9780137622153

Adobe InDesign Classroom in a Book (2022 release)
ISBN: 9780137622962

Adobe Dreamweaver Classroom in a Book (2022 release)
ISBN: 9780137623303

Adobe Premiere Pro Classroom in a Book (2022 release)
ISBN: 9780137625123

Adobe After Effects Classroom in a Book (2022 release)
ISBN: 9780137623921

Adobe Animate Classroom in a Book (2022 release)
ISBN: 9780137623587

Adobe Photoshop Lightroom Classic Classroom in a Book (2022 release)
ISBN: 9780137625154